Post-Punk and Philosophy

Pop Culture and Philosophy®

General Editor: George A. Reisch

For full details of all Pop Culture and Philosophy® books, and all Open Universe® books, visit www.carusbooks.com

Pop Culture and Philosophy®

Post-Punk and Philosophy

Rip It Up and Think Again

Edited by

JOSHUA HETER AND RICHARD GREENE

OPEN UNIVERSE
Chicago

Volume 13 in the series, Pop Culture and Philosophy®, Series Editor George A. Reisch

To find out more about Open Universe and Carus Books, visit our website at www.carusbooks.com.

Printed and bound in the United States of America. Printed on acid-free paper.

Post-Punk and Philosophy: Rip It Up and Think Again

ISBN: 978-1-63770-057-0

This book is also available as an e-book, 978-1-63770-040-2.

Library of Congress Control Number: 2023942148

For Kasey Mohammad

Contents

Thanks

Working on this project has been a pleasure, in no small part because of the many fine folks who have assisted us along the way. In particular, a debt of gratitude is owed to David Ramsay Steele at Carus Books, the contributors to this volume, the School of Humanities at Jefferson College and the Department of Political Science and Philosophy at Weber State University. Finally, we'd like to thank those family members, students, friends, and colleagues with whom we've had fruitful and rewarding conversations on various aspects of all things Post-Punk as it relates to philosophical themes.

Well, How Did We Get Here?

The Sex Pistols played their final show at San Francisco's Winterland Ballroom on January 14th 1978. The performance was—by almost all accounts—a bit underwhelming.

Beyond the fact that lead singer Johnny Rotten appeared mostly disinterested in the festivities and bassist Sid Vicious's primary contribution was his now infamous rebellious persona (as opposed to anything coming from his instrument), Punk in general was simply in a worrisome state.

Punk's British invasion wasn't taking hold in the US in the same way that rock'n'roll's British invasion had a decade earlier. Perhaps worse, rather than ushering in any sort of meaningful political change (as evidenced at least in part by the elections of Margaret Thatcher and Ronald Reagan), Punk was in the midst of being co-opted by corporate America and the culture at large (as evidenced in part by the release of a 1980 album of Punk covers by The Chipmunks). It isn't difficult then to understand what Rotten had in mind when he ended the Pistols' set on the evening in question by asking—somehow both earnestly yet cynically—". . . *ever get the feeling you've been cheated?!*"

With the state of Punk being what it was, you could be forgiven for thinking that perhaps Punk was coming to an end—not with the brash, furious exuberance for which it had become known but—with a faint, impotent whimper that threatened to leave it largely forgotten.

With the benefit of hindsight, we can see that Punk would be just fine. In fact, you could reasonably argue that even during this uncertain time, the genre had some of its brightest days ahead. Nevertheless, it was during and perhaps because of this somewhat bleak period that a new cadre of musicians and artists would emerge who would leave an indelible mark well into the next decade and beyond—not only on rock music but on popular culture in general.

Well before Punk's initial heyday would come to an end, a number of bands that would eventually be labeled *Post-Punk* were forming. As early as 1976, groups like Siouxsie and the Banshees, Wire, Joy Division, and a host of others were moving beyond the three-chord, two-minute tracks typical of Punk Rock. While a number of elements from Punk remained, the burgeoning genre was a bit more subdued and much more eclectic, drawing from a wide range of influences such as free jazz, dub, glam rock, folk, and even disco. Thematically, Post-Punk possessed an avant-garde aesthetic and lyrics drawn from perhaps more sophisticated mediums such as literature and cinema. And, while it didn't completely leave behind the anger and fury of Punk, Post-Punk delved into a wide range of themes such as love, existential despair, and questions of ultimate meaning.

The emergence of a movement like Post-Punk should not have been all that surprising. Beyond the fact that art is almost always in a constant state of change, by the mid-1970s, rock music was a quarter-century old and had, for quite some time, been the product of evolution and experimentation as made clear by the existence of Punk Rock itself. It was not only predictable but perhaps necessary that yet another unique iteration of rock'n'roll in general and Punk Rock in particular would be truly innovate and ground-breaking. And in that regard, those at the forefront of Post-Punk and the many who followed in their wake did not disappoint.

As Post-Punk gained credibility and a fair bit of mainstream success, even artists like Johnny Rotten (who reclaimed his original name, John Lydon) joined the Post-Punk mix with his new, post-Sex Pistols band Public Image Ltd., while a number of acts that originated as straightforwardly Punk allowed their sound to mature in a way that was a bit more in line with the new Post-Punk scene (think The Clash of "London Calling" as opposed to The Clash of "Give 'Em Enough Rope"). And, the experimental spirit that gave rise to the new sound only continued, eventually leading to the birth of subgenres such as new wave, goth rock, indie rock, emo, and countless new forms of music made for a Post-Punk world. Not unlike Punk Rock itself, eventual revivals would cement Post-Punk's legacy and influence decades into the future.

With all of this in mind, it should be of little surprise that such an explosion of creativity—from a wide range of artists drawing from a variety of outlets—gives rise to a number of intriguing philosophical questions. What sort of thing *is* Post-Punk? Is it merely a musical genre, an artistic movement, or something else altogether? What is the proper role of emotion in the intellectual life? Is any attempt to be cool an inherently losing battle; should I embrace my eccentricities? Does a counterculture need to care about change, or can it simply focus on its art? Are nihilism and love compatible? Is the best way to deal with a bleak worldview simply to embrace it through art? How much should we care (if at all) about the moral failings of the artists whose work we love so much? What exactly is authenticity, and how important is it?

As a result of so much thoughtful artistry and music-making, the editors of this book were fortunate enough to bring together the talented authors whose work comprises it as they raise, clarify, and even attempt to answer some of these questions. Thankfully, their creativity and innovation are worthy of the Post-Punk creatives about which they've written. And, their varied and eclectic perspectives are akin to the variety of influences that led to and help make Post-Punk such a unique and beloved art form.

So, that is how we got here; through and past the downward spiral of Punk's initial wave, alternative rock music came out stronger and even more diverse and compelling with the advent of Post-Punk, and we are now in a position to reflect deeply on the movement as a whole. Perhaps if we think carefully enough about it all, we might even be able to discover where we go from here.

I

Post-Punk
and the
Human Person

1
Post-Punk's Melancholy Melody

CANDACE MIRANDA AND WALTER BARTA

Post-Punk explores the emotions of melancholy, resentment, and despair. These moods, and their corresponding themes, are exemplified by chart-hitting singles that shot up to the top of the "pops" such as "Love will Tear us Apart" by Joy Division, "Heaven Knows I'm Miserable Now" by The Smiths, and "No Weak Men" by Gang of Four, amongst many other songs.

Melancholy, to many philosophers, from the Renaissance onward, has been characterized as the intellectual's emotion, bred perhaps from knowing too much. Resentment and despair, on the other hand, are emotions theorized about by many modern philosophers—Kierkegaard, Nietzsche, Scheler, and others. These feelings have been associated with the politics and psychology of disempowerment and nihilism. As explored through Post-Punk music, these emotions and their corresponding philosophies are interesting as mental states and modes of thought.

The Mind, Melancholy, and Music

Philosophers and artists alike have long been interested in the way that states of mind relate, including cognitive states like thoughts and beliefs but also non-cognitive states like emotions. In general, there is a strong intuition that our thoughts and feelings are connected. Emotions often come associated with certain beliefs and attitudes and philosophies about the world. As such, different genres of music may have lyrics that express certain types of thoughts, and these thoughts may be connected to the emotional tones and moods of the songs. To use an obvious example, if you sing about darkness and death, you may be depressed and if you sing about sunshine and springtime, you may be joyful.

So, it's easy to see how the ideas in Post-Punk lyrics may connect deeply to the tone, mood, and overall sound of the music. As illustration, compare Post-Punk songs with songs of other genres during the same era and you can observe that much of the difference in genre is a difference in mood. It becomes very apparent, even after only listening to a handful of Post-Punk songs, that they include pretty dark themes, especially when compared to other popular music of the same period. For examples of dark themes, consider the following Post-Punk songs by Public Image Ltd. (also known as PiL) with blatant titles such as "Death Disco," "The Order of Death," "Disappointed," and "This is Not a Love Song". Also, even more explicitly, there is a song by Bauhaus straightforwardly called "Dark Entries." Now juxtapose that to other songs in the zeitgeist of the time with upbeat titles like "Disco Nights" by GQ, "Too Much Heaven" by the Bee Gees, and "Love is the Answer" by England Dan and John Ford Coley. Ironically, the Post-Punk band Gang of Four wrote about the unique and contrasting tones of the Post-Punk genre as compared with other popular genres of the period in their song titled, "Love like Anthrax," stating in the song, "most groups make most of their songs about falling in love or how happy they are to be in love."

On a deeper level, intelligent pursuit itself, as a state of mind, has its own associated attitudes and emotions. Because the intellectual dares to think deep thoughts, they are often led towards topics that are uncomfortable and even tragic. Such is the idea that the truth is hard, harsh, or sad. Or, as they say in reverse, ignorance is bliss. So, philosophy and poetry (not to mention Post-Punk music), as intellectual pursuits, can often be associated with or lead towards negative beliefs and attitudes.

"Melancholy" has long been one broad catch-all term for these kinds of negative attitudinal and emotional states. The idea dates back to the original Greek philosopher of medicine, Hippocrates (460–370 B.C.E.), who proposed that "melancholia" was one of the four humors governing the human body and mind, manifesting in the sad and longing disposition we now think of as melancholy. The seventeenth-century book, Robert Burton's *Anatomy of Melancholy,* became one of the clearest statements of the connection between melancholy and its intellectual expressions. According to Burton, "he that increaseth wisdom, increaseth sorrow" (p. 46).

Artistic expression itself has also long been associated with feelings of melancholy. The history of literature is littered with melancholic philosophical authors and characters. Perhaps the most famous melancholic philosophical type in literature remains William Shakespeare's *Hamlet*. Similarly, Johann Wolfgang von Goethe's *Sorrows of Young Werther* became notorious for its depiction of a suicidal young poet whose representation is said to have caused a suicide-fad in its readership. Edward Young's *Night-Thoughts*, a book of poetic meditations, was another famous representation of melancholy through poetry, the tone and style of which arguably developed into the genre of the Romantic poets, famous for their personal, wistful, and thoughtful poetry. Some of these poets, like Lord Byron and Percy Shelley, were arguably the pop stars of the nineteenth century, before mass-marketed music was possible, since the only mode of mass media was text. Many such poets likely would have been Punk and Post-Punk artists if they had been born a few centuries later.

Indeed, we may even be able to imagine the front men of Post-Punk bands—such as Ian Curtis of Joy Division, Steven Morrissey of The Smiths, John "Johnny Rotten" Lydon of PiL, and Robert Smith of The Cure—as akin to the Romantic poets reincarnated during Britain's Post-Punk scene, circa 1978 to 1984. These musicians frequently wrote with morose poeticism, just as Shelley and Byron did. For example, verses in PiL's song "The Order of Death" feature themes of death and dying:

> here now,
> ending,
> one life,
> one knife. (Public Image Ltd., "The Order of Death")

Another verse from The Cure's song "Killing an Arab," similarly about killing, parallels this:

> I'm alive.
> I'm dead.
> I'm the stranger
> killing an Arab. (The Cure, "Killing an Arab")

These two songs characteristically express tones and themes of melancholic ennui, like those of the melancholic poets before them.

All of this provides a philosophical and artistic tradition to which some modern musical movements like Post-Punk can be traced, which both place Post-Punk as a genre that expresses a philosophical disposition, and as an especially melancholic and thus intellectual genre.

What other specific negative attitudes and associated philosophies most characterize the Post-Punk movement?

Punk, Resentment, and Resistance

One such characteristic Post-Punk attitude is that of resentment and resistance. To better understand the way that resentment plays out in Post-Punk music, we must first delve into the genre's predecessor, Punk, also known as "garage rock." Punk originated in the late 1960s with strong influences of a do-it-yourself culture, and lyrics that projected feelings of resistance towards the choices of politicians of the era, especially in light of the Cold War. Examples of these political attitudes are present in the lyrics of songs such as "Big A little a" by Crass, where they speak critically of government leaders and religious figures that society conforms with, in order to maintain the status quo:

> The system might have got you,
> but it won't get me.
> 1–2–3–4
> External control
> are you gonna let them get you?
> Do you wanna be a prisoner in the boundaries that they set you?
> You say you want to be yourself,
> by Christ, do you think they'll let you?
> They're out to
> get you get you get you. . . (Crass, "Big A little a")

The interrogatory format of this song introduces us as listeners to the philosophies of Punk by allowing us to think about what our own feelings, especially trepidations and disagreements, may have been towards those in power at the time it was written. This questioning of the government was often committed to full on *anarchy*, the rejection of all systems of authority and power, which was and is still a strong message of those who identify with Punk. The Sex Pistols wrote multiple songs expressing sentiments of anarchy towards the government. These songs were blunt and honest with little to hide behind with titles such as "Anarchy in the U.K." and "God Save the Queen." There is even a subgenre of Punk called Anarcho-Punk with bands such as Crass, Conflict, and Poison Girls popularizing this style of music with their political messages and out-of-the-box ways. These bands made themselves heard via their outlandish album titles (such as *Penis Envy*) and eclectic clothing along with their to-the-point lyrics. As another example, The Slits, an all-girl Punk band, also utilized Punk's musical platform to express their disdain towards female stereotypes in order to shed light on the ongoing gender divide via their song titled "Typical Girls" which provided sarcastic humor, stating:

[typical girls]
Don't create.
Don't rebel.
Have intuition.
Don't drive well. (The Slits, "Typical Girls," 1979)

Through these kinds of interrogations and rejections of power, the genre of Punk Rock not only resisted political standards with the use of their loud guitar riffs and lawless lyrics, but they also rebelled against the nouveau genres in music, such as rock, pop-rock, and what the world knew as rock'n'roll. The Clash described this new form of rock perfectly in their song titled "1977," stating, "No Elvis, Beatles, or The Rolling Stones."

Most Punk artists, and their Post-Punk successors, have a negative emotional tone directed against some real or perceived source of oppression. Thus, the signature Punk musical mood, which makes it a distinctive genre, seems to be this spirit of resistance expressed in a tone of resentment. Resentment itself, often used in the French form *"ressentiment,"* is an emotion that many philosophers—including the greats like Søren Kierkegaard, Friedrich Nietzsche, and Max Scheler— have had interesting things to say about.

Søren Kierkegaard (1813–1855) described resentment in terms of the artistic individual and consuming community. To Kierkegaard, the modern age is a passionless one, in which the unifying emotion is resentment rather than enthusiasm. It is not difficult to apply Kierkegaard's idea to the Punk artist. The Punk artist finds their community, usually those in explicit or implicit opposition to the Punk scene, lacking in the enthusiasm that they themselves feel they must express, and that stifling feeling expresses itself as a resentment towards conformity. Likewise, the community resents and resists the artist for daring to do anything different.

Friedrich Nietzsche (1844–1900) posited resentment as central to his theory of power and morality. Nietzsche pointed out that lambs surely resent the birds of prey that eat them; in contrast, the birds of prey do not resent their prey, but actually

love the tasty lambs. Thus, to Nietzsche, resentment is an emotion felt by the disempowered towards the empowered. Nietzsche
further extended this into the counterintuitive idea of moral good-
ness as derivative from resentment (*The Genealogy of Morals*).

Nietzsche imagined the powerless ascetic pauper calling
himself "good" and the powerful king "bad" as an expression of
resentment. It is not difficult to apply Nietzsche's theory to the
Punk artist as well. The Punk resents The Man, the system,
the government, the status quo, the neighbors who tell them to
turn down the music, and the police who come to turn it down
forcibly. The Punk artist resents anyone in a position of power,
and they resist by expressing that resentment in music. In
turn, once an artist has gained popularity and esteem, there is
a corresponding resentment towards Punk's newfound cultural
power in the reactionary anti-Punk attitudes of the more conservative members of society.

Max Scheler (1874–1928) also made resentment one of his
central philosophical ideas. Scheler took the Nietzschean concept of resentment but pathologized it, believing that resentment ultimately undermined and poisoned a person's ability to
appropriately value. The resentful person becomes obsessed
with, identified through, and defined by their negative emotion
towards the powers that be. We might apply Scheler's idea
to Punk artists as well. The Punk artist comes to enact and
embody their resentment in their music and performance.
Through this, resentment becomes a dominant feature of their
self-presentation and identity, a type of cycle that cannot be
escaped, because it becomes solidified into their "Punk" brand-
ing, potentially leading to self-destructive life choices.

Likewise, the anti-Punk conservative doubles down on their
own form of resentment, committed to the view that the Punk
is destroying society, unable to see anything valuable in the
emotion that the Punk attitude is giving voice to. We can witness these attributes as an audience, as Punk Rock is seen as
the stereotypical genre of music that living rooms of parents
would rather have turned off than turned up all over the world.
For example, speaking of parents, the song "Mommy Can I Go
Out and Kill Tonight" by the Misfits comically expresses feelings of conformity and rebellion. The song begins by describing
ways in which we conform, like "getting straight A's" and "doing
my homework, so I'll be smart", but it then gradually morphs
into more sinister lyrics of rebellion, starting with the threat of
"I'll laugh last . . ." and leading to the gruesome verse, "Rip the
veins from human necks . . ." (The Misfits, "Mommy Can I Go
Out and Kill Tonight," 1982).

In addition to being expressed explicitly through the lyrical content of Punk music, resentment is also often expressed implicitly through musical form. Several formal elements contribute to this resentful feeling: the angry vocal tone, the loudness, the active and even aggressive timbre. Real life also provides examples of the resentful emotional valence of Punk and Post-Punk, as well as that of anti-Punk reactionaries. One of the most notable of these live events was Iggy Pop's so-called *Murder of a Virgin,* around 1974, an example of his extreme, self-destructive on-stage presence, best exemplified by him being whipped on stage by his guitarist, Ron Asheton, until he bled while provoked by his equally rambunctious audience.

Post-Punk, Despair, and Resignation

Another characteristic Post-Punk attitude is that of despair and resignation. In contrast to the pure Punk aesthetic, Post-Punk can be seen as a continuation of the trajectory of the Punk emotion, but a continuation of the same feelings with less sense of direction. It was a year after the namesake of "1977," circa 1978, that Punk began to dissipate to make way for Post-Punk. Trends set by those in the Punk scene remained and increased in popularity until they became a part of what was mainstream, and it was this rise of "posers" over-wearing safety pin earrings and leather garb that seemingly caused Punk to die.

As Crass said, Punk is "just another product for the consumer's head . . . Punk is dead" ("Punk is Dead," 1978). This attitude and the belief that the rebellion was over, co-opted by the system itself as just one more consumer product, informs much of the Post-Punk sensibility. The signature Post-Punk move, which makes it generically different from Punk, seems to be the attitudinal development from resentment towards despair. Like Punk songs, most Post-Punk tracks have a negative emotional tone, but rather than continuing to direct this emotion into resistance against some power, the emotion is more diffused and directionless, leading to a feeling of more general monotonous resignation, often bordering on *anhedonia*, the complete lack of pleasure or joy.

This form of resistance-turned-resignation has a strong presence in philosophy, especially in theories of nihilism, the philosophical stance that nothing is meaningful and that everything is therefore meaningless. The nihilist is prototypically the philosopher who, having rebelled against every possible belief and rejected every value, now has nothing to believe in or value

(Alan Pratt, "Nihilism"). Both Kierkegaard and Nietzsche had philosophical conceptions of nihilism and lamented its pervasiveness in modern culture.

Kierkegaard believed that existential despair may be intrinsic to the artistic process itself (*Either/Or*). Kierkegaard imagined the artist, what he terms the "aesthete," as a person trapped in the human condition of hedonistically seeking pleasure, but that this itself is only a distraction from the decline towards existential despair. The Post-Punk artist seems to reflect this Kierkegaardian diagnosis in some ways.

After the exhaustion of the hedonistic Punk party, Post-Punk music feels more like the emotional sensibility of the hangover the day after. All of the pleasures were pursued, but some level of baseline emotional despair remains—making Post-Punk "more musical. . . more intellectual, and more cerebral" comparatively to its predecessor (Amplified, "Joy Division: The Poster Children of Post-Punk").

On the other hand, Nietzsche imagined a passionless future in which all grand ideas and beliefs had been debunked, in which the vacuum left behind was a nihilistic wasteland (*The Will to Power*, Section 585). The general attitude in such a world would be something like a resignation to the meaningless of it all. Post-Punk falls into the emotional trough of this Nietzschean resignation as well. Much of Post-Punk feels like Punk that has worn itself out, that has fought the fight but fallen, too tired to continue, that now doubts the dreams it once had, and has resigned itself to mourning over its previous incarnation of passion and verve.

This pervasive sense of nihilistic resignation also makes Post-Punk an especially philosophical genre, because it allows itself to consider deep and uncomfortable thoughts and has the corresponding emotional valences, not unlike what is required of the truth-seeking philosopher.

Consistent with the feelings of resignation, the characteristic Post-Punk sound corresponds to the dampening of several Punk elements: the somber vocal tone, the softer and more monotonous noise, the more passive timbre. These qualities play an integral part in Post-Punk's almost depressed sound.

Several other formal elements also contribute to this resigned feeling as well. The flat notes give the music a tonal dissonance. The bass guitar's low pitched range captures feelings at the lower scales. And the frequent decrescendos, descending scales from high to low, provide a feeling of descending into sadness. Furthermore, the monotone voice, the use of a piano's una corda pedal, instrumental mufflers, and other similar devices add more similar effects.

Perfectly exemplifying each of these attributes is PiL's album titled *Metal Box* as it embraces and embodies the melancholic Post-Punk persona of resignation with song titles such as, "Graveyard," "No Birds," and "Bad Baby." As an overall record, it is viewed as "dank sounding," according to Scottish musician, Robert "Bobby" Gillespie. "It's dark. It's damp, and it's slightly depressed" making the album the quintessential combination that is: Post-Punk (BBC Four). As Pat Gilbert, former *Mojo* editor, put it "if you're not trying to make rock music, you often end up kind of slightly monotonous, repetitive bass lines and backing tracks like Joy Division started out doing" (Amplified). All of these give a tonal feeling that a Post-Punk band has expressed feelings of having given up.

The lyrics of their songs also often explicitly represent thoughts of a defeatist or nihilist, further contributing to this resigned feeling. For example, the title and lyrics of "Heaven Knows I'm Miserable Now" give a sense of abiding resigned misery, even in contrast to the promise of heaven. Similarly, "Love will Tear us Apart" gives an ambivalent account of the positive emotion of love, by suggesting that even such a powerful positive emotion will "tear us apart." The verb tense "will" also gives a sense of inevitability to the claim, adding to a sense of resignation. The song "Please, Please, Please, Let Me Get What I Want" by The Smiths with the refrain, "For once in my life, let me get what I want," has a similar tone. The refrain does not resist, but begs, to be given something, but with the acknowledgement that it is probably not going to happen, as it has never happened before. Other examples include lyrics like "little orphans in the snow with nowhere to call a home" per Siouxsie and the Banshees and "Whatever happened to all the heroes? All the Shakespearoes? They watched their Rome burn" by the Stranglers.

Real life also provides examples of the despairing nature of the Post-Punk mentality. The ironically named band Joy Division boasts a graveyard on the cover of its final album *Closer*. Furthermore, not long after its publication, the lead singer, Ian Curtis, committed suicide. It is also real-life experiences that provide the inspiration to these melancholy melodies, and vice versa. For example, following his mother's death, John "Johnny Rotten" Lydon of PiL wrote the song in his mourning titled, "Death Disco." Another notable real-life example of Post-Punk's tragic nature is the death one of the most referenced couples of the twentieth century, Sid and Nancy (Sid

Vicious and Nancy Spungeon), after their heroine-fueled (alleged) murder-suicide became a euphemism for the toxically self-destructive couple.

A Post-Script on Post-Punk

The emotional forms of songs in various genres, Punk and Post-Punk included, are reflected in and often derived from the ideas, beliefs, and attitudes that are expressed in their music. The tradition of Punk music can be identified with its characteristic emotional valence of *ressentiment* and its corresponding political rebelliousness and personal rejection of norms. And, whether inspired by precipitating factors such as unrequited romance or the political climate of the time, Post-Punk music can be identified with the continuation of these Punk feelings, but more despairing, reorienting the same negative feelings towards personal resignation, nihilism, and the internal struggle of the artist.

The combination of anarchy and anhedonia makes Post-Punk a distinctively philosophical genre, and these musical forms and the philosophies that they express continue to trace into the genres of modern song to this day.

2

Love in the Time of Post-Punk

CATHERINE VILLANUEVA GARDNER

In the mid-1970s, Punk Rock tore onto the UK music scene, with jagged vocals, screeching chords, and a deliberately ugly visual esthetic; indeed, the visual imagery of punks—ears and cheeks pierced with safety pins, bondage trousers, and day-glo spiked hair (sometimes held in place by super-glue)—reflected the frustrations and sense of oppression for young people of that time.

The music of Punk Rock exposed the alienation and anger of 1970s white UK youth, with songs about anarchy, riots, and general mayhem that left little space for songs about romantic love, which has been a dominant theme in popular music, reaching as far back as the ancient Sumerians.

But what of love in the time of *Post-Punk*? Was it possible to explore the vicissitudes of romantic love in an era that was simultaneously both nihilistic and increasingly politicized? Margaret Thatcher became the British prime minister in 1979 during a recession and a period of extreme unemployment. So, could we express love in the time of rule by an Iron Lady? Or, to put it more colloquially, if music were the food of love, *could* we still play on?

Certainly, the actual subject matter of love and heartbreak returned to the songs and song titles of Post-Punk, but did these supposedly *universal* human concepts and emotions remain the same after Punk or had they undergone transformation in some way? As both a witness to and participant of the Post-Punk era, and as a philosopher, I would argue that this musical era ushered in *new* narratives of human romantic relationships. Informed by the authenticity and anti-commercialism of Punk, Post-Punk bands offered new types of songs about romantic love that rejected the prior conventions of popular music.

13

In such Post-Punk classics as Gang of Four's *Damaged Goods* EP, Joy Division's "Love Will Tear Us Apart," The Associates' "Party Fears Two," The Cure's "Boys Don't Cry," Human League's "Don't You Want Me," and Echo and the Bunnymen's "Rescue," we can hear new narratives of isolation-within-a-relationship, fractured masculinity, and commodification of humanity, at play in Post-Punk. Even the covers of beloved 1960s soul classics by, for example, Talking Heads ("Take Me to the River") and The Slits ("I Heard It Through the Grapevine") were performed without their original passion and vocal tensions, a loss of "soul" that spoke to the loss of musical innocence following the Punk era.

Introduction to Post-Punk

As Punk Rock lost some of its original impetus in the late 1970s and before the image-driven music of the "New Romantics" (such as Duran Duran, or Spandau Ballet) of the early 1980s, Post-Punk found an eager audience in the UK. Yet the music that followed Punk in time was not a monolithic sound, nor did it have a shared aesthetic.

Some young white men in the UK were listening to "Oi" bands, like Sham 69 and the Cockney Rejects. The skinhead aesthetic was typically a Fred Perry with drainpipe jeans and 16-eyelet cherry-red Doc Marten boots. Buying boots one or two sizes too large (and stuffing the end with newspaper) gave their wearer a "hard" look.

Based on my own knowledge of the pulp fiction at that time, aimed at skinheads and suedeheads, this subculture glorified violence towards outsiders, both rival gangs and people of color. Inside the subculture, female roles dictated that *true* "skin girls" supposedly engaged willingly in gang bangs (group sex) with the male gang members. (In the late 1970s, the progressive Labour council of my home city wanted to attract these youths to the libraries by offering books that catered to their interests. I was employed by the local library to read the relevant works.)

Skinheads were not a new subculture, having originated out of Mods in the late 1960s. Timothy Brown has shown that by about 1980, the skinhead identity had become more or less interchangeable with right-wing, anti-immigrant views, whereas if Post-Punks did express a political view point, it was usually left-wing. In contrast to the hyper-masculinity of the skinheads (beer-violence-meaningless sex), Post-Punk bands and their followers tended to be emotionally fragile, vulnerable in their masculinity, and alienated in their intimate relationships. Overall, bands were predominantly male. Post-Punk lyrics were often gender-ambiguous, leaving the song open to non-heteronormative interpretation for queer listeners. A classic example of this new type of song would be "Rescue" by Echo and the Bunnymen.

Echo and the Bunnymen—"Rescue"

The band was formed in Liverpool in 1978, and their debut album, *Crocodiles*, was released in 1980. The song "Rescue" was the second single from this album, charting at number 62 on the UK Singles Chart, which does not reflect the critical praise of and loyal fanbase for the band. I attended a concert in 1980 which the Bunnymen were headlining, with the lesser-known U2 as their support band. It was not a fairytale first gig in England for U2. The lead singer, Bono, got stuck on the sound system, having climbed up there for dramatic effect. Helped down by roadies, his trousers split, and the band played out their set to the sound of jeers and objects being thrown. The crowd only settled down once the Bunnymen appeared.

"Rescue" should be appreciated against the social and political turmoil of life in the UK at that time: the "Winter of Discontent" (November 1978 to February 1979), multiple strikes and a sense of impending economic doom, followed by the election of Margaret Thatcher as prime minister in 1979. Despite the urging of the Bunnymen, romantic love was not enough to rescue Britain's youth from life under Thatcher, from increased unemployment to the poll tax to Conservative attacks on education. Echo and the Bunnymen sing of being lost and confused in "Rescue," asking if the other person will rescue them: "If I said I'd lost my way / Would you sympathize . . . Things are going wrong / Can you tell that in a song . . . Won't you come on down to my rescue?" Here it would seem that the singer is not singing of the problems with his relationship; instead, he is singing of living in a world of isolation and alienation that he hopes the non-gendered person he is addressing can rescue him from.

It's this world that forms the background for many Post-Punk songs of romantic or sexual love; Gang of Four, for example, was another Post-Punk band inhabiting this alienating world.

Gang of Four—Damaged Goods EP

Gang of Four are an English Post-Punk band formed in Leeds in 1976. Their breakout recording was the EP *Damaged Goods*

(1978) on the independent Fast Product label, and their debut album, *Entertainment*, was released in 1979 through EMI records. On the A-Side, the song "Damaged Goods" engages in multiple plays on the pun of being "damaged goods"—someone who is no longer desirable or valuable, typically, because of their emotional baggage or some other kind of character flaw— in a doomed relationship, with the singer asking to be returned and the money refunded. Why is the relationship doomed? In a 2009 interview with *Clash* magazine, singer and lyricist Jon King says that it is one "where legover [sex] had become, maybe, too much of a good thing. Or at any rate, a thing." In other words, the value of the relationship appears to have decreased when there was more supply than demand.

In this way, more than anything else, "Damaged Goods" is a song comparing a doomed romance to capitalist exchange relations. The singer wishes his partner "goodbye" at the end, which we also hear as "good buy." He says that the change will do them good: money/change in the relationship. Even though this partner said they were cheap (sexually available), they cost too much. *Allmusic* critic, Tom Maginnis, stated that the lyrics "could summarize the collective attitude of the Post-Punk era, bidding adieu to the more optimistic music of the '60s and self-absorbed '70s with a singalong chorus" (Maginnis, 2023).

The really disturbing song, "Love Like Anthrax," was on the B-Side of the EP. In the original lyrics for the song, it has Andy Gill talking about the mechanics of how the track was recorded, and began with someone coughing (stricken with anthrax?). This separation of content—the infection of romantic love—from the mechanism of writing and singing about love produces a song that is as alienating as it is about love-induced alienation. Subsequently, King said that this split-audio/ running commentary "seemed like a modern way to describe things, how stories can't always be decoded from a single point of view and, among all the conflicting narratives, a story's sense changes depending on where you sit."

When the track was re-recorded for the *Entertainment* album, the content of Gill's contribution had changed, and this changed version is perhaps the better known. Ultimately, the song requires an old stereo player for the full effect, so that one speaker has Jon King's lyrics about the almost Kafka-esque horrors of romantic love and the other has Andy Gill simultaneously speaking a monologue about why bands sing about love.

According to King, he feels "like a beetle on its back and there's no way for me to get up," as love will "get you like a case of anthrax" and "that's something I don't want to catch."

Meanwhile, Gill tells us that bands write and sing about love, about falling in love, or how happy they are to be in love. Towards the end, Gill speaks for both of them when he says, "I don't think we're saying there's anything wrong with love, we just don't think that what goes on between two people should be shrouded with mystery." And it would seem that a brutal and public dissection of a human relationship was one of the hallmarks of the Post-Punk era; indeed, never more so than with the next two songs I shall consider.

Joy Division—"Love Will Tear Us Apart"

When people think of what sound epitomizes the Post-Punk musical era, they most likely think of Joy Division, a band formed in Salford in 1976, and the melancholic bitterness of "Love Will Tear Us Apart," released in 1980 by the independent Factory Records. Supposedly, the lyrics were inspired by the marital problems of Ian Curtis and his own health problems. (I attended one of Joy Division's last concerts in England, unfortunately cut short by Curtis collapsing on the stage.)

As in Gang of Four's "Damaged Goods," Curtis sings here about a failing relationship, only this time the lyrics are about the resentments and tensions between a couple as they experience a loss of love. However, even among the dying embers of the relationship, we're told "there's still this appeal that we've kept through our lives," and that their love is "something so good, just can't function no more." These paradoxes, obviously, lead to the equally paradoxical chorus and title of the song that love—a supposedly good thing—is tearing them apart.

In many ways, such lyrics were far too mature for the majority of their adolescent audience. Curtis was not singing about a bitter-sweet romance in any traditional sense, nor is he singing the praises of love as an emotion. Instead, Curtis is posing the more existential question of whether human beings can maintain a romantic relationship within a cold and alienating world, one full of both emotional and social pain. The music of Joy Division itself paints a tonal picture of that world.

In contrast, the Post-Punk band Human League sang "Don't You Want Me" about a failed relationship in more standard terms, reflected in the production and music. The song offers a split commentary on the relationship, with the male and female singers taking turns to offer their narrative perspective, but without the emotional complexity of Joy Division or the modernist production values of Gang of Four. However, the song is significant for a discussion of narratives of Post-Punk romantic love in that the male singer appears remarkably oblivious to his contribution to the relationship's failure, even though the female singer explains it to him in her verses.

Human League—"Don't You Want Me"

Formed in 1977 in Sheffield, Human League had their biggest hit with "Don't You Want Me" released on Virgin records in 1981. On the surface, the synth-heavy pop song appears to be simply about a five-year relationship that has ended unhappily for the male singer (Philip Oakey), as he pleads with the female singer (Susan Ann Sulley), "Don't, don't you want me? You know I can't believe it when I hear that you won't see me . . . You know that I don't believe it when you say you don't need me." Closer attention to the lyrics, however, shows an unhealthy gender dynamic in the song, and the use of both voices to tell the narrative of the relationship and its ending produces a dual perspective on the failed relationship.

Oakey sings that he discovered Sulley when she was a wait-ress and transformed her into a success (as what is unspeci-fied, but the audience assumes as a pop singer). Sulley agrees in part with his version of their relationship origin story, but claims "But even then I knew I'd find a much better place either with or without you." Sulley states that she still loves him, but needs to live on her own.

So, what then is the problem? He says he loves her. She says she loves him. Is it another case, like their contempo-raries Joy Division, of love tearing them apart? A closer look at the lyrics sung by the male, Oakey, says otherwise: "But don't forget, it's me who put you where you are now, and I can put you back down too . . . You'd better change [your mind] back or we will both be sorry." Thus, this song is not about romantic love in any authentic sense of the word, but about male control being mistaken for love. The use of the female voice to tell part of the narrative, rather than functioning merely as back-up—subordinate—vocals, allow us to see that this is a narrative about problematic gender roles in a romantic relationship, with the man as dominant to the point of controlling and failing to under-stand that this is not love. The woman claims she still loves him, but recognizes that she needs to get away from his kind of emotion. In this way, "Don't You Want Me," despite its frothy synthesizer overlay, is an early critique of the trope of male-love-as-obsession that sometimes underpins intimate partner abuse.

Masculinity and Romantic Love—
The Associates and The Cure

Just as Post-Punk marked a critical awareness of the stereotypical expectations of masculinity, so it also pushed against these gender expectations to the point of their fragmentation. One example of this pushing against gender boundaries is the Associates, formed in 1979 in Dundee, with their biggest selling single, "Party Fears Two" in 1982. Initially written in 1979, the band decided the song was too pretty for a music scene that was the ending of Punk and released it three years later (Tom Doyle, *The Glamour Chase*). The lyrics tend towards the ambiguous, but it's clear that the singer is struggling with anxiety about a relationship.

Is he good enough for the other person?, he asks. He says he feels inadequate and ugly, while we're told that the other person thinks he dresses too well, which appears to be less of a compliment and more of a comment on the singer using clothing to disguise his own social and emotional fears. With hindsight, pop-culture commenters have suggested that the fear is partly about the singer's own sexuality: homosexuality could not be equated with stereotypical masculinity.

However, the era of Post-Punk did leave openings in its songs for same-sex love that were, thankfully, not about self-hatred and were simply about good, old-fashioned heartache and misery, but framed for the particular sensibilities of the Post-Punk generation. The Cure's "Boys Don't Cry" was much loved by straight and gay folks alike, allowing for the expression of a fragile masculinity that would not have been able to find a home in the macho posturing of Oi bands or the raucous aggression of Punk music.

Formed in Crawley in 1978, The Cure released "Boys Don't Cry" as their second single in 1979 on Fiction Records. The song was written by all three members of the band—Michael Dempsey, Robert Smith, and Lol Tolhurst—with Smith on vocals. In an interview with the *New Musical Express*, Smith said that "as an English boy at the time, you're encouraged not to show your emotions to any degree. And I couldn't help show my emotions when younger. I never found it awkward showing my emotions." In the same interview from 2019 Smith discusses how at a recent concert he realized how the song still spoke to people of all generations and identities when he saw all the rainbow flags flying in the audience.

Lost Innocence

Post-Punk's world of alienation and isolation for romantic relationships can, almost paradoxically, be brought out by listening to its covers of beloved classic 1960s soul tracks, even though covers are often seen as an artistic kiss of death. (Originally, reports Ray Padget, David Byrne of Talking Heads did not want to release a cover song). Sung by Al Green, "Take Me to the River" is a heated, ambiguous mixture of baptism and teenage desire. Sung by Talking Heads (1978), the tempo was slowed down to the point that the passion and immediacy completely dissolved.

Whereas Marvin Gaye wrenched out every ounce of emotion from his version of "I Heard It through the Grapevine" (1968) by singing slightly higher than his usual range, The Slits sang an emotion-free version that almost mocked the meaning of the original song while also functioning as a message of female empowerment (Island, 1979). Significantly, "Grapevine," was the B-side of their single "Typical Girls," which listed in grim detail all the stereotypes young women lived with, such as being bad drivers, avid consumers of magazines, overly sensitive and emotional, and constantly focused on looking for the typical boy. Importantly, these two songs (and others like the Flying Lizards cover of "Money") were performed *without* their original passion and vocal tensions, a loss of their original "soul" which speaks to the loss of musical innocence in the Post-Punk era.

3
Post-Punk Authenticity and the Public Image

MICHAEL RINGS

> Public image, you got what you wanted
> The public image belongs to me
> It's my entrance, my own creation
> My grand finale, my goodbye.
>
> —Public Image Ltd., "Public Image"

May 15th 1981, New York: John Lydon stands behind a massive video screen on the stage of The Ritz. He is joined by fellow bandmates of Public Image, Ltd. (PiL), guitarist Keith Levene and performer-videographer Jeanette Lee, along with Sam Ulano, a sixty-something jazz drummer they had met in a bar and hired earlier that day.

The band has just paused after the cacophonous opening to their show: a torrent of squalling guitar noise, pounding drums, and Lydon playing their new album, *The Flowers of Romance*, on an onstage turntable. They do all this behind the screen, only their silhouettes visible, as giant images of them are simultaneously projected on the screen. Lydon is taunting a rowdy, disgruntled crowd: "sil-ly fuck-ing audience, sil-ly fuck-ing audience," mocking them for paying the twelve-dollar admission to be subjected to this. The audience is chanting "raise the screen, raise the screen," throwing bottles and becoming increasingly hostile. His response: "We're not going to raise the fucking screen!" (Ed Caraballo, "There's a Riot Goin' On").

In our received version of John Lydon's life story, the intertwined themes of personal identity and authenticity have played a crucial part. The idea of a public self is of course front and center in the name of his seminal Post-Punk band and its eponymous debut single. The song's lyrics evoke the legal struggle Lydon endured (and lost) over the use of the name "Johnny Rotten," to which Sex Pistols manager Malcolm McLaren had claimed exclusive rights (*The Public Image Is Rotten*).

For John Lydon, identity is something always in danger of being lost, co-opted, or corrupted. This can be traced back to his childhood, when a bout with spinal meningitis at age seven led to severe amnesia that left him unable to remember his own parents and even his own identity (it took him four years to restore his memory entirely). In a recent biopic he comments on his persistent life-long anxiety with this loss of self, which led to his abuse of substances like cocaine that kept him from sleep: "the longer I'm awake, the less chance of waking up from a sleep and not knowing who I am" (*The Public Image Is Rotten*).

This anxiety is accompanied by his constantly avowed and demonstrated commitment to the values of honesty and integrity. In interviews he attributed his notoriety to "being honest," to refusing to be a "puppet" or "act out somebody else's pantomime." Film director Julien Temple has remarked that you only had to spend a half-hour with Lydon to discover that "he wasn't inventive—his personal history and his life was all that he was about."

On the other hand, there is the side of Lydon's public persona that is overtly theatrical and constructed: "I can tell you I was a piece of work, I *worked* on being Johnny Rotten!" (*The Public Image Is Rotten*). This adamant assertion of control over his own public persona is there in the closing lyrics of "Public Image"—it's his "own creation," as well as (and more enigmatically) his "grand finale" and "goodbye."

Even though his struggles with identity are personal and idiosyncratic, Lydon nevertheless occupies a central place in Post-Punk's historical narrative. The ways in which Lydon, PiL, and other Post-Punk artists grapple with the paradoxes of expressing an "authentic" identity through popular art demonstrate a very complex and fraught relationship with this fragile ideal.

What Is Post-Punk Authenticity, Anyway?

Authenticity is a controversial concept in both philosophy and popular music. In philosophy, personal authenticity has long been regarded as an ideal that is highly prized but also elusive, chimerical, even downright paradoxical. It has been formulated in many ways, but usually involves the notion of being true to yourself. Somogy Varga offers a sketch of the authentic individual as "a person who acts in a way that we think of as faithful to herself and her principles," one who "acts on impulses and ideals that are not only hers (insofar as they bear her authorship), but that are also expressions of who she really is" (*Authenticity as an Ethical Ideal*, p. 2).

In the context of Punk, authenticity is traditionally associated with a set of related values and ideals, including unvarnished self-expression, originality, individuality, and staunch artistic integrity. However, as we move from the strident politics and shock tactics of first-wave Punk to Post-Punk's more experimental and politically oblique artistic strategies, the relationship that many artists seem to have with authenticity becomes more complex.

Markus Kohl argues that Post-Punk sees a shift from the "outward" model of authenticity manifested in punk's fairly straightforward agit-prop to a more "inward" model. This inward form of authenticity—which he argues is motivated in part by skepticism regarding Punk's political commitments, as well as disillusionment with how easily they can be commercially co-opted—is characterized by a "detached stance of experimental individualism" reminiscent of that found in existentialist philosophers like Nietzsche and Kierkegaard. This new stance is exhibited outwardly by a shift "away from the crude, stifling three chord guitar rock-punk ethos towards more experimental forms of musical self-expression" ("The Post-Punk Struggle," p. 94).

Kohl's inward model of authenticity is not unlike the ideal of the *strong poet*, a concept that philosopher Richard Rorty borrows from Harold Bloom's notion of the poet who manages to step outside the shadow of her influences and forge a unique and original voice of her own, creating art that "uses words as they have never before been used" (*Contingency, Irony, and Solidarity*, p. 28). In Rorty's conception, the strong poet is a heroically autonomous individual who artistically expresses a character that is utterly novel and unprecedented.

While this may be an ultimately unattainable ideal (no artist works in a vacuum, entirely free from all outside influences) it is certainly one that many artists strive to achieve. It's an aspiration reflected in the work of the most fiercely original and radically *new* sounding Post-Punk bands: Pere Ubu, The Pop Group, Devo, Mars, DNA, Talking Heads, Throbbing Gristle, and (in their early days, at least) PiL.

Pere Ubu lead singer Dave Thomas, for example, worked under self-imposed rules in order to remove all trace of the blues from his voice—"I would refuse to bend a note or extend a syllable past one beat"—and ended up crafting a singular vocal style (*Rip It Up and Start Again*, p. 33). We can credit Lydon with a similar achievement, as he forged a distinctive voice throughout his career, evolving from his hectoring snarl in the Pistols to the otherworldly "muezzin wail" heard in his work with PiL (p. 281). PiL's Keith Levene pledged that he was "not going to play anything that's ever been played before" when crafting the alien post-rock sounds of *Metal Box* and *Flowers of Romance* (p. 275). The world of Post-Punk is full of artists who approach their instruments—or even *non*-instruments employed as instruments—in completely new ways, in some cases reshaping the whole vocabulary of rock music.

So, Kohl's inward model of authenticity seems to have some legs—but is this all there is to the story? First, Post-Punk's multifaceted and heterogeneous nature must be acknowledged. It is perhaps best understood as an umbrella term that encompasses a set of diverse genres that bloomed in certain UK and US musical scenes in the wake of Punk's first wave: punk-funk, goth, No Wave, industrial, 2-Tone ska, synth pop, mutant disco, and so on. Therefore, any broad generalizations that treat Post-Punk as a unified category are unlikely to withstand close scrutiny.

Second, even if we put this concern aside, Kohl's authenticity model also ends up making Post-Punk seem a lot less radical in relation to what came before it: as an ideal, his version of authenticity sounds remarkably close to a traditional romanticized ethos of rock music, an "aesthetic ideal that elevates the artist's originality, emotion, spontaneity, and invention as the measure of aesthetic success" (*Rhythm and Noise*, p. 175). This is the romantic ideal that lionizes the "dinosaurs" that most Punks and Post-Punks were trying to knock over: Led Zeppelin, Pink Floyd, Jimi Hendrix, Janice Joplin, Bruce Springsteen, and others. All these canonical names have long been praised in the terms of the strong poet—as trailblazing artists who transcended their influences and crafted new sounds in their own inimitable voices. Should Post-Punk be understood as merely a continuation of that same well-worn tradition?

Post-Punk versus Authenticity

For all the staunchly individualist musical experimentation we find in Post-Punk, we also find artists more intent on critiquing or deflating the myth of the "authentic individual" than worshipping it. Indeed, some are even avowedly anti-individualistic. London Music Collective (or LMC), for example, was a loose, open-ended group of musicians that blended free improvisational music with an anarchistic punk sensibility and emphasized collective music-making over the expression of specific individuals (*Rip It Up and Start Again*, pp. 207–08).

Other groups, like Gang of Four and The Mekons, endorsed a similarly collective and democratized approach to music-making, though with a more overtly political and anti-individualistic stance. Gang of Four's Dave Allen once declared that his band "doesn't believe in the individual," and their deliberately "democratic" music was designed so that all instruments (guitar-drums-bass) were balanced in an egalitarian fashion (p. 114). Similarly, The Mekons took an approach to music-making that avoided singling out any individual, stressing that "anybody could do it [make music] . . . we were nobody special" (p. 114). They took this as far as insisting on no photographs or surnames of the band being published with a *New Musical Express* interview, declaring "we don't want to push ourselves as INDIVIDUAL PERSONALITIES!" (p. 115).

Here then were Post-Punk artists who did not see their music in terms of on individualistic self-expression, and who even went so far as to *reject* the ideal of personal authenticity as something politically suspect. As Simon Reynolds argues, bands like Gang of Four and Scritti Politti "abandoned tell-it-like-it-is denunciation for songs that exposed and dramatized . . . the ways in which seemingly spontaneous, innermost feelings are actually scripted by larger forces" (*Rip It Up and Start Again*, p. xxiii). We can see this demonstrated in Gang of Four's track "Love Like Anthrax," in which front man Jon King sings an acerbic lyric about love in one ear, while in the other guitarist Andy Gill flatly delivers a monologue documenting the technical details of the song's recording process. The effect of this on the listener is disorienting and distancing, undercutting the conventional idea of the rock song as a personal expression communicated directly from artist to listener.

Reynolds likens the band's strategy here to the "alienation effects" employed by Bertolt Brecht in his highly political anti-naturalistic theater, and to similar devices in the cinema of Jean-Luc Godard, in which disruptive effects (e.g., disjointed editing, lapses in continuity, mismatched image and sound) make viewers hyper-aware of the film's artificial nature (p. 117). Scritti Politti deploys a similar tactic in the sleeve-art of their first single, "Skank Bloc Bologna," which features an itemized run-down of the recording, mastering, and pressing costs of the record. These artistic strategies are designed to destabilize and "wake up" the bewitched audience member, and in the process "offer a glimpse of the deep structures that organize our lives" (p. 117).

The romanticist notion of the artist as a free, autonomous individual who transcends society's strictures by expressing her innermost thoughts and feelings is replaced in these artists by a more skeptical (and perhaps cynical) viewpoint that sees the individual as a non-autonomous agent embedded within power structures that have shaped her thoughts and feelings, even if she is not conscious of it.

Implicit here is a critique of authenticity that is similar to that presented by Theodor Adorno, who sees authenticity's idea of "turning inward" and granting full authority to the "true self" as both theoretically ungrounded and politically suspect (*The Jargon of Authenticity*). Adorno argues that authenticity's "liturgy of inwardness" is founded on a flawed idea of the self-transparent individual who is capable of "choosing herself" (Varga, *Authenticity*, p. 26).

According to Adorno, the ideal of authenticity is not an antidote to the negative social impacts of capitalism, but is instead merely their "other. In other words, the attempt to retreat into an "authentic inner self," which is always already embedded in and conditioned by sociopolitical structures, cannot serve as a way to oppose those power structures because that "self" is already a part of them (pp. 26–27). If Adorno's critique is on point, then the inward model of authenticity is just as vulnerable to capitalist co-optation as the more overtly political outward model that Kohl finds at work in first-wave Punk.

Returning to Lydon and PiL, we can find several satirical artistic and marketing strategies throughout their career that parody and critique the corporate nature of commercial pop music and the idea of the "authentic" artist working within that structure. This starts with the very identity of the band itself. The "Ltd." in the name Public Image, Ltd. was added when the band was incorporated as a company in 1978, and Lydon and Levene repeatedly insisted in interviews they were a not a *band*, but a "communications company" that produced various kinds of media (video, graphics, and others) in addition to music. When asked by Tom Snyder in a contentious 1980 interview if PiL were a band, Lydon replied: "We ain't no band, we're a company. Simple. Nothing to do with rock'n'roll. Doo Da" (*Tomorrow Show* 1980).

As a satirical acknowledgment and embrace of the commerce side of rock music, foregrounding it rather than disavowing it or covering it up, the band's posture is also a rejection of the romanticized authenticity ideal that Theodore Gracyk and others see at work in rock music. Gracyk observes the long-running tradition of rock artists being marketed as "authentic" Dionysian individuals in calculated and often spurious ways (for instance, the middle-class members of the Rolling Stones presented as street-tough bad boys, the Sex Pistols literally created by manager Malcolm McLaren according to the gritty "Punk" template). "Once Romantic stereotypes are part of their marketing strategies," Gracyk states, "the line between the real and the artificial is hopelessly muddled" (*Rhythm and Noise*, p. 183). PiL, seemingly motivated by a similar realization, dropped the pretense of producing authentic art-versus-commerce, and instead openly embraced the idea of art-*as*-commerce.

This playfully provocative stance is especially prevalent in PiL's Eighties albums. Their 1984 follow-up to *Flowers of Romance* had the working title of *You Are Now Entering a Commercial Zone*, self-consciously reflecting their music's turn in a markedly more accessible, radio-friendly direction. Lead single "This Is Not a Love Song" (which garnered the band its highest chart ranking to date) was written by Lydon in response to the label's requests for a "hit," and openly expresses its author's ambivalent relationship to commercial pop. Lydon commented on the song:

> At the time people were saying that I'd joined big business and become a bourgeois shit. So I thought the best way of tackling this would be to pump out a song saying 'That's exactly what I am!' Tongue firmly in cheek. And that kind of stopped that nonsense—so it worked. (Neil Spencer, "Public Image Limited." *Volume Three*).

A similarly satirical approach is taken with 1986's *Album*, which was packaged in a manner inspired by the cheap generic brand products sold in supermarkets. PiL even extended this conceit to other material related to the album—the first single "Rise" was titled "Single," and its video started with a title card "Video."

The band's intent here is clearly critical of the record industry and its reduction of art to mere "product," scrubbed of all identity and individuality. This genericization extends to the album's personnel: Lydon's backing band was composed largely of professional studio musicians and hired guns, some of whom (such as guitarist Steve Vai and drummer Ginger Baker) hailed from far outside the Punk underground.

You could argue that this turn to more professional music-making was not so much the artists' intentional commentary on generic rock, but instead a sign that they were "selling out." This ambiguity led to much criticism of Lydon and PiL at the time, especially in Punk circles, even as the band enjoyed some of the biggest commercial success of its career.

The Ritz Riot Show, Revisited

Bearing all this in mind, let's return to the notorious 1981 Ritz show. PiL had been booked at the last minute as a fill-in for a cancelled show by Bow Wow Wow (a band managed by Lydon's old nemesis Malcolm McLaren), and tickets immediately sold out (*The Public Image Is Rotten*). The show was promoted by the Ritz as "Johnny Rotten's PiL," and fans came expecting to see their Punk hero deliver a straightforward rock show (Jack Whatley, "Riot at the Ritz"). The band had something else entirely in mind, though. Conceived mainly by Levene and video technician Ed Caraballo, the show was to be a kind of performance art event that took full advantage of the Ritz's high tech video projection capabilities and massive forty-foot-wide movie screen ("There's a Riot Goin' On").

The idea was for the band to remain behind the screen for the whole show, as Lydon describes it, "pantomiming, playing along with the record, creating images" (*The Public Image Is Rotten*). In Caraballo's words, "The concept of the show was that it was like a mask. PiL would have this show playing behind the video and you could never actually get to see them live" ("There's a Riot Goin' On"). In presenting the idea to the Ritz's promoters, Levene declared, "Rock'n'roll is fucking dead. We're not a band, we're a company. We're here to do performance art. This is going to be a show" ("Riot at the Ritz").

By the time the show started, the audience was already rowdy and disgruntled, having been made to wait outside in the rain until 1:00 A.M. They were initially receptive to the sight of Lydon's and Levene's silhouettes behind the illuminated screen, as Ulano laid down a tribal beat to Levene's harsh guitar noise, and Lydon just put on the *Flowers of Romance* record and stood there. The crowd became less hospitable as it became clear the screen was not going to be raised, and Lydon began taunting and baiting them, asking them if they thought they were getting their money's worth. Giant images of Lydon, Levene, and other band members were projected on the screen as they continued to make their amorphous racket behind it. The audience became more furious and hostile, throwing bottles and chairs at the screen, and even trying to pull it down, along with a white tarp that covered the stage's floor. Things quickly came to a head as police arrived to quell the riot and evacuate the venue. The show was over.

Though Lydon certainly saw it as disastrous in the moment—it led him to promptly fire the rest of the band—he has remarked years later that it was "probably one of the best gigs I've ever done" (*The Public Image Is Rotten*). As haphazard, chaotic, and under-planned as the whole thing was, the event obviously resonated deeply with Lydon, and at least some of those in the audience; among them was Sonic Youth's Thurston Moore, who has also claimed it was one of the greatest shows he had ever seen (*The Public Image Is Rotten*).

Though it's unclear that it was deliberately conceived as such, this event could be analyzed as a performance art piece that deconstructs or challenges the ideal of the authentic rock artist who expresses and presents their "real" unique personality to their audience through their art. The screen between PiL and their audience could function, on the one hand, as a stand-in for the various media platforms on which the artist's public image is projected, and on the other as a *barrier* that stands between artist and audience, hiding the "real" artist behind it. In refusing to raise the curtain to reveal themselves, Lydon and co. highlight this obscuring nature of the artist's publicly presented, artistically mediated self. We could read Lydon's inciting the audience to tear the screen down as a provocation to reject and destroy these inauthentic modes of public presentation, to get to the "real" people behind the façade.

This reading would fit in with Kohl's account of the Post-Punk authentic, corresponding with the idea that Post-Punk's artistic innovations are meant to tear down the accumulated conventions, clichés, and banalities of rock and pop, and to reveal the authentic individuals obscured behind them. However, there's some ambiguity here: what if, after the listeners are invited to tear down the artist's projected "self," they discover there's *nothing* behind the screen at all? What if tearing down the screen is not so much an invitation to uncover the artist's "real self" as it is a tearing down of the *whole idea* of such a self? Perhaps the screen is what French theorist Jean Baudrillard called a "pure *simulacrum*": a simulation of reality that "bears no relation to any reality whatever" (*Simulacra and Simulation*, p. 170). Baudrillard's idea is that such a simulation (which, in his view, comes to take the place of "reality" in a postmodern society) is not so much a *mis*representation or masking of some underlying reality, but a pure fabrication that has no connection to any such reality.

Applying this to our central topic, if the authentic self is a simulacrum, then the screen is *all there is* to the self—it is merely a socially constructed fiction, all the way down, with no basis in some fundamental reality. This interpretation would connect PiL's position to a long-running thread in philosophy that is deeply skeptical of the idea that we each possess a real cohesive and persistent "self." This critique runs from David

Hume's theory of the self as a loose "bundle" of ever-shifting conscious states, through Nietzsche's view that the only "self" that could exist is the one we create for ourselves, to Nietzsche-influenced post-structuralist philosophers, like Michel Foucault, who deconstructed the whole idea of the "self" or "subject," declaring it a "mythology" (*Authenticity as an Ethical Ideal*, p. 27).

So, which interpretation of the Ritz show should we favor? It's unclear. There seems to be a real tension in the work of PiL and other Post-Punk artists, between what Greil Marcus has characterized as *negationist* and *nihilist* tendencies (*Lipstick Traces*, pp. 1–24). The *negationist*, according to Marcus, is one who challenges, rejects, or tears down our received conventional notions of the world in order to construct a new and better society in their place. Applied to the idea of the self, the negationist position would be that we should challenge or reject our traditional received notions or models of the "self" in order to get at a *more real* and meaningful notion of what it means to be an authentic individual.

On the other hand, *nihilism* is, in Marcus's words, "the belief in nothing and the wish to become nothing; oblivion is its ruling passion" (p. 9). The nihilist tears down but does not rebuild on the cleared ground; the destructive act is the final point, not the prelude to reconstruction. Regarding the self, the nihilist would strive to tear down the artificial masks and false social pretensions that masquerade as the "true self," but proposes nothing in place of those falsities—the cleared ground remains cleared, and the vacuum left behind after the self is demolished remains just that, a vacuum.

When considering these contrasting perspectives as artistic strategies, however, it can be difficult to differentiate them. As Marcus observes, the tools the negationist uses—"real or symbolic violence, blasphemy, dissipation, contempt, ridiculousness—change hands with those of the nihilist." The anarchic transgressions and artistic pranks found throughout Lydon's and PiL's work all seem to serve equally well as tools of both negationism *and* nihilism, leading to the complex and ambiguous relationship the band maintains with the ideas of authenticity and identity.

The Man Behind the Screen

Whether we should take artists' intentions or biographies into consideration when interpreting artworks (and if so, how we should do it) is a point of long-running controversy in the philosophy of art. However, it is tempting to consider the significance of the Ritz show in light of Lydon's biography and his life-long grappling with questions of personal identity and authenticity. Considering how he first wrestled with the loss of his identity due to childhood amnesia, then recovered it arduously over several years, only to lose ownership of it again in his fight with McLaren over the "Johnny Rotten" stage name, it is tempting to interpret Lydon's refusal to raise the curtain at the Ritz as a protective move, a refusal to relinquish control over his true self, or to surrender to the public's consumption of it.

Taking such a position may imply that the best way for an artist to retain her authentic identity is to *refrain entirely* from sharing it via an act of soul-baring free expression, which would open it up to the various forces of market co-optation and manipulation that will inevitably compromise and distort it. Refusing to raise the curtain, to opt out of the showbiz games of rock'n'roll and pop culture at large, is perhaps the only way to stay authentic, in the end.

Lydon was and remains a very public and outspoken figure, both prior to the Ritz show and long after it, so this raises the question of just how dedicated he ever was, or is, to such self-protective strategies. At the very least, his work and persona reflect a deep distrust and ambivalence toward the whole enterprise of trying to make art and stay authentic in a commercial sphere, a fraught relationship with rock culture that is not exclusive to Lydon but resonates across the world of Post-Punk, and beyond.

What Post-Punk artists like Lydon did (and continue to do), is interrogate and challenge, in a particularly pointed way, the mechanisms of personal mythmaking that drive the construction and consumption of artists' images in popular music and other media. This is just one aspect of Post-Punk's rich legacy, and one that remains both relevant and vexing for musical artists working today.

4

We're Through Being Cool!

MITCH HANEY

In 1981, Devo called to young people, whether they lived in a "small town" or a "big place," that conformity wasn't necessary. The Spudboys called to the misfits, the "aliens," and those of the "many factions underground" that they "dare to declare . . . we're through being cool!"

For those of us at that time who found the predominant socio-cultural norms hard to meet, or repugnant, or who were simply rejected by those who embraced them, this proclamation of a new nonconformity felt revolutionary.

The theme of welcoming and celebrating nonconformity or simply rejecting the prevailing norms was not unique to Devo. It was an attitude shared between Punk and Post-Punk overall. It had even been shared with the history of rock'n'roll generally, but much of popular rock'n'roll had itself evolved into a matter of being mainstream and conformist with its own successful commercialization over the 1960s and 1970s.

Part of what made Punk and Post-Punk "edgy" was precisely its intentional breaking the norms that had settled into rock'n'roll as a popular form of music—its dominance, conformism and commercialization that pervaded much of youth and young adult culture. Punks and Post-Punks both prescribed a posture of rejoicing in nonconformity that would allow people to be different from "everyone else." The message to listeners was that if they felt rejected, odd, or out-of-step with mainstream society that this was not something to bemoan, rather it was something to celebrate and cultivate. (Although sometimes it even celebrated the bemoaning—think of Goth Punk.)

Punk and Post-Punk may be distinguished sonically and along some artistic, visual dimensions, but they really cannot be clearly distinguished all that much, chronologically or thematically. Both the sounds and visuals of these movements were enmeshed with each other in the late 1970s to early 1980s. They both felt a disdain with a certain status quo in Euro-American culture, and they both desired to make a culture outside the mainstream and under their own control. The theme of celebrating nonconformity or anarchy or individuality, however you may want to name it, runs deeply through the scenes of punk and Post-Punk. However, the scenes nicely expose, sometimes reflectively and sometimes performatively, that in order to be a nonconformist or be an individual over and against prevailing social norms, you still need a community. You need a "faction underground" or "a dozen or two alien types to step up and say . . . "We're through being cool!"

Punk and Post-Punk both reflectively and performatively through the music and practices of the scene demonstrate that the achievement of individuality is intimately intertwined with community. The idea that we are each atoms that are self-contained and that we're not positively in need of others to "be ourselves" is not the experience of the scene. The message may have often seemed to be one that we need nothing more than non-interference from others, but the situation, as the very milieu demonstrated, was more complex than that.

The Do-it-Yourself (DIY) culture that was intimately part of punk and Post-Punk hides the fact that DIY is a community-based phenomenon where individuals flourish, as unique individuals, due to the aid of and camaraderie with like-minded others. And the DIY ethic that was central to Punk and Post-Punk and intersects with the social achievement of individuality generally, reveals that the scene was the embodiment of (sometimes reflectively, but definitely practically) of what many refer to as anarchism—a theme that was often embraced but may not have been fully understood by the kids themselves.

I'm Not the Same as When I Began

An often-told story in early days of reflection on the period was that the baptismal moment separating Post-Punk (New Musick or Art Punk) from Punk was the coming together of John Lydon (Johnny Rotten), Keith Levene, Jah Wobble, and Jim Walker to form Public Image Ltd after the US tour that utterly decimated the Sex Pistols. Such a story leads to many a debate among aficionados of the music, art, culture, and politics of the scene about whether or not Public Image Ltd was the first Post-Punk band, or attending debates about what makes a band, song, look "Post-Punk" rather than "Punk." These debates can be illuminating about what we mean when we deploy these concepts and interpret what the scene meant.

The fact that John Lydon and company wanted to express themselves with some more musical breadth and expertise, to be able to be free to produce their own creations out from under the management of others, and to experiment with sounds and ideas beyond what had been crystallizing as Punk "canon" has itself congealed as a set of features regularly associated with Post-Punk. And, it appeared that since the very Johnny Rotten himself was resisting being pigeon-holed into a sound and look that he helped create, this was a sensible place to mark a transition from Punk to Post-Punk. Even in Public Image Ltd there were still sonic, lyrical, and attitudinal similarities which generated the sounds, styles, and aesthetic overlap with Punk. This remained true for much of what qualifies as Post-Punk in the late 1970s and into the 1980s.

Post-Punk shared with Punk a disdain for the status quo, and each scene sought to reflect a youth culture that wanted to express itself on its own terms rather than what was acceptable to others in the wider cultural, commercialized milieu. Thus, Post-Punk continued the DIY ethic of punk rock, and they took seriously the idea that as individuals that they could pick up instruments, find their sound, find their message, and create. What Post-Punks seem to add was that this did not have to be even constrained by what was becoming labelled as acceptably "Punk."

In Public Image Ltd's song "Public Image," some saw John Lydon declaring that he was striking out on his own from the manicured image of Johnny Rotten that Malcolm McClaren had clipped, filed and shaped in order to create a specific Punk profile. As Lydon sang,

> You never listened to a word that I said
> You only seen me from the clothes that I wear
> Or did the interest go so much deeper
> It must have been to the color of my hair . . .
> Public Image . . .
> Two sides to every story
> Somebody had to stop me
> I am not the same as when I began
> I will not be treated as property
> Public Image . . . (Public Image Ltd, 1978)

The declaration in a song that stepped beyond the three-chord format of canon Punk, on an LP which explored other musical styles still fused with a Punk energy many see the passage through which Punk traveled into Post-Punk. However, about this claim, I want to make a little trouble—although others such as David Wilkinson and Alex Ogg have already prepared the ground.

New Musick, Art Punk, or (as it was finally named) Post-Punk has been discussed as a musical, artistic, political, and overall sub-cultural (even sub-sub-cultural) movement with the apparent following features: Rooted in the Punk affinities for sounds that agitate the commercial rock'n'roll norm and embrace a DIY ethic, Post-Punk sought to explore possibilities beyond the three-chord garage sound, black leather jacket, Kool-Aid colored hair, and the ransom note style show flyers and fanzines that were coming to define Punk. They experimented with mixing world music, electronica, folk, Dadaist, Futurist, and other artistic imagery, into the Punk energy while continuing to resist yielding control to commercial entities.

Here's the trouble. If these are the characteristic features of Post-Punk, then there was nothing "post" about it, and there is no way that the formation of Public Image Ltd is the baptismal moment. (This is not to say that Public Image Ltd wasn't an amazing band and their formation, as well as message, wasn't a meaningful event in its discernment from Punk.)

The "Post" of "Post-Punk" is certainly not a chronological designation, if it is the features noted above that make a band, song, or style, Post-Punk. Even if the fact that Johnny Rotten, a seminal figure of Punk, transitioned back to his birth name, "John Lydon," and expanded his sound and look with Public Image Ltd was momentous, he was not the first punk to embrace a wider aesthetic and sound. The Clash had already incorporated reggae and ska. Siouxsie and the Banshees, The Slits, Pere Ubu, Talking Heads, Devo, and Joy Division had already been mixing Punk sensibilities with a greater range of artistic and philosophical expressions, as well as mixing of other musical influences alongside some of the themes that emerged from garage or pub rock, as well as a showing a desire to demonstrate greater instrumental virtuosity. As such, Post-Punk was not really post at all. It had been emerging alongside Punk Rock all along. Siouxsie and the Banshees and Joy Division were playing alongside the Clash and the Sex Pistols in the UK. Devo, Blondie, and The Talking Heads were playing alongside the Dead Boys and Ramones in New York City.

It may be that the "post" of "Post-Punk" was a rejection of something that was becoming understood to be fundamentally or essentially Punk. If the concept Punk must remain confined to the three-chord guitar, high speed tempo, and aggressive lyrics, along with the torn jeans, self-adorned T-shirts, and leather jackets, piercings, and certain DIY haircuts, then maybe Post-Punk is a rejection of Punk in that sense.

However, in the crucial period from the mid-1970s to, especially, 1980 or so, those bands that had been experimenting beyond that narrower formula were generally embraced by many in Punk circles for the fact that they were still rejecting conformity, a general resistance to commercialization, styles and lyrical content that still hit a raw and honest youth point of view of the period (even though it may have often contained less vulgarity or what was vulgar tended to wax poetic—for instance the contrast in speaking of violence between The Talking Heads' "Psycho Killer" and the Ramones' "Beat on the Brat.") Thus, it is not clear that whether Punk was rejecting artistic virtue or Post-Punk was rejecting such a rejection, but at the time they were all in the mix and these are categories that we have imposed back on the time to track some subtle distinctions in sounds and artistic choices. These categories may be useful for certain aesthetic purposes, but whether or not they are making clear historical claims about bands and times and places, about who was in or who was out, this might put too much pressure on the concepts.

What we do see in John Lydon, but also Siouxsie Sioux, Mark Mothersbaugh, Debbie Harry, and numerous others in the scene were individuals who first and foremost wanted to be themselves or create themselves, and they did so within a community of fellow bandmembers and fans, within a DIY community, that both supported and challenged each other in their own evolutions. There was a strong form of individualism that wove its way through the Punk and Post-Punk scene, but it was not a simple individualism.

It was not the formula that each person does as they desire and others should simply not interfere. It was not a simple libertarianism. Instead, being and becoming an individual deeply relied on having a community of persons who voluntarily aided one's projects to express oneself (even as those expressions transformed—whether they be sonically or philosophically). I don't want to suggest that this was only true for those whose names have gone on famously or infamously in the history of the scene. A well-supported individualism occurs in community supportive of individuals being and expressing themselves not just in terms of morale but often a community that would regularly provide material, logistic, creative, and other resources as well. This was an attractive element about the scene. This was especially true for those who felt unacknowledged and unsupported by the wider culture and other communities of which they were or had been a part—family, schools, and other organizations.

In the Punk/Post-Punk scene, and maybe this was what was so symbolically significant in John Lydon's shedding of Johnny Rotten, was an acknowledgement that he would not be constrained even by the expectations of the emerging norms of Punk, and that his goal of individuality needed community recognition and support (*Rip It Up and Start Again*, pp. 45–47). He announces that the self does not happen in a vacuum. As the anarchist theorist Murray Bookchin so nicely puts it, "The making of a human being, in short, is a collective process, a process in which both the community and the individual participate" (*The Modern Crisis*, p. 31).

Bookchin argues for this on the basis that we are inherently social creatures. That we are vulnerable in isolation. By ourselves, he notes, we become "warped." He states,

> the making of that 'whole' we call rounded, creative, and richly variegated human being crucially depends upon community supports for which no amount of self-interest and egotism could substitute. Indeed, without these supports, there would be no real self to distort—only a fragmented, wriggling, frail, and pathological thing that could only be called a "self" for want of another word to describe it. (*The Modern Crisis*)

Bookchin is thinking here of the maturation of individuals across their entire development, and any given person in the Punk or Post-Punk scene has usually shifted communities where they likely found a previous community wanting of sufficient support (but they had previously some modicum of support nonetheless—at least in many cases). However, part of what made the Punk and Post-Punk community so attractive was for those who felt insufficiently supported or excluded by other communities, a community of people who had confronted such exile and embraced individual self-expression as an ideal that was both encouraged and supported from within.

The upshot is that Punk and Post-Punk practiced a form of individualism that very much adhered to a social or relational idea of the self (Gergen, "The Self as Social Construction," pp. 642–47). That for an individual to genuinely create and express themselves and to be free of the bonds of a dominant culture with which they clash or with which they are ill-at-ease, they need to find those other "alien types" or "factions underground" with which to commune and engage in mutual support in order to achieve one's individuality. This sense of individualism was definitely in practice in the scene, but it may or may not have been so much understood in the rhetoric of individuality and anarchy that tended toward atomistic senses of the self that best fit slogans on jackets, buttons, and in some of the short articles of fanzines.

DIY, Anarchism, and Post-Punk

In the heyday of Punk and Post-Punk, the mid-1970s to around 1980, the scene was completely intermixed in the US and UK urban centers and they spread out from there. From the beginning there was always a wing of Punk that willfully challenged the necessitation that Punk be rooted to historic, simpler sounds and a populist street look in order to flip their noses at the commercial rock and commercialized youth culture of the time.

Post-Punk was a wing of Punk that agreed that the status quo of a homogenized, commercial rock'n'roll was awful; agreed that hippie ideology was dead and the emerging yuppie ideology was a sham, and that all this should be announced and contested, but that one could do so with sights and sounds that need not even pay homage to a past to which what was emerging as canonical Punk had tied itself through garage and pub rock. As such, they thought they could do all this with an individual flair that sought musical and artistic experimentation and virtuosity while maintaining a link to Punk's edge.

Like Punks, Post-Punks either did not find themselves represented in the mainstream youth culture or they decided that they wanted to define themselves in ways where they were not told how they should be. Thus, Punk/Post-Punk culture was a place where the margins of youth culture, "burnouts," "nerds," and "freaks," built or discovered communities (even communities within the wider community as the movement extended). At its beginnings, it was a community where David Byrne, Mark Mothersbaugh, Debbie Harry, Joey Ramone, and Stiv Bator could share a stage and venue. Or it was a venue where Sid Vicious, Captain Sensible, Siouxsie Sioux, Viv Albertine, and Mick Jones could all cohabitate and share audiences (*Pretty in Punk*, pp. 32–48). On both sides of the pond there was the shared sense of youth who felt excluded or wanted to rebel against the status quo, and where they could both simultaneously celebrate in as well as revolt against that exclusion.

To what extent it was fully understood or not at the time, the DIY ethic shared by both Punk and Post-Punk kids (categories which I hope we might see becoming more and more difficult to meaningfully distinguish beyond their aesthetic usefulness) and their often-shared symbolism of anarchy is important. Intersecting with the DIY ethic are core ideas of anarchism and a conception of individuality which perhaps emerges from the practices of the community, but which may sometimes have been hidden by its own rhetoric or may not have been as fully appreciated by members of the community at-large.

Much approbation by kids of the scene was that it allowed them to express themselves as individuals. As Ian MacKaye (Minor Threat, Fugazi, and owner of Dischord Records) said in an interview about his introduction to Punk, "What I was hearing from that, what I gleaned from it, was self-definition. They (the bands) were doing something so completely radical. There was a sense that you could celebrate self-definition, you could do whatever you want to do" (*Global Punk*, p. 2).

Kids were attracted to the scene because it allowed them to be themselves without the constraints of such things as proper etiquette or mores that might burnish dirty truths that they wanted to bring to the light. They also wanted to have fun in ways that were more generally frowned upon. There was a deep celebration of individuality in the scene, although it may have lacked the optimism that one had found in the previous era of the hippies. In all this, you might see a simple idea of individualism that the kids sought a mere freedom from restraint. And many of the kids may have seen it that way too. They wanted the liberty of simply being left alone to express themselves as they saw fit, to be themselves, and to create themselves without interference. Sometimes the meaning of anarchy that moved throughout the scene seemed to be such a base individualism. However, it appears that the practice of the kids illuminated a much more social form of individualism, as was argued earlier, but it also embraced a real sense of political anarchy as well.

If we turn to the DIY ethic, we can see the rudiments of a social anarchism and even how it may intersect with social or relational self that some anarchists have embraced. These views appear completely compatible with the practices we see in the Punk/Post-Punk community. The DIY ethic is the ideal that you may successfully complete some task that you desire, without the aid of a paid expert, outside the confines of a capitalist authoritative regime (*Global Punk*, p. 13). It is especially true when it comes to the fact that it is a task where society has come to generally rely on some division of labor of a paid expert as a necessity. In our arena, musical and artistic expression of popular music had come to rely almost exclusively on a specialized groups of artist and repertoire representatives (A&R), show promoters, commercial recording studios, radio stations, to find artists, record, and market their work for fees.

The DIY ethic embraced by Punk and Post-Punk largely meant that bands and fans in the community itself controlled these operations. It allowed musical artists, writers, show promoters, and others to express themselves directly without the imposition of expectations and standards from "paid professionals" outside their community. It did allow people to rely on each other's specific talents, as a matter of voluntary co-operation, to get things accomplished and to spur creative growth, but it allowed them to be free of being beholden to interests outside their community while doing so.

Crass's embrace of a DIY ethic which fueled the establishment of their anarcho-commune, Dial House, in Epping, UK, through which they supported their efforts, is a good example where this was absolutely explicit. Other bands did cross over to commercial record deals, however, many were initially handled in a very laisser-faire fashion, because the commercial companies hoped that they could capitalize on that DIY ethic which drove the bands' success within the community. Here I think of Devo and Public Image Ltd's early contracts with Warner Bros. and Virgin Records that gave them much room to harness what they had previously achieved through their DIY ethic. However, this appeared to be a relatively short-term feature of the early days of commercial cross-over of Punk and Post-Punk music in the commercial record scene.

DIY communities, so principal to the Punk and Post-Punk scene, were voluntaristic associations of individuals with common interests who worked together either in small collectives or who were individuals who would reach out to compatriots for support, feedback, resource support, etc. in order to engage in the lifestyle and practices that they mutually loved and in which they believed. This was from individuals and small groups running fanzines, recording labels, as well as those organizing shows to the bands themselves. This is how anarchism, as an operative form of political organization, is often described by theoreticians and defenders of the ideology, such as Mikhail Bakunin and Pierre-Jean Proudhon. Iain McKay summarizes Proudhon's anarchism, using a phrase from Martin Buber, "All associated and all free" ("Anarchist: FAQ"). The DIY ethic that permeated the Punk/Post-Punk scene of the mid-1970s into the early 1980s propelled a moment where we can see anarchism in practice.

Anarchists defend the idea that human goal seeking activity may best be achieved by voluntary associations of individuals or voluntary societies that remain communities without hierarchies. Bands and fans formed loose voluntaristic communities and roles emerged out of necessity and talent that had been previously assigned to paid experts in order to fulfill members' artistic and political expressions of their youthful experiences so as not to be captured or massaged by a wider corporate echelon that often wasn't of their generation and had a distinct motive to capitalize on that expression (*Global Punk*, pp. 11–15).

Individuals were exploring with other like-minded persons what they wanted to express without any filters that might be imposed by generational and other cultural ideals that weren't their own. There were no bureaucratic leaders, although some may have tried to become said leaders, the very scene resisted the crowning of any monarchs. Instead, the punk and Post-Punk scene was a loose society of kids that wanted to explore being able to define, experiment, and express themselves, within a community that would both tolerate difference and, when asked, provide each other support, because members wanted to see themselves and their scene thrive (*Pretty in Punk*).

Although it may have been quite conscious that some members of the community were embracing anarchist ideology in a deep way, it was nonetheless true that the DIY ethic with the attendant social individualism which pervaded the practice, really made the Punk and Post-Punk scene of the 1970s to 1980s an excellent example of anarchist political organization made real whether this was reflectively grasped or not.

We can debate its success in how well it provided for all its members, because there were certainly numerous tragedies amid the scene. However, there were also the triumphs, where misfits of the world found community, learned to be creative and productive members, who learned to be themselves as well as to thrive in the world. Rich knowledge, skills, and genuine discovery of a sense of self were found by members who actively engaged in a community of nonconformists, daring to declare that they were "through being cool!"

II

Post-Punk
and the Ghost of
Philosophy

5
Art Will Tear Art Apart
. . . Again

CASEY RENTMEESTER

"I hate the fucking Eagles, man!" Whether or not you agree
with The Dude's assessment of the band in that memorable
scene from *The Big Lebowski*, you can't deny that there's something "off" about the whole genre of soft rock that The Eagles
represent.

Isn't George Carlin spot-on in *Brain Droppings* when he
calls "soft rock" an oxymoron? Take, for example, The Eagles'
song "Life in the Fast Lane," which is a staple of the soft-rock
genre that dominated the mid-1970s. While it is a song about
living excessively—chronicling lives wrought with pills, parties, and lines of cocaine—it's hard not to find the mellow
melody at odds with its edgy content. Where those lyrics *really*
belong is in a harder Punk Rock context like The Stooges' trailblazing *Raw Power* album from the same era along with
"Search and Destroy" and "Gimme Danger."

We can't help but think that vocalist Don Henley is somehow *lying* about living life in the fast lane, even if he'd be
exposed with a sixteen-year-old drug-addled prostitute rendered unconscious in his home a mere four years after the
song's release, an episode that partially inspired his solo
release "Dirty Laundry." In contrast, when Iggy Pop refers to
himself as "a street walking cheetah with a heart full of
napalm" to kick off *Raw Power*, we don't so quickly question
whether that is how he really feels. What are we to make of the
relationship between soft rock's simple, easy-listening, melodic
sound and Punk Rock's hard-edged, fast-paced, in-your-face
style? And how might we frame Post-Punk as somewhere in
between in that they polished the energy of Punk into a much
more harmonious sound as seen, for example, in the band Joy
Division that evokes a level of seriousness and believability

45

while leaving out the abrasive and untamed elements found in Punk?

In the realm of philosophy, the most obvious answer to these questions lies in Hegel. Yes, Hegel—you know, the philosopher nearly universally regarded as brilliant but whose philosophy hardly anyone actually reads due to its sheer difficulty. I primarily work on Heidegger, who once stated that "making itself intelligible is suicide for philosophy" (in his most difficult work, *Contributions to Philosophy*) and tried to live up to this through his obfuscating jargon. In comparison to Hegel, Heidegger is child's play. Indeed, Bertrand Russell rightly called Hegel "the hardest to understand of the great philosophers" (*A History of Western Philosophy*, p. 730). And yet, Hegel's entire philosophy is informed by a certain method called "dialectical reasoning" that helps to explain the progression of ideas, which is precisely the method that can help us understand the relationships between soft rock, Punk Rock, and Post-Punk.

Dialectical Reasoning through the Eagles to Joy Division

Hegel's dialectical reasoning begins with an initial proposition, which we can refer to as the thesis. This is the status quo that gets the process going. For our purposes, the thesis that guides soft rock is the claim that music should be pleasant to the ears. While in terms of personal preference, I'm prone to agree with the Dude's assessment of The Eagles, even I can't deny their talent for harmony. Although soft rock sucks and The Eagles are the perfect embodiment of the movement, The Eagles do *sound* good. We can easily recognize this in their 1972 debut single "Take It Easy," a song with a catchy rhythm that reminds people that even when life doesn't go as planned, it's important to "take it easy" and embrace being "loose, fun, and free" (*To the Limit*, p. 82).

The song may as well be a motto for the soft-rock music movement, as it asks us to go with the flow and enjoy the superficial-yet-pleasant sound. "Take It Easy" comes as a stark contrast to the countercultural hippie music of the 1960s that literally attempted to change the world through the youth movement that prioritized freedom over the corrupt government order that reigned at the time. Rather than worry about all that heaviness, the Eagles intentionally opted for the superficial, easy listening sound that came to iconize them, with an explicit attempt to "appeal to an older, wealthier, less fickle demographic" (*History of Rock and Roll*, p. 223) than the hippies. In doing so, they became one of the best-selling bands in history, which provides a hint as to the musical preferences of the masses.

Despite their massive success, we can't "take it easy" all of the time. Sometimes life is downright brutal; moreover, there are times in which we must have the courage to say so. Thus, from a Hegelian perspective, the thesis of soft rock must be met with the antithesis of Punk Rock, whose essence is "gimme some truth," no matter how much it hurts. For Hegel, art forms like music serve as expressions of human freedom (*Introductory Lectures on Aesthetics*, p. 7), and freedom of expression is one of the most coveted ideals of the Punk scene.

A fitting contrast to the "Take It Easy" narrative of The Eagles can be found in the 1978 single "I Wanna Be Sedated" by The Ramones. Rather than a go-with-the-flow, easy-listening melody, we get a hard-edged, heavy-hitting, stripped down expulsion of truth asserting that life can be so downright overwhelming at times that what we really want is to be sedated to escape from all the chaotic suffering. This dedication to truth and authenticity epitomizes Punk Rock. Indeed, Johnny Ramone explains their approach to Punk as follows: "What we did was take out everything that we didn't like about rock and roll and use the rest, so there would be . . . nothing that would get in the way of the songs" (*Commando*, p. 11).

The Punk Rock scene of The Ramones embodied authentic expressions of emotions through the mode of music, which led to some gut-wrenching songs, even for fans. Johnny Rotten's viscerally charged lyrics "Fuck this and fuck that / Fuck it all and fuck a fucking brat" in "Bodies," for instance, the graphic song about a terminated fetus that kicked off their only album, *Never Mind the Bollocks*, a staple of that genre, is just too abrasive for some people. Punk rock may be authentic, but some emotions are downright unpleasant and thus the music that captures them ends up being unpleasant as well.

The beauty of Post-Punk is that it takes up some of the values of Punk—authenticity, truth, freedom of expression—and integrates them into music that *is* pleasant to the ear. In Hegel's dialectic reasoning, just as a thesis is met with an antithesis, an antithesis is met with a synthesis, which somehow molds together both ideas to form something new. This, in our context, is Post-Punk, which combined the melodic sound of soft rock with the truth and authenticity of Punk. The Post-Punk band *par excellence*, in my opinion, is Joy Division, whose name—true to Punk form—refers to the sex slave wings of the Nazi concentration camps in which the German soldiers exploited young Jewish women.

Joy Division was influenced by the authenticity of the Sex Pistols, as the band was formed after many of the members attended a Sex Pistols concert, but, unlike the Sex Pistols, Joy Division was also determined to make music that was beautiful. Their bassist Peter Hook explains their early roots as follow: "the Sex Pistols . . . is what we aspired to: that volume and attitude. Our first songs were like that, all just punk-copy songs" (*Unknown Pleasures*). However, by the time Joy Division was formed, Punk Rock had run its course.

Even Johnny Rotten was getting sick of the Punk scene: at their last concert at Winterland in San Francisco, he asked the audience, "Ever get the feeling you've been cheated?" (quoted in *Rip It Up and Start Again*, p. 15). He soon abandoned his image of Johnny Rotten and took up his own persona of John Lydon to form the Post-Punk band Public Image Ltd (PiL) as a response. Punk rock became more about chaos and aggression for the sake of chaos and aggression and less about authenticity and truth. It therefore had to die. In line with this, Hegel recognized that all things, in fact, have the "germ of death" built right into them: in true Hegelian style he stated that "the hour of their birth is the hour of their death" (*Science of Logic*, p. 101). Thus, in order to succeed, Joy Division had to stop copying Punk and make their own authentic sound. This is the sound of Post-Punk.

Authentic Living through Nietzsche's Eternal Recurrence

Joy Division's unique sound was formed largely by frontman Ian Curtis, who was heavily influenced by Nietzsche's doctrine of eternal recurrence: the idea that you should live your life as if it were to be repeated over and over for eternity (*Touching from a Distance*, p. 90). For Nietzsche, this was a litmus test to determine if the life you are living is truly the life you want to live. The affirmation of eternal recurrence is "the triumphant Yes to life beyond death and change" (*Twilight of the Idols*, p. 120). For Nietzsche, this meant philosophizing with a hammer and leaving no stone unturned: he boldly criticized religion, cultural values, and even truth itself. For Curtis, this meant a deep commitment to authenticity, especially in the realm of music. In his journal he asks the Nietzschean question, "is this the role you want to live?" (*So This Is Permanence*, p. 87), a question that guided his musical and personal life.

Aligned with Hegel's sense that music is an expression of freedom, Curtis used music as a mode of processing and expressing the issues he was facing personally. A good example of this is "She's Lost Control" from their debut album *Unknown Pleasures*, a song about a woman Curtis knew who had epilepsy, which disrupted her ability to find steady work and ultimately killed her, as she had a fatal seizure in her sleep. Since Curtis also had an epileptic condition, he was deeply disturbed by her fate that he thought might portend his own. Instead of running from that fear, Curtis, in true Nietzschean form, attempted to confront it head-on through song. The result is a fitting phenomenological account of what it means to be dedicated to self-expression but continue to be haunted by the epilepsy that leaves one on the verge of losing control of oneself, noted, for instance, in the lyrics: "she expressed herself in many different ways . . . until she lost control again." We're left with a mix of authenticity and beautifully rendered angst, a combination that Joy Division mastered through the muse of Curtis. In the context of Hegel's dialectical reasoning process, this synthesis of truth and beauty can be understood as the essence of Post-Punk.

If a beautiful confrontation with the truth strikes to the core of Post-Punk, then Joy Division's "Love Will Tear Us Apart" is the paragon of this movement. This harrowing song chronicles the sense of loss and alienation Curtis felt as his marriage was falling apart. Having released *Unknown Pleasures*, Curtis was struggling to maintain his family life while on tour and increasingly suffering from seizures, sometimes on stage. "Love Will Tear Us Apart" is about how "something so good, just can't function no more," as Curtis was recognizing that he and his wife were drifting apart, partially due to the pressures of success. You can hear the pain Curtis is going through in his voice as he belts out the lyrics. This is aligned with the highest form of art for Hegel in which art "has become simply a mode of revealing to consciousness and bringing to utterance . . . the deepest interests of humanity" (*Introductory Lectures on Aesthetics*, p. 9).

"Love Will Tear Us Apart" is an honest confrontation with emotion via the mode of music. This is at a glaring contrast to ungenuine art for Hegel, which is merely there for "killing time in entertaining fashion" (*Introductory Lectures on Aesthetics*, p. 5), which, as it happens, is a fitting characterization of soft rock. The point of soft rock is not to engage in an authentic confrontation with the truth but rather to distract us from that very confrontation. This is why the singer-songwriter Gram Parsons famously dismissed The Eagles' music as "bubblegum" before his untimely death (*Hickory Wind*, p. 175): it lacks soul, just like the entire movement of soft rock. In contrast, "Love Will Tear Us Apart" is anything but bubblegum as it evokes a deep sense of earnestness.

Tragically, this became clear on May 18th 1980, when Ian Curtis took his own life. His wife informs us that Curtis was listening to Iggy Pop's 1977 album, *The Idiot*, before he hung himself, an album named after Fyodor Dostoevsky's novel of the same name about "the positively good and beautiful man" (*Dostoevsky: A Writer in His Time*, p. 577) who suffered from epilepsy and is driven mad by the alienating nature of modern society, a narrative that aptly fits the life of Curtis (*Touching from a Distance*). Curtis asked his wife to drop off divorce papers that day, and the angst and depression that accompanied his failed marriage, as well as his increasingly overwhelming sense of alienation, led to his untimely death. "Love Will Tear Us Apart" was released just one month after his suicide, a torturous reminder that all good things must come to an end. In the case of Curtis, Hegel's "germ of decease" was planted far too soon.

The Legacy of Post-Punk beyond Joy Division

Joy Division simply couldn't go on without Curtis, their primary muse, which is why they changed their name to New Order after his passing and shifted their sound. Joy Division's legacy, though, does not end with their music, as the group proved highly influential to various bands, including The Cure and U2. The Cure carried the torch of Post-Punk into the 1980s, which culminated in their 1989 album *Disintegration*, a Post-Punk masterpiece including their two most famous songs, "Pictures of You" and "Lovesong," both of which are beautiful expressions of emotions—that of loss in the first case and unconditional love in the second.

And U2 crafted their Post-Punk roots to go on to become perhaps the biggest band in the world in the late Eighties with *The Joshua Tree*, an album that proves popular music can be serious. The album starts with back-to-back-to-back songs we've all come to memorize: "Where the Streets Have No Name," "I Still Haven't Found What I'm Looking For," and "With or Without You," all of which express a search for meaning in the modern world and thus uphold the ethos of Post-Punk's engagement with the truth, albeit in a more pop music sort of fashion.

Although Post-Punk's momentum fizzled out by the late 1980s, it left us with the reminder that music is not meant to be something that falls into the background as superficial easy listening but rather should be a confrontation with truth and meaning. Hegel would put the point the following way: if music doesn't acquire "spiritual content and expression," then it fails to be "a genuine art" (*Aesthetics: Lectures on Fine Art, Volume II*, p. 936). Our contemporary music scene is dominated by Top 40 radio in which the goal is to push out catchy songs that sound good but that lack substance in a similar way that soft rock did in the 1970s. Max Horkheimer and Theodor Adorno argued that the "culture industry" of pop music is inherently leveling in that songs sound the same and can be heard anywhere and at any time, leaving them unable to move us in significant ways (*The Dialectic of Enlightenment*). We might consider this to be par for the course in pop music, but this leveling effect has spread to genres beyond pop, as country music has now adopted the same model and transgressed their primal roots of Country and Western. Even Punk became poppy through Green Day in the 1990s. The legacy of Post-Punk is that music should be a combination of truth and beauty if we are to regard it as a genuine art. Although Post-Punk as art eventually tore itself apart, as all art forms do in the Hegelian system, this legacy of truth and beauty remains.

6

The Existential Drama of "Once in a Lifetime"

Scott Gordon

And You May Find Yourself

You have found yourself reading this book. How did you get here? Perhaps a friend recommended it to you. Perhaps you received it as a gift. Or perhaps you chanced upon it on a bookstore shelf. Either way, you have found yourself reading this book, and specifically this chapter (lucky you!) But we are always *somewhere*, doing *something*; it is a basic part of the human condition. And it is with this fact that the narrator of "Once in a Lifetime" begins our journey.

You may find yourself thinking, "Well, duh! Of course, we're always somewhere doing something. There's nothing profound about that." And in a sense, you would be right to think that; it's a rather mundane and even obvious observation. And yet behind it lurk much deeper waters. For if there's any answer that the song "Once in a Lifetime" provides, it's that the things we take for granted in life are uncannier than they may seem.

This is also an essential insight common to many philosophers grouped together under the label "existentialism." For these so-called existentialists, philosophy is about questioning the basic assumptions we make about who we are, what we do, and why we do it. However, there is no agreed upon definition of existentialism, nor is there an official credo; as such, we will primarily be referring to the work of the German philosopher Martin Heidegger (1889–1976), one of the most influential (and difficult to read) exemplars of the existentialist approach to philosophy.

How Did I Get Here?

David Byrne's narrator, with signature evangelical fervor, lists possible places we might find ourselves: living in a shotgun shack, in another part of the world, behind the wheel of a large automobile, or in a beautiful house with a beautiful wife. The key here is that we "find ourselves" in these situations. Most of the time, we're absorbed in whatever activities and projects we happen to be engaged in at the given moment, and we neglect to ask the question of how we've gotten to where we are. Lives are complicated: the factors that contributed, either directly or indirectly, to you, for example, reading this book at this moment are innumerable. And the vast majority of those factors are out of our control, or even outside our awareness. This is part of why we might ask, "How did I get here?"

But there's another element to this question. For along with the question of how and why we find ourselves where we are, we can also ask the question, "Why do I find myself in *this* situation? Why is my life the way that it is, *and not some other way?*" This question touches on what philosophers call "contingency": our lives are contingent in the sense that they depend on certain causes and conditions. If those causes had been different—if we had been born at a different time, if we had different parents, if we had made different choices—then our lives would've been different. But because humans have the power of imagination, we can—and often do—imagine what the world and our lives would be like if certain things were different. Because of this, many of us are tempted to find a special meaning that explains why things are the way they are. For Heidegger and other existentialists, however, there's no special meaning to the way things are; the world is as it is because that's how we happen to find it. If behind the question of "how I got here" lies the question of "Why am I here?" then the existentialist's response is that there is no answer to that question. In the words of a song sung by British soldiers during World War I, "We're here because we're here."

This Is Not My Beautiful House!

The primary refrain of the song's chorus is, of course, "Letting the days go by." For the most part, we let ourselves get carried along by whatever we're doing and whatever situations come up, rarely reflecting on why we do most of the things we do. But in addition to this, we also tend toward social conformity. This not only or even primarily happens when we consciously try to fit in with the people around us; as Heidegger observes, everything from the way we get on a bus, to the way we read the newspaper, to the way we greet each other, are all dictated by social scripts that are not unique to us and that we perform automatically, without any conscious thought. Heidegger's term for this is, in German, *"Das Man,"* which can perhaps best be translated as "the one." We speak *as one speaks*, using clichés and other common turns of phrase; we read books *as one* reads books, sitting down and flipping through the pages; we eat *as one eats*, following whatever rules of etiquette our culture upholds; we even shower *as one showers*, rubbing shampoo in our hair and lathering soap over our body (and some of us may throw some singing into the process).

Even the failure to act in the way one is supposed to act is part of *Das Man*. The failure to, for example, follow proper driving etiquette is not only defined by what the rules are, but is also done in certain typical ways. One is not supposed to cut another person off on the highway, though one often does; one is supposed to use one's turn signal when turning, but one often does not. Even the violation of the rules happens in standard, typical ways. The same goes for failing to *understand* rules and norms, for such lack of understanding is, again, defined and characterized against an understanding of the rules and norms. We may find ourselves puzzling at how to "succeed" at the "game of life," which can lead us to ask questions such as "How do I work this?" But the question itself only makes sense on the basis of there being some way "one" is supposed to "work this."

For the most part, we do not do things in a unique way at all, and insofar as we're absorbed in the mundane activities of our lives, there is a very real sense in which we "forget" ourselves and our individuality. Heidegger refers to this forgetting of ourselves as "fallenness": we "fall into" the day-to-day without thinking about *who we are* and what distinguishes each of us from the rest. Even something that you might identify with as a core part of your identity—such as, say, being a fan of the Talking Heads—is often done in the way *you identify with that thing*. In the case of liking the Talking Heads, you might listen to their music via vinyl, CD, or streaming; you might find yourself watching the *Stop Making Sense* concert on your couch; or you might find yourself putting "Burning Down the House" onto a CD to share with your children, thus fostering a new generation of Talking Heads fans who might, for example, write book chapters such as the one you're reading right now. But for all the uniqueness and eccentricity of the Talking Heads fanbase, these actions are all quite typical of a fan, and it is in their typicality that they show how even choices and behaviors which seem quite unique to us are, nevertheless, part of how "one" does things.

If "Once in a Lifetime" is about anything specifically, it is about a midlife crisis. Arguably one of the main contributing factors to such crises is the realization, seemingly too late, that one has been living a life unreflectively, just doing what they were "supposed to" do. One is "supposed to" get married and have children; one is "supposed to" find a career that brings financial security and at least some social status; one is "supposed to" take out a mortgage and buy a house in which to raise one's children with one's spouse. But for many people, once they have achieved all these things, they find that there is still a hole at the center of their life—something is *lacking*. And for many, they discover that this lack is a lack of, in a very real sense, living one's own life. If someone has spent their whole life doing all the things they were "supposed to" do, then it only makes sense that, once they have done all those things, they find that they had neglected to do the most important thing of all: to be *themselves*, and no one else. Upon realizing this, one may look at the beautiful house and the beautiful wife they have and say, "this is not my beautiful house! This is not my beautiful wife!" And in a certain sense, they may be right. But like anything, that is just the way *one* has a midlife crisis.

Where Does That Highway Go To?

Nearly every moment of the day, you are making choices. The choices could be as mundane as how long to brush your teeth in the morning or which route to take to get to work; but they could just as well be significant choices, such as whom to marry, whether to have children, or whether to move to a new city. Regardless of the magnitude of the choice, however, it's an inescapable fact of life that we're always making choices.

Heidegger emphasizes this aspect of our existence and refers to it as our "always-being-ahead-of-ourselves." We are essentially future-oriented beings; we do things because we plan to achieve some outcome, whether we consciously have it in mind or not. You may habitually make a cup of coffee in the morning without thinking about it at all, yet you do it *in order to* have coffee to drink. And you want to have coffee to drink in order to wake yourself up at the start of the day, which in turn is in order for you to be as productive at work as possible, in order to earn as much as possible, in order to . . . Thus, even something as simple as your morning cup of coffee is part of a much larger web of action that centers around your plans for the future.

But, of course, the future hasn't happened yet. This may seem like another trivial point of little interest to anyone. But if we're essentially future-oriented beings whose lives are characterized by choices aimed at outcomes that have not yet occurred (and indeed might not), then there is a very real sense in which our lives are *open-ended*. Perhaps the most central insight of existentialist philosophy is that the question of "who I am" is not one with a definite answer; with every choice we make, we're engaged in the project of defining who we are, what we're like, and what we care about. The future, then, is not simply all the things that haven't happened yet; it is, rather, the horizon of our identity. And, like the actual horizon, it is always "ahead of" you; just as you can never "arrive at" the horizon, you can never "arrive at" your own identity. The self is a project that we never complete.

But, you might protest, doesn't death complete our lives? If there is any moment in which we "arrive at" ourselves, then surely it is the moment of our death. This may be part of the explanation for the timing of midlife crises: once we have reached middle age, we realize that the time we have left is less than the time we've already lived. And with that thought naturally come reflections on one's own mortality and what our life has amounted to.

Heidegger thought that death was much more than just the end of our lives; for him, death is the one possibility that is utterly unique to us. As we saw, we always engage in activities as "one" does them. But in death, we face the finitude of our own individual existence *as an individual existence*; your death is yours alone, and no one else's. And because of this, reflecting upon our own mortality can lead us to "snap out of" our fallenness and distractedness and remind us of the limited time we have, a time that is ours alone to live. This is why so many people who have near-death experiences undergo profound changes in their life in terms of their personality and priorities. There's nothing that reminds us of life quite like death does.

My God! What Have I Done?

"Snapping out of" our fallenness and becoming aware of our own finite existence is liberating, but it is also deeply frightening. And it's not just because we're thinking about death. Imagine that you find yourself in the midst of a midlife crisis; you have done everything you were supposed to do in life, and now that you've achieved all the conventional markers of success, you're left with a dreadful feeling of lack at the center of your life. You examine this feeling and its causes, and you realize that you have been living as anyone but yourself; you have always followed conventional wisdom, doing all the things that the society around you told you to do, but you never stopped to think about what it means to be *you*. But now that you have passed the halfway point of your life, you begin to realize that this life of yours is all you have; it is the only thing that is, at the deepest level, yours. And because it's yours, you're *responsible* for it; just as no one can die for you, no one can live for you either. This combination of realizations leads you to one final, dreadful realization: *I have neglected the most important thing for my whole life, and now more than half of it is gone.* If that realization doesn't send shivers down your spine, I don't know what will.

Heidegger refers to this state as "guilt": we are "guilty" of neglecting our own existence and forgetting ourselves. We take on numerous responsibilities—as employees, as spouses, as children, as parents, as citizens—all the while forgetting that we only have this one life to live, and without it none of our projects would be possible. In order to be responsible for anything at all, we must be responsible for ourselves, and in a much deeper way than simply being a "responsible adult." By neglecting this responsibility, according to Heidegger, we're choosing to live "inauthentically," thereby losing ourselves in the anonymity of the "one." This guilt only gets stronger as one gets older and closer to death; and yet, at only twenty-eight years old, David Byrne seemed to capture it perfectly when he uttered perhaps the most famous words in "Once in a Lifetime": "My God! What have I done?"

Same as It Ever Was

If you're suffering a midlife crisis, you're not alone; or, more accurately, you're not alone in being alone (wait a minute, that's from a different song). Nor do you need to be in a midlife crisis to appreciate and relate to the lyrics of "Once in a Lifetime." After all, the facts of life that we've examined here—situatedness, choice, distractedness, mortality—are true for all of us by virtue of our being human. What you do with all of this is, like all things in your life, up to you; there is no "right" way to live authentically. You could very well decide, after your midlife (or quarter-life) crisis, that you must start over completely anew and redefine yourself; or you may decide that you're happy with the life you have made for yourself and leave it the same as it ever was. Neither choice is more or less authentic than the other—the measure of authenticity is whether you're making the choice *as yourself*, and no one else.

Philosophy and art are both, taken on their own, uniquely equipped to address these topics; taken together, their powers of expression and revelation are unsurpassable. That's what makes "Once in a Lifetime" such an enduring song, because in truth, it is so much more than just a song: it's a revelation of the most profound kind. It is thus quite fitting that David Byrne sing-speaks as if he were an evangelist. But the revelation he provides is not an answer; rather, it is a chance for us to finally start asking the real questions. Here comes the twister: where will you take it?

7
Post-Punk Under the Shadow of Nihilism

Markus Kohl

Some major figures of early Post-Punk, such as Joy Divison's Ian Curtis or The Fall's Mark E. Smith, were strongly influenced by existentialist themes they encountered in the writings of philosophers such as Camus and Nietzsche.

Part of the unique aesthetic appeal of early Post-Punk stems from the pioneering ways in which the most original artists expressed existentialist ideas through the dark lens of late twentieth-century Western society and culture. A central concern for early Post-Punk is the struggle with *nihilism* in a godless, disenchanted, materialistic world.

Nietzsche's New Dawn

Modern nihilism is a prevalent theme in Nietzsche's philosophy and poetry. For Nietzsche, nihilism is at its core a powerful, negative emotional reaction to humanity in its modern guise, which involves feelings of weariness and disgust. "The sight of the human being now makes us weary—what is nihilism today, if not that? . . . We are weary of the human being" (*On the Genealogy of Morality*, Essay I, 12). Our modern "fatality" is a deep-seated "distaste for the human being" (Essay I, 11).

If these feelings are constantly repeated and reinforced in our everyday reality, they are prone to make a profound, lasting impact on our psychology by undermining any sense of real purpose, depriving us of all genuine ambition, thereby paralyzing our capacity for imagining and wholeheartedly pursuing long-term creative projects. This habitual stance of resignation, consternation, and inaction eventually morphs into a deep-seated indifference or even antipathy towards our life as a future-oriented, goal-directed process. Such indifference is often accompanied by an increasingly addictive wish to seize short-term measures for muting our consciousness of an unbearable reality (such as alcohol or TV-escapism). For stronger natures, it can prompt a will to negate a life one deems hopelessly worthless through suicide.

Nietzsche views this nihilistic condition as a distinctively modern form of decadence and degeneration, as an increasingly widespread "sickliness of the type of human being . . . the physiological struggle of humanity with death (to be more exact: with disgust at life, with exhaustion and with the wish for the 'end' . . . for being otherwise, being elsewhere)" (*Genealogy of Morals*, Essay III, 13).

A further characteristic aspect of the modern nihilistic experience is a deep sense of disorientation and aimlessness. We are especially prone to feel such *horror vacui* (fear of emptiness) if we realize that the dwindling of all sincere religious belief must lead to the collapse of the authority that certain basic moral norms used to possess for human beings due to their presumed divine origin.

While traditional norms and purposes have lost their grip on us, nothing seems left to replace them—hence we lack any clear direction. What we should do with our lives, which ends we should pursue, how we should relate to others and to our socio-political communities—these basic questions increasingly strike us as unsolvable riddles where we can only haphazardly fish for arbitrary answers or follow the course of entrenched but equally arbitrary social conventions. Likewise, with the loss of any sincere belief in an afterlife, we're forced to come to terms with our finitude, the finality of our fast-approaching death.

This evokes a disconcerting impression of personal insignificance: the course of time will wash away any trace of our existence like a mere speck of dust. Nietzsche famously expresses these sentiments in the voice of a "madman" who proclaims that "God is dead" but then anxiously wonders: "Whither are *we* moving? Away from all suns? Are we not plunging continually? Backward, sideward, forward, in all directions? Is there still any up or down? Are we not straying as through an infinite nothing?" (*The Gay Science*).

Contrary to popular misconceptions, Nietzsche merely diagnoses but does not promote modern nihilism. He hopes that some select few humans may see the absence of binding universal norms and the collapse of olden theistic authorities not as a stifling obstacle but rather as a thrilling opportunity for exercising their individual creative powers without constraint in conceiving new values, purposes, and modes of human existence. When Nietzsche and other "free spirits" who retain an inner strength not yet fully consumed by modern degeneration "hear the news that 'the old god is dead'" it is "as if a *new dawn* shone on us; our heart overflows with gratitude, amazement, premonitions, expectation." For those who "feel illuminated by a new dawn," "the horizon appears free . . . at long last our ships may venture out again, venture out to face any danger . . . the sea, our sea, lies open again; perhaps there has never yet been such an 'open sea'."

A New Dawn Fades

Although early Post-Punk is a complex phenomenon, it is fair to say that (generally speaking) Post-Punk leaves behind the shallow political-leftist orientation that was characteristic of early Punk. Many foundational Post-Punk artists turned inward, away from political issues, focusing instead on the existential questions and struggles that shaped their personal life experience (as I explained in my chapter, "The Post-Punk Struggle for Authenticity" in *Punk Rock and Philosophy*).

One crucial aspect of this inward turn in Post-Punk and related genres is that it frequently induces an uncompromisingly pessimistic worldview, a stance of succumbing to nihilism. Far from embracing Nietzsche's cheerful sense of thrill about venturing into the great unknown in complete freedom from religious and moral constraints, Post-Punk artists often experience and express a sense of dread, defeat, and self-disgust, the impression of drifting aimlessly and hopelessly in the sea of (post-)modernity. They write and sing from a profound sense that the modern degeneration diagnosed by Nietzsche has now reached unprecedented lows so that our "disgust at life," our "exhaustion and . . . wish for the 'end' . . . for being otherwise, being elsewhere" has become inescapable.

Let's look at what is arguably the most influential and best Post-Punk band of all time, Joy Division. The real focus here is on lead singer Ian Curtis. He stood out amongst his more simplistic bandmates, who confessed that they never really engaged with or even listened to his song lyrics, as having profound aestheticist and intellectual tendencies. (This is a major theme in many books on Joy Division written by Curtis's contemporaries: see, for instance, bassist Peter Hook's *Unknown Pleasures* and especially Lindsay Reade and Mick Middle's *Torn Apart*.)

The concern with existential problems that is evident in his lyrics was clearly sparked and constantly reinforced by his personal troubles (although part of the lasting appeal of Joy Division is that Curtis could express these issues in ways that transcended his individual situation, that expressed a more universal modern crisis and thus connected with the lived experiences of others). He had married too young and then had a child with his wife whom he did not love and who lacked any appreciation for his more refined tastes and interests (Deborah Curtis vividly if somewhat unwittingly confirms this in her *Touching from A Distance*).

He then fell in love and had a Platonic relationship with another woman who shared his deeper interests and could relate to his problems; but he felt guilty for (as he saw it) betraying his wife and child, to whom he already felt responsible for not "providing" enough in the way of financial security. Furthermore, he suffered from increasingly severe and frequent epileptic fits which made touring and performing on stage especially difficult—this heightened his sense of inadequacy and made him feel guilty for (as he saw it) leaving his band mates in the lurch. Curtis's consciousness was also shaped by the grim realities of 1970s Manchester, by all accounts a cold, alienating, and materialistic post-industrial desert. The suffering of its inhabitants was a further sting for Curtis's sensitive, compassionate nature—he was deeply aware of this suffering, partly because of his job as a social worker for unemployed and disabled people.

It's easy to imagine how this constant battery of unsettling experiences would lead to something like the overwhelming sense of weariness, self-disgust and disorientation that Nietzsche singled out as key aspects of modern nihilism. Curtis repeatedly dealt with this theme in his lyrics. I don't claim with any certainty that these lyrics definitely arose from his conscious engagement with Nietzsche's writings. Although various contemporaries have confirmed that Curtis avidly read Nietzsche alongside figures such as Sartre and Dostoyevsky (*Touching from a Distance*, p. 90), I don't know which texts he engaged with. Nevertheless, some crucial themes in Curtis's lyrics can be illuminated by considering them against a broadly Nietzschean background.

I think it's a reasonable (albeit speculative) conjecture that Curtis was familiar with Nietzsche's "new dawn" metaphor, since the relevant passage alongside the "God is dead" passage from *The Gay Science* is among the most iconic writings of Nietzsche that would have been included in any typical Nietzsche reader or anthology. Specifically, I conjecture that the Joy Division song "New Dawn Fades" (from *Unknown Pleasures*) can be understood as a reaction to Nietzsche's account of nihilism and his invocation of a "new dawn" that shines on strong free spirits as the hopeful harbinger of a post-nihilistic future invested with new, anti-theistic, life-affirming values.

The song begins with a seemingly hopeful intimation of a new beginning, a resolve to discard the past: "A change of speed / A change of style / A change of scene / With no regrets." To be sure, the wary listener is unlikely to take this sense of forward-looking resolve at face value, since it's expressed in a less-than-enthusiastic voice that is caught between a sluggish drumbeat and a faltering, forlorn melody (carried by Peter Hook's characteristically high-pitched bass guitar). Deborah Curtis initially disliked the album and specifically songs like "New Dawn Fades" because they struck her as "morbid dirges" (*Touching from a Distance,* p. 85).

Ian Curtis continues: "A chance to watch, admire the distance / Still occupied, though you forget." This line features several ambiguities, inviting reflection and interpretation from the listener. What exactly is being watched, what distance is being admired? Is it a literally *physical* distance, as when we stand on top of a steep mountain and take pleasure both in the scenic sight from the top and the awareness that we have *mastered* the mountain through a long arduous climb? Or is this rather a *psychological* metaphor for the mental act of surveying how far we have already come in our life journey from the point where we resolved to start anew, deriving satisfaction from the progress we have made and the obstacles we have overcome in our quest for some unspecified goal?

The latter, psychological reading is suggested but also complicated by "Still occupied, though you forget"—words indicating psychological occurrences, but not exactly feelings of gladness or satisfaction. This line instead suggests that the apparent sense of resolve, the seeming conviction that we have effected a proper change of speed, scene, and style *without* regrets involves some degree of insincerity or self-deception. What *seems* to have been left behind still occupies, even as we forget it to some extent and in some level of detail.

Who is the subject of emotion and memory in "Still occupied, though you forget"? "You" might be a second-personal way of addressing an interlocutor of the narrator or lyrical subject, such as the listener; it might refer to the lyrical subject, if that subject narrates a dialogue with itself; or it might be the impersonal "you" (the German *man*).

The song continues: "Different colors, different shades over each mistakes were made"—again a physical metaphor for a psychological process, namely, the process of sugarcoating your past errors and bad choices: either by trying to put a positive spin on them, as in the tiresome commonplaces of current entertainment culture ("Our mistakes help us to grow!", "I wouldn't be where I am right now if I hadn't . . .", even worse, "Everything happens for a reason"); or by pretending that you bear no responsibility since you couldn't help acting as you did and couldn't foresee the bad consequences; or, by spinning some fanciful, self-delusional tale in which the apparent error was really no error at all.

The ultimate futility of all these coping mechanisms is diagnosed when the lyrical subject—now unequivocally revealing itself as the personal narrator—reports: "I took the blame" for the past mistakes overanalyzed through different "colors" and "shades." According to his girlfriend Annik Honoré, Curtis "means it . . . When he says, 'I take the blame,' . . . He does exactly that, he thinks everything is his fault" (*Torn Apart*, p. 245).

This confession makes clear that the previous, seemingly high-spirited declaration of making a new beginning (in current parlance, "reinventing" yourself), of admiring how far you have progressed since your departure from the olden days and ways was a mere charade, a sham. There has been no real progress, no genuine departure, no successful coming to terms with and leaving behind your past: this past still continues to haunt the person struggling to move forward via bad memories, shameful remembrances of bad decisions and their embarrassing, hurtful consequences, reflected in the disappointed looks and accusatory words of your parents, peers, and (former and current) partners.

The crippling, paralyzing effect of memory is a recurrent theme in Nietzsche. Via memory, man "braces himself against the great and ever greater pressure of what is past: it pushes him or bends him down or bends him sideways, it encumbers his steps as a dark, invisible burden"; thus, "forgetting is essential to action of any kind" (*On the Advantage and Disadvantage of History for Life*). Without forgetting, "there could be no happiness, no cheerfulness, no hope, no pride, no present"; so, "forgetting represents . . . a form of robust health" in human beings (*On the Genealogy of Morality*, Essay II).

Life-affirming, forward-looking agency requires a robust sense of *resolve* that depends on your ability to effectively cancel from your consciousness (and *sub*-consciousness) the whole big bag of modern self-negativity which includes: past failures, disappointing others' expectations and (thus) becoming the object of critique, discipline, blame, and rejection (in Sartrean terms, recognizing yourself as the object of others' judging "look"), and associated stinging feelings of shame and inadequacy.

But, as Nietzsche notes, modern human beings are raised in a civilized social setting that overflows with written and unwritten codes, rules, norms, and expectations designed to hamper our vital passions, our individuality and spontaneous self-expression. We suffer from the pathology of the bad and (much worse) the *guilty* conscience that perpetually recalls our past failures and inadequacies. Since our capacity for proper forgetting is perpetually blocked, our potential for affirming life in a forward-looking manner, with pride and cheerfulness, is fatally undermined.

Accordingly, the change of speed, scene, and style invoked at the outset of "New Dawn Fades" does not mark a fruitful new beginning that involves a genuine resolve to move forward but merely a frantic, uninspired hashing for new directions and goals: the narrator's path is "directionless" and this lack of aim or purpose is "so plain to see" if you manage to grasp your existential situation without self-deceived sugarcoating. And not just currently directionless but without any hope to eventually find a new direction, since you remain instead fixated on your past mistakes, accepting the shame and accusations arising from these mistakes and their bad consequences, hence despairing over who you are and cannot help being to the point where you seriously consider abolishing yourself via suicide. "Directionless, so plain to see / A loaded gun won't set you free" (another effective pause)—"so you say."

Especially in light of our knowledge that Curtis did eventually choose the road of ultimate escape (though by utilizing a clothesline rather than a gun), we cannot help hearing "A loaded gun won't set you free" as the commonplace plea of an interlocutor, either some concrete person or the universal faceless mass-you (*das Man*), that suicide is not truly an escape, not really the *proper* way of breaking free from your despair and hopelessness. That is, even though Curtis puts the emphasis on "say" ("So you *say*"), thus indicating that he as the lyrical self does not buy into the commonplace plea, the later listener is strongly inclined to hear him pronouncing the "you" ("so *you* say"—this is Middle and Reade's take on the line in *Torn Apart*, pp. 133–34). The implication is of course the same.

After this line, "New Dawn Fades" takes a musical break and then merges into the final part where the singer's desperation and hopelessness erupt without compromise. Thus far Curtis has mostly been recounting or observing (mostly himself) with a calm, collected voice (though with more than a hint of resignation), but now he is in the thick of things, a full participant in social life's ugly scenes: "We'll share a drink and step outside, an angry voice and one who cried." He begins to shout out his anger and frustration over the numbness he feels after having exhausted himself in (unspecified, perhaps mostly internal) turmoil: "We'll give you everything and more / The strain's too much, can't take much more / I've walked on water run through fire / Can't seem to feel it anymore." Then he gives voice to what Nietzsche deemed the core of modern nihilism, namely, "exhaustion and . . . wish for the 'end' . . . for being otherwise, being elsewhere": "It was me, waiting for me / Hoping for something more . . . Me, seeing me this time / Hoping for something else." Nietzsche's new dawn fades away as the song concludes with despondent guitar—and basslines reinforcing the sense of hopeless and ultimate resignation.

The other songs on *Unknown Pleasures*, particularly those on the (vinyl) A-side, express the same post-Nietzschean stance of pessimistic-nihilistic resignation. The first song on the album, "Disorder," immediately announces the theme of disorientation and alienation from common social guidelines and habits ("I've been waiting for a guide to come and take me by the hand / Could these sensations make me feel the pleasures of a normal man?"). The brilliantly ambiguous report in "Day of the Lords" give us a taste of the Nietzschean sentiment that weakness is a sign of decay and degeneration which, in a godless world without allegedly given "inalienable" rights, undercuts the legitimacy of human existence ("I guess you were right, when we talked in the heat, there's no room for the weak").

"Candidate" stresses the impact of debilitating memories corrupting one's vital powers ("Corrupted from memory / No longer the power"), inducing a weariness with life and a wish for the ultimate end ("It's creeping up slowly, that last fatal hour"); this loss of vital powers is linked, specifically, with the abandonment of any deeper ambition, such as the ambition to effectively challenge traditional social values and thereby to heed Nietzsche's call for the "revaluation of values" that is needed to escape the threat of suicidal nihilism ("I don't know what made me, or what gave me the right, to mess with your values, and change wrong to right"). "Insight" picks up on these themes ("Guess your dreams always end / They don't rise up, just descend, I don't care anymore / I've lost the will to want more"); its final, repeated insistence "I'm not afraid anymore" presumably means something like, "I'm not afraid anymore to face up to my last fatal hour and act on my wish for the end."

This expression of lack of fear of death connects with the abovementioned point in the ensuing *New Dawn Fades* (concluding the A-side), "A loaded gun won't set you free, so you *say*" or "so *you* say."

Joy Division's final album *Closer* resounds and intensifies these topics (and presents them in a more complex, refined musical style). It culminates in the band's central masterpiece (besides "New Dawn Fades") "Decades," recounting the experiences of young but already world-weary, depleted nihilists ("Here are the young men, the weight on their shoulders . . . / Weary inside, now our heart's lost forever"—according to Honoré, this was "the way" Curtis "was talking in his last days," *Torn Apart*, p. 214). The young men take up a semi-detached standpoint in the theatre of modern nightmarish memories which reveals to them, with brutal clarity, their deep-seated despair and lack of affirmative power ("Watched from the wings as the scenes were replaying / We saw ourselves now as we never have seen / Portrayal of the trauma and degeneration / The sorrows we suffered and never were free") as well as the fatal hopelessness of their endeavors ("Each ritual showed up the door for our wanderings, open then shut, then slammed in our face").

It is worth noting how many of the lines and sentiments expressed in these lyrics are repeated in Curtis's private correspondence, even years after he had written them. In his letters to Honoré, we find him saying, for instance, "Indeed the strain had become too much" (compare "New Dawn Fades": "The strain's too much, can't take much more") or "There is no room for the weak and emotive" (compare "Day of the Lords") (*Torn Apart*, p. 223). Honore emphasizes Curtis's compassion, how he deeply felt "especially for the weakest" (*Torn Apart*, p. 190). But from a Nietzschean perspective, excessive compassion and identification with the suffering of others is already a sure sign of nihilistic decay, a symptom of the degeneration of life's affirmative vital forces.

The resulting stance is, as in Curtis, frequently one of shame, self-blame, and self-disgust (from another letter: "I feel so ashamed of myself…I now feel a deep self-hate"; *Torn Apart*, p. 243). This sparks a growing will to exit a life condition one finds unbearable. Honoré reports that after his first suicide attempt, Curtis told her, "It wasn't a cry for help—I actually want out" (*Torn Apart*, p. 239). He eventually got out when he killed himself on May 18th 1980.

It's customary to end a discussion of Curtis's trajectory, or of any human fate ending in suicide, with some presumptuously edifying reflection on how terrible suicide is, how it could and should have been prevented, sometimes coupled with a quasi-Christian appeal to the sanctity of human life. But one might also take a different outlook from which suicide is just the logical-practical consequence of clearly seeing one's existential situation for what it is, and judging that a life filled with suffering, hopelessness, and despair is simply not a life worth living. Curtis's friend Vini Reilly (leader of the Durutti Column, who joined Joy Division for many concerts) felt that "Perhaps it was his time to go" (*Torn Apart*, p. 242). As Camus points out: "One kills oneself because life is not worth living, that is certainly a truth" (*Basic Writings*, p. 445).

III

Post-Punk
Politics

8

From Velvet Underground to Velvet Revolution

Marty Sulek

Post-modernism shares a close relationship with both Punk and its Post-Punk successors—much like Punk itself, though, as Charles Boone has said, "precise definition of what may (or may not) be a postmodern period is difficult" (p. 207).

Post-modernism's indeterminate character stems from two inter-related factors. To begin with, it's a fluid concept still in the process of being defined. There isn't even much agreement over whether post-modernism constitutes a definitive break with modernism, is an extension of modernism into a new phase, or is an attempt to recover a more "authentic" mode of being from the pre-modern past.

The other factor stems from post-modernism's embrace of the non-rational character of being, which tends to elude modern analytical philosophy.

Despite its indeterminate nature, we can identify four aspects of post-modernism which relate to Post-Punk:

- **the death of master narratives and loss of faith in ideology**
- **simulacra and simulation**
- **the blurring of the distinction between artist and audience**
- **absurdism**

Punk, Post-Punk, and Post-Modernism

"Master narratives" are those conceptions of the ultimate ends of humanity that once granted direction, meaning, and legitimacy to the pursuit of knowledge. The modern Western narrative has traditionally taken the form of "relieving the human estate" and attaining utopia at the "end of history" through the application of reason, science, and technology. This master narrative has underwritten faith in the two major political ideologies of our time: liberalism and communism. It has lost credibility due to the rise of nihilism, modern anti-teleological science, anti-metaphysical logical positivism, and technological advance, all of which shifted attention away from the ends of action and exclusively toward means (Lyotard, *The Postmodern Condition*, pp. 35–36).

Punk is highly skeptical of modernity's master narratives. The Sex Pistols' chorus "No future for you / no future for me" in "God Save the Queen" neatly sums up this outlook. We live in a "fascist regime," a surveillance state where "there's always someone looking at you" (Boomtown Rats). The most powerful creation of modern technological science—the H-bomb—threatens us with extinction. The only purpose of "career opportunities" is to "keep you out the dock" (Clash). There are "no more heroes any more" (Stranglers).

The post-modern idea of simulacra is closely tied to modern technology's mechanical means of reproduction and the simulated realities it creates. In Jean Baudrillard's account, the images produced by art have passed through four distinct phases in human history. At first, the image was conceived as the reflection of a profound reality (pagan idol worship). Then the image was seen as masking and denaturing a profound reality (Christianity's obfuscation of nature). Then the image masked the *absence* of a profound reality (logical positivism's anti-metaphysical stance). And finally, the image has no relation to any reality whatsoever: it has become its own pure simulacrum (*Simulacra and Simulation*, p. 6).

Punk is deeply entwined with the idea of simulacra. The music industry against which Punk so famously railed is based on selling the products of mechanical reproduction. It also employs the media to market its products, creating public images that bear little relation to reality. In the case of Punk, they peddle the image of rebellion without an appreciation of its underlying reality. As the Clash sings:

Ha! You think it's funny
Turning rebellion into money..

Or, in the words of Johnny Rotten:

And you thought that we were faking
That we were all just money making

You do not believe we are for real
Or you would lose your cheap appeal.

The post-modern blurring of the distinction between artist and audience largely derives from literary theory. Roland Barthes sees the central status assigned to the author as an invention of the modern era that has diminished the role of the reader. In the interests of writing, therefore, he calls for the suppression of the author and a corresponding elevation of the reader. Jacques Derrida (*Writing and Difference*) further develops this line of reasoning, asserting that the interpretation of a text in post-modern discourse cannot be determined by the intentions of the author. The text is completely independent of the author the moment it's committed to paper. The only valid determinant of a text's meaning is that supplied by readers, with their particular history, needs, modes of interpretation, and stipulations imposed on recreating the text's images in their mind.

Punk emulates the post-modern ideal of eliminating barriers between performer and audience through its "Do It Yourself" (DIY) ethos. It incites the audience to be more than passive listeners, to participate in the performance and even pick up instruments and create their own music. Punk's DIY ethos is greatly facilitated by its "de-evolutionary" aesthetic (Devo), which strips music down to its essentials. When the Ramones toured the UK in 1976, they inspired legions of musicians who emulated their elemental style and became the vanguard of the UK Punk movement. This DIY ethos has extended into Post-Punk. Yee Loi, two girls from Liverpool, initiated their musical careers performing Ramones covers. (See Dunn's chapter in *Punk Rock and Philosophy*.)

Absurdism, a post-modern concept that grew out of *avant garde* theater, sees life as inherently irrational, illogical, incongruous, and without reason (*Theatre of the Absurd*). In the modern age, the imposition of rational order and the suppression of the irrational, rather than resulting in a greater rationality, has led in practice to particularly virulent forms of irrationality. Differently put: to err (act irrationally) is human, but to really screw things up takes something ordered on purely rational principles such as a computer or bureaucracy.

Punk zestfully embraces the irrational aspects of post-modern life. The modern ideal of living in "perpetual peace" within a "safety culture" is completely anathema to Punk, which relishes the conflict and dangers of the mosh pit and living on the fringes of society. Punk also repudiates the idea of a supposedly rationally ordered society and the tyranny of "complete control"

(Clash) that necessarily entails. Finally, Punk casts the "pretty vacant" (Sex Pistols) absurdities of modern life into high relief. While styles have changed in the transition from Punk to Post-Punk, these post-modern elements have remained.

Post-modern politics and the Velvet Revolution

Post-modernism arose primarily from literary theory, but quickly spread into the realm of politics. One of the more prominent examples of this transmigration is Czechoslovakia's "Velvet Revolution" of 1989, the first truly post-modern revolution. The Velvet Revolution was also decisively inspired by Punk, from its proto- to Post-Punk forms, due to the influence of Lou Reed and the Velvet Underground ("VU") on the Czechoslovak dissident movement in the 1970s and 1980s. To understand post-modernity's and Post-Punk's influence on the Velvet Revolution, we need to recount the events leading up to that time.

Between May and June of 1968, a young upcoming Czech playwright named Václav Havel spent six weeks in New York for the English language premiere of his play *The Memorandum*. Staged at The Public Theater in the East Village, as part of the New York Shakespeare Festival, the play went on to win a prestigious Obie award, which cemented Havel's reputation in the US. Barely below the surface of this absurdist comedy lurked a trenchant critique of ideology and the accompanying dangers of centralized power and control. While in New York, Havel also imbibed the *avant garde* art scene then flourishing in the East Village, including the music of Frank Zappa, Captain Beefheart, and, of course, the VU. Havel bought their records, including the newly released album *White Light / White Heat*, brought them back to Czechoslovakia, and shared them with his friends.

On the night of August 20-21, 1968, Warsaw Pact armies invaded Czechoslovakia and installed a new hardline regime under Gustáv Husák. The liberalizing reforms undertaken by the previous Communist leader, Alexander Dubček, were quickly rolled back under the banner of "normalization"; repression and censorship were reimposed. Less than a month later, Milan Hlavsa formed a band called the Plastic People of the Universe ("the Plastics"). It was primarily inspired by the VU, but also covered the songs of other American groups: the Fugs, the Doors, Captain Beefheart, and Frank Zappa. The name of the band purportedly derived from Frank Zappa's song

"Plastic People" (Yanosik, "The Plastic People of the Universe") but it was likely also inspired by a series of multimedia events organized by Andy Warhol in 1966 and 1967 titled "The Exploding Plastic Inevitable," featuring musical performances by the Velvet Underground and Nico.

In 1969, the Plastics were joined by Ivan Jirous, who became its artistic director, performing a role analogous to Andy Warhol with the VU. As the process of normalization progressed under the Husák regime, many bands changed their look and sound to survive the transition. Most quickly adopted the "aesthetics of banality" (*Disturbing the Peace*, p. 18) that sought not to provoke or disturb, but rather to reiterate ideologically conventional ideas in soothing tones. The Plastics refused to change, though, leading authorities to revoke their musician's license in 1970. As a result, they could no longer be paid for performances, and lost access to state-owned instruments, and rehearsal and performance spaces.

The Plastics continued as an amateur outfit, using second-hand and improvised instruments, prefiguring the DIY ethos of punk. As Jirous was still a member of the Union of Artists, he was able to obtain permits for convention halls. There, he "would lecture on Andy Warhol for a few minutes, show a few slides, and then the Plastics would 'demonstrate' the songs of the VU for a couple of hours." Eventually, though, the authorities caught on and these shows were banned as well. In 1972, a concert in downtown Prague featuring the Plastics was cancelled after a drunken militia clashed with fans. The Plastics were thereafter banned from performing in Prague. Around this time, Vratislav Brabenec, a free jazz saxophonist, joined them on the condition that they only play their own original music and sing in Czech.

Effectively prevented from performing in public, the Plastics resorted to playing at weddings. Whenever friends got married, the wedding party provided an occasion to rent a hall and stage a private concert. Even so, these "concerts" had to be held in rural locations and under conditions of extreme secrecy, as the Plastics continued to be hounded by authorities. In March 1974, over a thousand fans traveled by train to one such concert in the small town of Ceské Budjovice. Awaiting them was a police contingent that beat them with clubs and sent them back to Prague. Six students were arrested and dozens more were expelled as a result.

In response to this police brutality and repression, Jirous organized the First Music Festival of the Second Culture. His idea was to create a separate and vibrant culture entirely independent of the banal and totalitarian "first culture" supported by authorities. In so doing, he became the first Czechoslovak intellectual to formulate and practice the concept of a "second culture." This approach would play a critical role in the formation of dissident opposition to the Communist regime:

> Although at first he was thinking chiefly of nonconformist rock music and only certain literary, artistic or performance events close to the sen'sibilities of those nonconformist rock musical groups, the term "second culture' very rapidly came to be used for the whole area of independent and repressed culture, that is, not only for art and its various currents but also for the humanities, the social sciences and philosophical thought. (*Disturbing the Peace*, p.101)

The first of the Second Culture festivals, dubbed "Hannibal's Wedding," was held on September 1, 1974. The second, on February 21, 1976, was dubbed "Magor's Wedding" after Ivan's nickname, Magor, slang for "crazy." In response, on March 17 the Secret Police arrested twenty-seven musicians and friends who participated in the festival, including the Plastics.

Music on Trial

On September 21st 1976, four of the musicians arrested went to trial, including two of the Plastics, Jirous and Brabenec. They were charged under article 202, section 2, of the Czechoslovak criminal code for "disturbing the peace," a catchall law commonly invoked by Communist authorities to suppress public demonstrations against the government. The ostensible reason was "obscene lyrics" in their songs, but their real crime was "the adoption of 'their own stance toward life,' which in its very independence constituted a challenge to the [Communist] Party" (*Charter 77 and Human Rights*, p. 7).

Several months before the Magor's Wedding concert, a mutual friend of Jirous and Havel had arranged a meeting between them. Each was initially suspicious of the other, they having met only briefly a couple of times in the mid-Sixties. Havel had since heard some wild stories about Jirous, who for his part considered Havel "a member of the official, and officially tolerated, opposition—in other words, a member of the establishment" (*Disturbing the Peace*, p. 126). Despite this mutual initial apprehension, they immediately hit it off. When Jirous played recordings of the Plastics and other bands involved in the planned concert, Havel was struck by their authenticity and sense of life:

Suddenly I realized that, regardless of how many vulgar words these people used or how long their hair was, truth was on their side. Somewhere in the midst of this group, their attitudes, and their creations, I sensed a special purity, a shame, and a vulnerability; in their music was an experience of metaphysical sorrow and a longing for salvation. It seemed to me that this underground of Jirous was an attempt to give hope to those who had been most excluded. (p. 127)

When Havel learned of the arrests and trial of the Magor Wedding musicians, he decided something had to be done, not only on principle, due to the injustice of the case, but also because of its special significance.

At this time, many prisoners found guilty of political dissent during the show trials of the early 1970s were being released from prison. People had grown used to the spectacle of political show trials. But the situation of these musicians, Havel felt, was entirely different.

What was happening here was not a settling of accounts with political enemies, who to a certain extent were prepared for the risks they were taking. This case had nothing whatsoever to do with a struggle between two competing political cliques. It was something far worse: an attack by the totalitarian system on life itself, on the very essence of human freedom and integrity. (p.127)

The Communist regime was turning the focus of its repression from political dissidents to cultural dissidents. The Soviet Bloc's military had forcefully brought the Czechoslovak state back under control, the judicial system had punished the regime's political enemies, and the state propaganda outlets had largely pacified the general population. But how to control the intellectuals and artists who now constituted the barely tolerated, unofficial opposition to the regime? The answer was to persecute a small group of "deviant" artists and intellectuals, situated at the very margins of society with little public sympathy, and hold them up as a warning to others not to stray from the Party line.

Havel played a key role in organizing support for the musicians, enlisting a small group of prominent individuals to advocate on their behalf. They began modestly, working behind the scenes to garner support. At first, they met with misunderstanding and resistance, but this evaporated as people came to recognize the changed circumstances. With a small but influential base of support, they pressed the government to drop the charges. It refused to do so, but it was nevertheless caught completely off guard by the public's defense of the Plastics. The State had expected to settle the case as a routine criminal matter. At first it counterattacked with a defamation campaign, but then retreated. Then it began releasing people from custody.

At trial, in September 1976, only four defendants were prosecuted. They were found guilty, but sentenced to relatively light prison terms, most receiving little more than time served. The exception was Jirous, who received eighteen months in Prague's infamous Ruzyně Prison. A month later, Havel composed a famous essay on the trial, titled "The Trial" after Kafka's nightmarish novel of prosecution by an anonymous bureaucratic judiciary. It was published in a book, *The Merry Ghetto*, included in the Plastics debut record album, *Egon Bondy's Happy Hearts Club Banned*, issued by Invisible Records in Paris in 1978.

A diverse group of supporters had attended the trial, including many prominent Czech artists and intellectuals. In the following months, they worked to establish a permanent human rights organization to combat political persecution. On January 1, 1977, they released a statement of principles and named themselves Charter 77. They quickly became the premiere dissident organization in Czechoslovakia, with Havel as their leader. By 1985, Charter 77 still only had around twelve hundred signatories, but it was sufficient to make it the *de facto* political opposition to the Communist regime.

The Velvet Revolution

The political situation in Czechoslovakia remained relatively static through most of the 1980s. It rapidly changed on November 17, 1989, though when students staged a demonstration in Prague, ostensibly to commemorate the anniversary of the death of student demonstrators at the hands of Nazi occupiers fifty years earlier. Police cracked down on the protesters, injuring several, and a student named Martin Šmid was reportedly killed. Reports of the death in the media sparked public outrage and further protests. In the days that followed, government officials vociferously denied that a student named Martin Šmid had ever been killed. The state media even conducted absurd interviews with two students named Martin Šmid (a relatively common name in Prague) who professed that they were still very much alive and well.

No matter. Within days an *ad hoc* organization named "Civic Forum" was formed to voice public opposition to the government. Charter 77's members played a pivotal role in its formation and direction. One of its first actions was to issue a list of demands to the government, including an investigation of the murder of the student, and the resignation of all the leadership who had invited the Warsaw Pact to intervene in 1968 (*Czechoslovakia's Velvet Revolution*, p. 76).

But even these strongly worded demands fell short, given the rapidly evaporating legitimacy of the Communist regime. On Friday, November 24th 1989, Havel gave a speech to a cheering crowd of 500,000 people in Wenceslas Square outlining Civic Forum's plan for transition from Communism to democracy:

> Civic Forum wants to be a bridge between totalitarianism and a real, pluralistic democracy, which will subsequently be legitimized by a free election. We further want truth, humanity, freedom. Henceforth we are all directing this country of ours and therefore all bear responsibility for its fate.

The political situation deteriorated so rapidly there wasn't even time to arrange democratic elections to legitimize a new government. On December 29th 1989, the Federal Assembly appointed Havel interim President of Czechoslovakia by a unanimous vote. An election was quickly slated for June 8th and 9th, 1990, to choose a new Assembly and President. In recognition of the peaceful and bloodless nature of the transfer of power, Western media dubbed it the "Velvet Revolution" at the suggestion of Havel's translator and spokesperson, Rita Klímová (*Revolution 1989*, p. 367).

It was later revealed that the story of Martin Šmid's killing was a merely a rumor, mostly likely started by the secret police to deter further protests (pp. 370–71). The Velvet Revolution had bee sparked by a simulacrum, a media copy without an original event. The exact origins of that rumor remain undetermined to this day, despite a formal investigation by the Czechoslovak government, further cementing the Velvet Revolution's post-modern status.

When Lou Met Václav

Lou Reed was experiencing something of a Post-Punk revival after the release of his *New York* album in January 1989, which evoked the raw Punk spirit of his early years. On April 17th 1990, he travelled to Prague at the invitation of Havel to interview the new president. At the beginning of the interview, Reed presented him with *Songs for Drella*, which he had just finished recording with his old VU bandmate, John Cale. Havel remarked how great it was that he could now listen to whatever music he desired, given previous conditions in the country: "For twenty years there was only the most banal pop music on our radio" (*Between Thought and Expression*, p. 150).

Having alit on the topic of music and repression, Havel described in detail the VU's seminal influence on the Plastics, and the resulting growth of political dissent in Communist Czechoslovakia:

> By this I mean to say that music, underground music, in particular one record [*White Light/White Heat*] by a band called Velvet Underground, played a rather significant role in the development in our country, and I don't think that many people in the United States have noticed this. (pp. 151–52)

At this revelation of the VU's seminal role in inspiring the Velvet Revolution, Reed meekly responded: "Really?" He had had no idea. They talked more about revolution and music, with Havel noting how the spirit of the Sixties, the rebellion against the establishment, significantly affected the spiritual life of his generation and younger people.

Havel then asked Reed if he could play at a special concert that evening featuring the band Půlnoc ("Midnight"), which included several former members of the Plastics (which broke up in 1988). Reed was hesitant, but reluctantly agreed as a personal favor to Havel after being assured it would be a small crowd composed of the inner circle of Charter 77. When Reed arrived at the venue, Půlnoc was already playing. The music sounded familiar.

> They were playing Velvet Underground songs—beautiful, heartfelt, impeccable versions of my songs. I couldn't believe it. This was not something they could have gotten together overnight. (p. 172)

Reed made his way to the green room to prepare to perform. Upon hearing that Havel had arrived, he went on stage and played a few songs from *New York* solo. As he was leaving the stage, the band asked if they could join him. He assented and together they blazed through some old VU numbers. Every song he called, they knew perfectly. It was as if his old bandmates were right there behind him.

Exhausted, Reed quit the stage and made his way to the balcony to join Havel. There, he was introduced to former dissidents, all of whom had been jailed, and many of whom told of having recited his lyrics for inspiration and comfort while in prison. Someone recalled a line from an essay he'd written years ago, "Everybody should die for the music." Reed concludes:

> When I had gotten out of college and helped form the VU, I had been concerned with, among other things, demonstrating how much more a song could be about than what was currently being written. So the VU albums and my own are implicitly about freedom of expression— freedom to write about what you please in any way you like. And the music had found a home here in Czechoslovakia. (p. 162)

Before they parted, Reed asked Havel, "Why did you stay, why didn't you leave? How could you stand the terrible abuse?" Havel replied, "I stayed because I live here. I was only trying to do the right thing. I had not planned for these various things to have happened but I never doubted that we would succeed. All I ever wanted to do was the right thing."

Reed concludes his report of the interview stating, "I love Václav Havel. And I'm keeping my fingers crossed. I too want to do the right thing."

9

Joe Strummer and Globalization

George A. Dunn

"Mondo Bongo" is an Italian phrase that means roughly "crazy world." It's also the title of a standout cut on Joe Strummer's 2001 album with the Mescaleros, *Global a Go-Go*. The song's musical style is evoked in the lilting phrase that Strummer rhymes with the title, "latino caribo," a beguiling fusion of Latin and Caribbean rhythms.

It's an acoustic tango with Spanish guitar, violin, accordion, congas, and bongos, with cryptic lyrics that hint at covert operations by the CIA, declare the singer's allegiance to the Mexican revolutionary band Zapatistas (a group whose anti-neoliberal ideology draws on such diverse sources as the Mayan tradition and Catholic liberation theology), and allude to presumably illicit activities involving a Japanese gambling machine called a Pachinko at a strip club ("nude noodle model parlor") in something called "the Nefarious zone." We also hear of working at a "bauxite mine" and taking a "monorail" to get home, which would seem to place the action in either Brazil or India, as they are the only countries with both bauxite mines and monorail systems.

This blizzard of incongruous images from far-flung locations rides atop a wistful melody that underscores the chorus's resigned sigh of "Nobody said it was fair." A crazy world indeed! Whatever sort of narrative we might tease out of these lyrics—and I'm not convinced that anything approaching a coherent narrative is even intended—the crazy world Strummer is evoking is the world of globalization, a world of diverse people and cultural signifiers colliding in a chaotic but often intoxicating way. The obscurity of the lyrics allows each listener to interpret the song after her own fashion, which also reflects the protean nature of our postmodern world, where plurality, discontinuity, and contingency, rather than universal truth, have become our new watchwords.

With its beautiful melody coupled with its quiet undertone of menace, "Mondo Bongo" evokes both the seductions and the dangers of our postmodern, globalized world. But the same could be said for Joe Strummer's oeuvre as a whole.

"Carnival Time"

Like their contemporaries the Sex Pistols, the early Clash were influenced by the Ramones, the pioneering New York punks whose 1976 tour of England launched the Punk scene in London, in addition to other New York bands like the Heartbreakers and the New York Dolls. But, from their very first records, the Clash also incorporated the syncopated rhythms of reggae, the music of London's Afro-Caribbean immigrant community.

The Clash's eponymous first album in 1977 featured a six-minute version of Junior Murvin's reggae song "Police and Thieves," fusing Punk and reggae in a way that later inspired Bob Marley to write the song "Punky Reggae Party." Including this song on their first album was the Clash's way of letting the world know from the start that they would not be hemmed in by people's expectations of a Punk Rock band. They were willing to color outside the lines as the spirit moved them. But the song was not just a musical statement but a political one as well, a declaration of their solidarity with the beleaguered Caribbean community in London.

With its high falsetto croon of "Police and thieves in the street / Scaring the nation with their guns and ammunition," the Junior Murvin record had been embraced as an anthem by Caribbean youth in the wake of the 1976 riot at the Notting Hill Carnival, an annual street party featuring calypso and reggae bands. Over a hundred casualties resulted from this hours-long battle with the police, who had been stopping and searching young blacks in a manner perceived as harassment. The back cover of *The Clash* album featured a photograph from the riot: police officers charging the crowd. Three years later, memories of the rampage would surface in the steel drum propelled "Let's Go Crazy" on their *Sandinista!* album. The festival mood of this energetic calypso number was belied by the lyrics: "Bricks and bottles, corrugated iron / Shields and helmets, Carnival time."

Indeed, the Clash would come to identify as much with London's Afro-Caribbean youth as they did with the white working-class punks who were the mainstay of their audience.

As Dick Hebdige writes in *Subculture: The Meaning of Style*, "Most conspicuously amongst Punk groups, the Clash were heavily influenced not only by the music, but also by the visual iconography of black Jamaican street style. Khaki battle dress stenciled with the Caribbean legends DUB and HEAVY MANNERS, narrow 'sta-prest' trousers, black brogues and slipons, even the pork pie hat, were all adopted at different times by various members of the group" (p. 29).

Songs like "Career Opportunities" and "London's Burning," which expressed the frustrations and grievances of working-class youth in general, became clarion calls for working-class unity across racial grounds when performed by white musicians who displayed their love of black music and culture so openly. The desire to emulate black youth, whom Strummer viewed as less timid than white youth in expressing their grievances, is expressed most directly in the song "White Riot," which Strummer wrote after he and bassist Paul Simenon found themselves in the middle of the Notting Hill riot: "Black man got a lot of problems / But they don't mind throwing a brick." Hebdige argues that the common thread connecting the white Punk Rock of Strummer and the Clash with the reggae subculture they so admired was their shared rejection of the symbols of British national identity. Reggae was the music of a poorly assimilated immigrant community that felt deeply alienated from its host nation, while punks were voluntary exiles from mainstream British culture, disenchanted with the false promises of what the Sex Pistols called "England's dreaming." The Clash and other punks attempted to forge a new counter-cultural identity for white working-class youth in part by identifying with—and even imitating aspects of the culture of—disenfranchised blacks.

Decades before the emergence of what we now call identity politics, the Clash were preoccupied with issues of identity. In an essay titled "Belonging," the social theorist René Girard notes that the word "identity" has a dual meaning: our identity is what makes us unique or one of a kind, but it can *also* denote a relationship in which two things are indistinguishable or identical (*All Desire*, p. 204).

The Clash were certainly interested in touting their unique ipseity, as evident in the many songs they wrote celebrating *themselves*: "Clash City Rockers," "Garageland," "All the Young Punks (New Boots and Contracts)," "This is Radio Clash," "We Are the Clash." But they also stressed their identity in the second sense, their essential commonality with the working-class Brits for whom they sought to be spokesmen. In the song

"Cheapskates," for instance, Strummer sang, "I have been a washer up / And he has been a scrubber up / And I seen him a picking up / Dog ends in the rain." But for the formation of a counter-culture of alienated white working-class youth, a shared experience of menial labor wasn't enough. As Hebdige argues, it involved rejecting the symbols of Britishness and the adoption of a new Punk aesthetic that "can be read in part as a white 'translation' of black 'ethnicity'" (p. 64). But the punks, with their deliberately torn tee shirts and jackets with stenciled slogans, could never have the same organic relationship to their adopted identity as Afro-Caribbean youth had to theirs. It could only be something laminated atop their disavowed British identity, like the Vaseline that spiked punk hair in imitation of "natty dreads." "Whereas urban black youths could place themselves through reggae 'beyond the pale' in an imagined elsewhere (Africa, the West Indies)," writes Hebdige, "the punks were tied to present time. They were bound to a Britain which had no foreseeable future" (p. 675).

Girard distinguished two types of community or "relations of belonging," based on their stance toward outsiders. In a more organic community, such as the Afro-Caribbean community that the Clash and many other punks sought to emulate, "the negation and refusal of the outside world is always subordinate to the affirmation of one's own genuinely lived values" (p. 215).

First and foremost, our sense of communal identity is bound up with a deep love of "our own" things, our own traditions, revered heroes, cultural practices, heritage, arts, styles of dress, and language, all of which are captured in the popular Jamaican word "roots," denoting not just the place but the traditions that nourish someone. The more the identity of a community is real and organic, the less need there is to adopt an antagonist posture toward outsiders in order to sustain a sense of identity. But that sense of identity is much more fragile in communities without deep roots, in artificial communities and among deracinated individuals with a weak sense of belonging to each other. "Ceremonies [and other identity markers] are no longer observed for the purpose of fostering unity or being oneself," says Girard, "but rather to distinguish oneself from those who do not observe them." The ceremonies and fashions of Punk Rock were a calculated rebuke to mainstream culture, a "negation and refusal of the outside world" that was meant to be the cornerstone of an alternative community, a new source of belonging. But the aggressiveness of these symbols only masked how fragile and artificial this community really was. It was in many ways just a caricature of the organic Afro-

Caribbean community. As Girard says, "It is precisely because they are collapsing that relationships of belonging try to dress themselves in a strength they no longer have" (p. 216).

But the same economic and cultural forces that had created the generation of alienated and disgruntled youth that figured so prominently in the Clash's early songs were increasingly being unleashed on the world at large. Globalization was uprooting communities and weaking relations of belonging in every corner of the world, while igniting all manner of ethnic, cultural, and religious conflicts.

"Westway to the World"

In 2000 Don Letts released his acclaimed documentary *The Clash: Westway to the World*, an overview of the band's history from its formation to the sacking of guitarist and founding member Mick Jones. In the song "London's Burning," from the Clash's 1977 album of that name, Joe Strummer sang, "I'm up and down the Westway, in and out the light," the Westway being the carriageway that ran through London, the city that figured so prominently in the songs of that first album as to practically be a character with a personality.

By the time *Combat Rock* released, their final album with Jones, the landscape of their songs had expanded far beyond London to encompass every corner of the globe. The highway they travel is now global and along its route we hear "stereos from Cuba" drowning out the singing of the *Missa Luba,* the Latin Mass set to a traditional Congolese arrangement ("Car Jamming"), the lament of an orphaned Vietnamese child, abandoned by his American soldier father ("Straight to Hell"), reports from a Middle Eastern kingdom about a king banning rock music and preparing to drop bombs on protesters ("Rock the Casbah"), the voice of Allen Ginsburg intoning "Guatemala, Honduras, Poland . . . death squad Salvador, Afghanistan," a small sampling of countries roiled by political violence ("Ghetto Defendant"), and objections voiced in "public bazaars" to unrelenting wars fought between unnamed neighboring countries ("Inoculated City"). And along with the worldwide compass of the band's lyrical themes came an increasingly globalized musical palette.

The Clash had already taken a giant step in that direction with their 1980 album *Sandinsta!* Of course, they had always been musically adventurous, experimenting not only with reggae and ska but also rockabilly, rhythm and blues, and even lounge jazz. Their eclectic musical outings on *London Calling* make it the first real Post-Punk album, but on *Sandinista!* they threw all of their remaining inhibitions to the wind and took a deep dive into world music, as well as hitherto unexplored genres such as funk, rap, and gospel, with even a lilting waltz and a fiery fiddle hoedown thrown in for good measure. Indeed, the Clash's *Sandinsta!*, coming years before Paul Simon's *Graceland* and Peter Gabriel's *So*, both released in 1986, was an early pioneer of what we later know as worldbeat, the fusion of Western pop or rock with traditional folk music from around the world.

Was this music still Punk? Was it even Post-Punk—or maybe even post-Post-Punk? Ever since the release of *London Calling*, the Clash had been waving away criticism from those they labeled the "punk police," whose narrow definitions of what could count as "Punk Rock" the Clash had been flouting from the beginning.

(Alas, the punk police are still with us! As of this writing, the young Punk band Yee Loi, consisting of teenage sisters Rose and Matilda Farrell, whose background is English-Irish and Chinese-Vietnamese, have just released their first professionally-produced single, "Dad's Money," written to answer the "punk police," who "judged us on our age, gender, race, and background.")

Like much of the Clash's previous work, many of the songs on *Sandinista!* were explicitly political, but now the politics was as international as the music. A standout cut was "Washington Bullets," which features the warm tones of a festive marimba supporting Strummer's lyrics, which flip through a series of snapshots of US imperialist engagements in Latin America over the course of the past few decades: from the CIA-backed coup that brought the bloody Pinochet regime to power in Chile, to the failed attempts to overthrow Castro in Cuba, to the successful (at the time) revolution by the Sandinista National Liberation Front in Nicaragua that toppled Anastazio Somoza after the US withdrew its support for his regime. The album's title is taken from the cry "Sandinista!" heard several times in the song. In a final verse, Strummer criticizes the Russian invasion of Afghanistan, the Chinese occupation of Tibet, and British weapon sales that arm mercenaries around the world.

But it wasn't just the lyrics that were political. The band's insubordination with respect to musical boundaries was itself a political statement, a reflection of their growing scorn for national borders, as if they were saying that the problems facing of British youth couldn't be separated from the struggles of dispossessed communities elsewhere in the world. If their aim in the earlier albums was to position themselves as the vanguard of a movement of counter-cultural British youth, they now dared to speak for a world in which lives in Asia, Africa, Central and South America, and the Caribbean were all mutually implicated. And just as this globalized world was one in which capital, labor, commodities, and (not least of all) weapons circulated freely without respect for territorial boundaries, so too the rhythms that originated on these distant shores bled into each other in the Clash's pioneering brand of world music. In *Westway to the World*, Strummer reflected, "We weren't parochial, we weren't narrow-minded, we weren't 'little Englanders.' At least we had the suss to embrace what we were presented with, which was the world and all its weird varieties, and we tried to reflect that into the tracks." And in 1982 Strummer told *Musician* magazine, "We're trying to make a universal music for a world without governments. Or a better way of putting it is to say for a world under One World Government. All this nationalism, these border wars, they're going to erupt into the death of us" (Gall, *Punk Rock Politics*, pp. 226–27).

Joe Strummer had become a self-proclaimed world citizen, something he had in common with the ancient school of philosophy known as Stoicism. The Greek philosopher Diogenes (412/404–323 B.C.E.), a forerunner of the Stoics, was once asked where he was from. He replied, "I am a citizen of the world [*kosmopolitês*]," thus giving us our word "cosmopolitan." Notorious for his irreverent and oddball behavior, Diogenes may have just been disclaiming allegiance to his birthplace Sinope, as well as to every other existing Greek city with their restricting mores and laws, but the ideal of cosmopolitanism came to have a more positive meaning for later Stoic philosophers.

Lucius Annaeus Seneca (4–65 C.E.) spoke of the "great and truly common" community to which we all belong, embracing every human being (and even the gods) due to our shared rational nature, which he distinguished from those much narrower communities "to which we have been assigned by the accident of our birth" ("On Leisure," p. 431). Quoting the Roman playwright Terence, he wrote, "That line of poetry should ever be in our hearts and on our lips: 'I am a man and think no man's lot foreign to me'" (*Selected Letters*, p. 202). Due to our shared humanity, our duties to others don't end at the borders of our local community. Almost exactly two millennia later, the Marxist-existentialist philosopher Alexandre Kojève coined the term "universal and homogeneous state" to describe the world toward which he believed history was inexorably propelling us, a world in which these two communities—one defined by our universal humanity, the other by accidents of birth—collapsed into one. This world without borders, in which all ethnic and class divisions would be overcome, seems a good match for Joe Strummer's aspirations when he spoke of the "world under One World Government" for which he and his bandmates were making "universal music."

Surveying the course of human history and the ambitions and needs that pressed it forward from one epoch to the next, Kojève concluded that the coming of the universal and homogeneous state was inevitable. But does that necessarily make it something to be affirmed? The philosopher Leo Strauss (1899–1973) was a lifelong friend of Kojève, but also one of his sharpest critics. A noted scholar of classical political philosophy, Strauss feared that the universal and homogeneous would be a tyranny of unmatched ferocity, since it would have at its disposal technologies of surveillance and control that were far beyond the wildest dreams of the most ruthless tyrants of antiquity. But his concerns didn't end there. "Classical political philosophy opposes to the universal and homogeneous state a substantive principle," he wrote. "It asserts that the society natural to man is the city, that is, a closed society" (*Liberalism*, p. x).

By closed society, Strauss means one that's organic in Girard's sense, satisfying the deep human need for belonging by uniting a community in a shared way of life. Strauss also feared that a universal and homogeneous state would foreclose the possibility of those human excellences that can be properly nurtured only within relatively closed horizons and are extinguished when what is distinctive about each historical community gets melted away into a universal stew of mediocrity. In musical terms, something precious seems to be lost when everyone the world over is tapping their toes in unison to the same banal pop hits, aimed at the widest possible audience because they've been calibrated to the lowest common denominator.

Later in his life, Strummer seems to have abandoned the dream of a One World Government in favor of more decentralized forms of human sociability, while exhibiting a greater willingness to acknowledge his own national identity. According to Gregor Gall, Strummer became an advocate of "an ethical form of decentralised, small-scale capitalism imbued with humanism," as well as a fierce critic of neoliberalism and the giant corporations that had bought and paid for governments around the world (p. 231). Yet, he remained an internationalist when it came to music. But if the local and the particular is the answer to the mediocrity of the universal and homogenous, as the early Clash's celebration of the culture of London's Afro-Caribbean community implied, how can the local be preserved in the era of globalization given the pitiless nature of global corporate power?

In his song "Johnny Appleseed," recorded with his last band, the Mescaleros, Strummer sang, "If you're after getting the honey, then you don't go killing all the bees." He explained the meaning of these lyrics in an interview: "This is what a lot of people feel about the corporate culture, how if it's good they'll find it and crush it out or they'll analyze what's good and bland it out. That was a yelp from the heart about, c'mon, you know, you can't go killing all the bees 'cause there ain't gonna be no honey left."

"World Service Bulletin"

Strummer's musical honey-gathering continued after the break up the Clash. Few popular musicians have availed themselves of the riches of world music quite as much as Joe Strummer. After the breakup, he turned for a time to the movies, composing the soundtrack to Alex Cox's 1987 movie *Walker*, a collection of acoustic performances that featured salsa, merengue, Afro-Cuban jazz, and hillbilly music. There followed several collaborations with the Pogues, the Celtic-punk pioneers who more or less singlehandedly reinvented Irish music. His 1989 *Earthquake Weather*, with his then-band the Latino Rockabilly War, was a tapestry of punk, rockabilly, reggae, folk, ska, funk, and Caribbean rhythms. Through it all, Strummer remained a musical marauder always in search of new beats to appropriate, stitching together a panoply of styles to create something unique in the world of pop music.

As Punk became more and more obsessed with building walls and policing its borders, dogged by concerns over what could and couldn't count as "authentic" punk rock, the Post-Punk career of Joe Strummer moved in the opposite direction, welcoming the whole world into his musical fold. If, as some have argued, hybridization is a fundamental characteristic of postmodernism, Joe Strummer's Post-Punk oeuvre is as postmodern as they come.

Yet, by the time the late 1990s rolled around, many people had written Strummer off as a spent force or were at best waiting for him to get back together with his former bandmates for a nostalgic "reunion tour." It was then that Strummer uncorked a new flask of creativity, as a DJ offering an eclectic array of music from around the globe on his BBC World Service "London Calling" radio program and as the leader of the

Mescaleros, a wild genre-blending band that served up a delicious gumbo of the wide variety of music in which Strummer had been marinating for the past decades. These two offices collided in the Mescalero's song "Global A Go-Go," from their 2001 album of the same title, which Strummer introduces by intoning "World Service Bulletin" before proceeding to thump his chest over how his "London Calling" broadcast reaches "all comers of the globe": "There is no hut in the Serengeti / Where my wavelengths do not probe."

The song offers a litany of artists whose songs Strummer is dispatching over his wavelengths, along with the far-flung destinations he imagines them reaching: "Big Youth booming in Djkarta / Nina Simone over Sierra Leone." He never asks whether such a deep and comprehensive global penetration is a good thing, which is perhaps surprising from someone who once decried American cultural imperialism in the Clash song "I'm So Bored with the USA." Like the "Yankee detectives" of the song, who are "always on TV," Strummer's wavelengths are an unstoppable force, laying siege to a world that's powerless to refuse them.

Of course, the content Strummer sends out across the airwaves is nothing as banal as *Starsky and Hutch* or *Kojak*. Yet, what he describes himself doing in his DJ booth at the BBC could still be seen as emblematic of global capitalism, which also leaves no place on Earth untouched, not even the humblest hut in the Serengeti. Strummer gathers up sounds from around the world, ushers them through his central distribution hub in London, and then dispatches them back out into the world to be enjoyed in places far from where they were made. Is our planetary culture enriched by the musical buffet Strummer sets before us? Maybe so, making his "Global A Go-Go" one of the upsides of globalization.

The inaugural episode of his "London Calling" broadcast featured artists from Jamaica, Columbia, Congo, Senegal, and Germany, as well the Mexican-American Trini Lopez from the boring old USA, whose music most of his audience would be unlikely to hear otherwise. But Strummer's playlist is hardly typical of the cultural offerings of global capitalism. Western music—whether rock, hip hop, or pop—has become one of globalization's most effective wedges, always conveying the same implicit message: the English language is cool, the English-speaking world is the source of everything hip and modern, and buying its products is how you can partake of its glamour.

Sitting in England with no leverage over heads of state and corporate CEOs, Strummer can do little more than celebrate the glory of human diversity that's still a reality, while it hasn't yet been completely plowed under by the homogenizing forces of the modern world. That's the theme of his Mescaleros' song "Bhindi Bhagee," in which Strummer acts as a local guide for a visitor to London from New Zealand, who is hoping to find some mushy peas. "No, we haven't really got 'em round here," Strummer replies, before rhapsodizing breathlessly for the next couple verses about the mad variety of world cuisines they do have ("Balti, bhindi, strictly Hindi, Dall, halal") and then segueing into the final verse's enthusiastic catalogue of the band's eclectic blend of styles ("Ragga, Bhangra, Two-Step Tanga").

The song depicts a world in which different cultures continually bump up against each other, but it's a world of hospitality rather than homogeneity. "Welcome stranger," purrs the chorus, "to the humble neighborhood." With his vibrant potpourri of musical styles, Strummer welcomes the stranger in an outpouring of hospitality that savors diversity, serving up a spicy gumbo of cultural richness rather than a pedestrian slop comparable to mushy peas. "Just check it out," he exclaims.

10

Gothicizing the Post-Punk Carcass

PETER J. CHURCH

By hook or by crook
You'll be first in his book
For an impaled affair
By hook or by crook
You'll be last in his book
Of flesh oh so rare.

　　—Siouxsie and the Banshees, "Carcass"

The 1976 Punk Rock revolution shattered the established order of British life through galvanizing a vibrant spirit of social conscience that condemned the wrongs of poverty, unemployment, and homelessness.

Punk erupted as a militant subculture to vocalize anger with the communal malaise and economic decline that pervaded 1970s Britain. But Punk Rock was inherently nihilist—a reaction—to social trauma, rather than a systematic rebellion and the reductive chimes of a nation with *no future* did not resonate with the youth, who demanded answers from the ruins of a broken society.

Gothic Rock surfaced through the faultlines of this damaged public consciousness as one attempt to resolve the political and psychological problems that festered in the Post-Punk carcass of British society in the late 1970s. The poetic sensibilities, brooding atmospheric melodies, and dark thematic lyrics enabled Gothic musicians to explore their personal fears and anxieties concerning the dehumanization of urban life in Thatcher's capitalist Britain. Early Gothic recordings by Siouxsie and the Banshees, Punishment of Luxury, Bauhaus, and Joy Division illustrate the decisive influence of the destructive legacy of Punk on the origins of Gothic Rock.

Idiots and Brainstorms

Last night I was down in the lab (Fun)
Talkin' to Dracula and his crew.

— IGGY POP, "Funtime"

Gothic is not an easy thing to define. Gothic evolves, mutates, destroys, and reincarnates. Everyone has a sense of what they mean by 'Gothic', but these thoughts are invariably different. Gothic can be viewed as an ideology, a philosophy, a lifestyle, an architectural–literary–musical genre, and a street fashion.

The first Post-Punk Goths rebelled against anything that acted as a sociological or artistic straitjacket including the Gothic! Steve Severin suggested that the Banshees were doing something entirely different to what their audience thought and expected, and lamented that as soon as Gothic "got latched onto as a label, and became a uniform of black dresses for everybody . . . that was a sad day for me."

There are some common signposts that cry out "Gothic!" Our Gothic ancestors were a barbarian tribe from Northern Europe, who rebelled against Augustan civility and crushed the uncrushable Roman Empire in the late fourth century. David Punter explains: "Where the classical was well-ordered, the Gothic was chaotic; where simple and pure, Gothic was ornate and convoluted; where the classics offered a set of cultural models to be followed, Gothic represented excess and exaggeration, the product of the wild and uncivilized" (*The Literature of Terror*, p. 5). Gothic re-emerged in the literature of the late eighteenth century with the publication of Horace Walpole's *The Castle of Otranto*, celebrated as the first Gothic horror story.

Today's Goths may be characterized by their black clothes, ghoulish make-up, and somber attitude; but their musical tastes have evolved from the distorted aesthetics of an early Gothic Rock that emerged from the hydra-headed Post-Punk monster. When the Punk head was chopped off, a far darker head was regenerated to scream menace and rage, to lament despair and hopelessness. This is the one common theme that blackens the Gothic. The Gothic discourse oozes through fractures in society as a disruptive force at times of civil unrest, distress, and fear. Pioneers of the late-eighteenth-century Gothic literary tradition, such as Ann Radcliffe and Matthew Lewis, were reacting to the *terrors* of the French Revolution. In the Victorian era, the common foes of Gothic writers were the Frankenstein monster of British industry and the Vampiric corruption of pure British blood. Contemporary anxieties around gender made Iain Banks waspish about the complexities of the male-female binary (*The Wasp Factory*, 1984). In 1978, Gothic Rock was as much a call for help, as a call to arms.

Punk may have been a catalyst for this new breed of dark music, but the DNA of Gothic Rock can be traced to the claustrophobic paranoia and lavish decadence of the Proto-Punk predecessors. Screamin' Jay Hawkins started the discs spinning with his 1956 cult classic, "I Put A Spell On You." The bewitching screaming and cannibalistic ritualism of the *ju-ju* man resulted in a widespread radio ban. Jim Morrison vocalized his deepest fears through the lyrics of The Doors' classic, "The End," which contemplated death as a release from the torment of living: "It's strange that they fear death. Life hurts a lot more than death. At the point of death, the pain is over. Yeah—I guess it is a friend" (*Creem Magazine*, 1968). Nico's *The Marble Index* (1968) has been described as the first Gothic album, with the Icelandic Valkyrie portrayed as a visual prototype for the Gothic Rock movement. Gothic music also absorbed the sexual ambiguity of Glam Rock pioneered by David Bowie, Marc Bolan, and Roxy Music.

Richard Kid Strange, the dangerous and decadent front man of The Doctors of Madness, was influenced by the "demented gothic theatricality" that defined the Crazy World of Arthur Brown (*Strange*, p. 25). The Doctors of Madness' first album, *Late Night Movies, All Night Brainstorms* (1976), veered into Proto-Gothic psychedelia with the atmospheric soundscape of the trilogy "Mitzi's Cure," "I Think We're Alone," and "The Noises of the Evening," depicting a descent into madness that Strange describes as "the gloomiest and darkest music" he has ever written (*Strange*, p. 58). And the Godfather of Punk was also the Godfather of Goth. Iggy Pop's solo masterpiece, *The Idiot* (1977), produced by Bowie, had a profound influence on Pete Murphy of Bauhaus. Siouxsie and the Banshees told producer Steve Lillywhite to replicate Iggy Pop's sound on their debut album, *The Scream*. The transcendent aesthetics of decay that color the last track on *The Idiot*, "Mass Production," were the final sounds that Ian Curtis heard before his tragic suicide.

The Blank Generation

Triangles were fallin' at the window as the doctor cursed
He was a cartoon long forsaken by the public eye
The nurse adjusted her garters as I breathed my first
The doctor grabbed my throat and yelled, "God's consolation prize"!

RICHARD HELL and the Voidoids, "Blank Generation"

Strange claims that Richard Hell's 1976 single, "Blank Generation," captured "the stuttering frustrated nihilism" of Punk better than any other vinyl, and "kicked a hole in the cultural wall" for the Sex Pistols and their Punk posse to storm through (*Strange*, pp. 81–82). As observed by Don Letts, Punk represented a "cultural ground zero," through which the disaffected youth could reinvent themselves with a refreshing DIY approach to music and fashion. Punk was an attitude more than merely a musical style. Griel Marcus notes "as an event in cultural time it was an earthquake, and it changed the landscape . . . Changing the rules of pop, insisting on new values, smashing old pieties . . ." (*In the Fascist Bathroom*, pp. 6–7). Jon Savage's celebrated account of the Sex Pistols glorifies the Punk legacy: "History is made by those who say 'No' and Punk's utopian heresies remain its gift to the world" (*England's Dreaming*, p. 541).

But Punks were lashing out at mainstream culture and authoritarian figures, rather than attempting to effect positive change. Their lyrics were confrontational and derogatory—a deliberate attempt to shock and offend politicians, royals, and conventional society. Punk was reactionary rather than rebellious. For Caroline Coon, Punk blew away the cobwebs, but "its nihilism and its anarchy were the seeds of its own destruction." This is the common message from those who witnessed firsthand the tumultuous sixteen months between The Damned's "New Rose" in October 1976, and what Howard Devoto describes as the night the Punk music died, when the Sex Pistols disbanded after a gig in San Francisco in January 1978. Punk imploded as a "seething mass of anger and frustration" (Adam Ant); it became "ugly, tawdry, dark, and desperate"'(Jah Wobble, PiL); and it was essentially "nihilistic" and "self-destructive" (Jerry Dammers, The Specials). Even John Lydon lamented in 1986 that "it could have been something very courageous, and an absolute change." Instead, Punk volunteered no solutions, no answers, and no future.

Yet the frustrated and downtrodden youth demanded answers. As Cosy Fanni Tutti of Throbbing Gristle remarked, "the climate of the time was pretty desperate." The economy was decimated by three-day working weeks, infrequent rubbish collections, and widespread strikes instigated by volatile trades unions. James Callaghan's socialist government was collapsing. The civil unrest in 1978–79 was exacerbated by an exceptionally cold Winter of Discontent, with severe storms isolating the more remote parts of Britain, resulting in difficulties with heating homes, obtaining basic supplies, and buying petrol. It was a time of rioting, racial tension, and the rise of the National Front.

When Margaret Thatcher was elected as the first female Prime Minister in May 1979, for the working classes this signified the ominous rise of capitalism. According to Jon King (Gang of Four), the country was tottering on the brink of what The Clash portrayed as an "English Civil War" (1978), with the most paranoid convinced the government was considering implementing martial law. Domestic trauma was heightened by the apocalyptic nightmare of World War Three. The Russian-American Cold War and the accumulation of weapons of mass destruction meant that nuclear war was a tangible threat to everyday life. This bunker mentality and fear for the survival of the human race was lyricized by the Welsh Post-Punk band, Young Marble Giants, in their 1980 release "Final Day":

Put a blanket up on the windowpane
When the baby cries lullaby again
As the light goes out on the final day
For the people who never had a say.

Post-Punk Hydra

One specific tentacle of the Post-Punk British rock octopus stopped flailing around in the wastes above its head, and burrowed instead into its blackest cave, there to contemplate . . .

—DAVE THOMPSON, *The Dark Reign of Gothic Rock*

Whether the most compelling analogy is heads of the Hydra or tentacles of an octopus, the reality is that Punk Rock fragmented into many diverse musical and cultural styles, including Oi!, 2 Tone, Indie, New Romanticism, Industrial, and Gothic Rock. The early Post-Punk vanguard revolted against Thatcher's capitalist masquerade and questioned the fundamental nature of society, materialism, and anodyne rock'n'roll. The restless youth needed an outlet, through which they could rationalise their growing pains and express deep-rooted anxieties about their lack of future prospects. The New Wave of British artistes rejected the raw simplicity of Punk, adopting a more experimental approach that leveraged the zeitgeist of the London and Manchester musical scenes and cultural hubs.

Working-class tension and urban violence were condemned in a second wave of Punk, with bands such as Sham 69 and the UK Subs, who sang about the reality of council estate Britain and the troubles on the streets. Oi! determined to escalate the fight to a more brutal level, as bands including The Exploited, Cockney Rejects, Angelic Upstarts, and Crass advocated *Anarchy* as a political ideology and call to direct action.

Gothic Rock offered something entirely different. It was introspective and personal. This was not a futile campaign to change society, but a forlorn attempt to change yourself. Gothic was somber and reflective: an escape from the harsh realities of life. Goths embraced fear and pain as essential in understanding the mechanics of existence. Goths wanted the world to change, but viewed social injustice as something to be exorcised by spirit, rather than destroyed by physical force. The contemplative and deeply personal lyrics of Gothic Rock demonized institutional authority with political leaders portrayed as puppet masters; lamented the deprivations of social trauma; and deployed a supernatural and eroticized imagination, expressed through a romanticized notion of death.

Early Gothic Rock was characterised by a darker sound, reverb and distortion, dramatic and brooding melodies. The lyrics were influenced by the traditional tropes, inherent in Gothic literature, of desolation, loss, mourning, suffering, and morbidity. The early bands did not identify with this Gothic label. But it is reasonable to say that their music was *Gothic*, even though they were not *Goths*.

Carcass

Drop some blues time to choose
Why your heart is just a stabbing
Bloody eyes can't describe
The nature of your hacking.

—The Damned, "Feel the Pain"

There were Gothic undertones in some of the earliest Punk recordings. Dave *Transyl*-Vanian, the former gravedigger and vocalist of The Damned, was a natural Gothic icon with his Dracula attire. The lyrics of "Feel the Pain" depicted suicide as a release from the agonies of living. Siouxsie and the Banshees were the first of the Post-Punk bands to completely absorb this Gothic mindset. Brian Johns epitomizes the *Gothicity* of the band when he writes: "The themes of alienation, despair and uncertainty that appeared with such gusto have become a trademark of the band ever since, and led directly to the 'gothic' tag" (*Entranced*, p. 31). Their debut album, *The Scream* (1978), was described by *Sounds* journalist Jane Suck, as "polar region rock," which sucked the life from the souls of its listeners, who were condemned to a gruesome death in a frostbitten apocalypse. Bassist, Steve Severin, claims *The Scream* combines black humour and twisted sexuality, with a strong dose of Hammer Horror, which was intended to sound like "a cross between the Velvet Underground and the shower scene from *Psycho.*"

The album track, "Carcass," originally titled "Limblessly in Love," explores the dehumanization of urban life in the late 1970s. There are parallels with the nineteenth-century penny dreadful *Sweeney Todd*, with Gothic images of self-mutilation and cannibalism, as Siouxsie wails, "Mother had her son for tea." On one level, the song is a macabre tale of slaughterhouse love, with a butcher's assistant, unable to get girls in the modern world, cutting of his arms and legs to enjoy a romance with a "dead pork," then skewering himself on a meat-hook to be near to the carcasses. On a metaphysical level, the lyrics could be interpreted as a struggle to find self, meaning, gender, and value, in the Post-Punk world:

> In love with your stumps
> In love with the bleeding
> In love with the pain
> That you once felt
> As you became a carcass.

There are philosophical similarities with the later *pandrogeny project* of Throbbing Gristle's vocalist, Genesis P'Orridge, who undertook extensive body modifications so that he and his lover, Lady Jayne, could resemble one another, based on their belief that the self is pure consciousness trapped in a DNA-governed body.

Puppet Life

> Wires stick through my soul, my actions are controlled
> Turning me from free man to puppet life suspended
>
> —Punishment of Luxury, "Puppet Life"

From the advent of puppeteers in the early 1600s, the puppet-master was perceived as a shadowy, metaphorical agent, who controlled things behind the scenes, manipulating people like a puppeteer operating a puppet. Oscar Wilde claimed, "Life cheats us with shadows, like a puppet-master." The notion of the puppet-master as an evil and manipulative figure has been carried into modern culture, such as Robert Heinlein's novel, *The Puppet Masters* (1951), which depicts aliens turning humans into puppet-like slaves; and Metallica's album *Master of Puppets* (1986), which aligns puppet-masters with the ruling political elite.

The Post-Punk band, Punishment of Luxury, portrayed the Gothic themes of control, suppression, and manipulation in both their recordings and gigs. The masked band members showcased a frenetic sense of psychedelic melodrama in their live performances, with songs such as "Puppet Life" conveying a cacophony of paranoia, chaos, and terror. The lyrics of "Puppet Life" depict a Gothic nightmare, with stygian images such as "wallowing around like an albino crocodile." But the underlying theme is a belief that suffering is temporary and there will be happier times ahead:

> Our day will come we pray, I'll be OK when I've
> Been mended, mended
> But until then I will be swinging on your rope
> With no hope.

The early Gothic Rock ideology challenged the Punk Rock anthem that there was no future. The journey might be lengthy, and the torment intolerable, but there were solutions, although salvation was highly individualized. This is integral to Gothic Rock, which was not tribal or homogeneous in the late 1970s, unlike its modern Goth stereotypes. The essence of early Gothic Rock was a mindset that challenged the mainstream, and rebelled against the constraints of any uniform fashion that suppressed the Gothic outlook of individuality. The Gothic championed the liberating DIY ethos of the new music scene, as the real legacy of Punk Rock.

Bela Lugosi's Dead

Guitars became coffin lids, creakingly opening, the bass became footfalls in a deserted corridor overhead, the drums was the flapping of a myriad bat wings and Murphy? Murphy was the Count, dead, undead.

—DAVE THOMPSON, *The Dark Reign of Gothic Rock*, p. 54.

Bauhaus, perhaps more than any other band of this era, appeared to both deride and embrace the Gothic mantra. Their lead singer, Pete Murphy, was desperate for an escape from his imprisonment in Northampton, which he described as living in the blank, grey, godless, "murder Mecca of the Midlands." Murphy claims that Bauhaus didn't easily identify with Gothic Rock, but were simply living out their musical fantasies and having a blast. Bauhaus were emblematic of Gothic being an attitude not a uniform: *Gothic* not *Goth*. Even their debut release, the Gothic pantomime classic "Bela Lugosi's Dead" (1979), was intended to be tongue-in-cheek kitsch, although the audience didn't get the joke!

However, "Bela Lugosi's Dead" was a pivotal record in the origins of Gothic Rock. Bauhaus attempted something unique in the late 1970s, which was to bring the lurid eroticism of contemporary horror movies into the music scene, extending the sexual ambiguity of Glam Rock into an emerging public discourse over the complexities of gender and self:

The virginal brides file past his tomb
Strewn with time's dead flowers
Bereft in deathly bloom
Alone in a darkened room
The count

Shadowplay

In the Shadowplay, acting out your own death, knowing no more
As the assassins all grouped in four lines, dancing on the floor.

—Joy Division, "Shadowplay," *Unknown Pleasures* (1979)

Manchester was a bastion of the Post-Punk movement. The smoky, fog-ridden city, described by Mark E Smith as resembling a film noir setting, was inherently suspicious of Metropolitan glamour. Peter Hook acknowledges that Manchester was a "pretty grim place," with the urban decay reflected in the dark music. Cultural commentator and *NME* journalist Paul Morley claims that 1970s Manchester was "haunted by the ghosts of the Industrial Revolution and hemmed in by hills, moors, and dull grey clouds" (*Joy Division: Piece By Piece*, p. 130). Joy Division epitomised the dark imaginative geography of Manchester with their brand of what producer Martin Hannett described as "dancing music, with Gothic overtones."

Joy Division's transition from the crude, inarticulate, and antagonistic Punk of their earliest manifestations as the Stiff Kittens and Warsaw, to the lyrical eloquence and sonic complexity of Joy Division, both paralleled and symbolized the progression from Punk Rock to Post-Punk. As Morley observes, the band's development from a "clumsy three-chord exuberance" into an "open spatial rock sound" epitomised how far the music scene had developed from "fast punk anguish" to "fast-slow post-punk anxiety" (*Joy Division*, pp. 100–104).

Bobby Gillespie of Primal Scream hits the nail on the head when he suggests that Joy Division took the externalized anger of Punk, but "the rage was internalized". Joy Division's corrosive music expressed despair, fear, and doubt, through dark brooding riffs saturated with the existential lyrics of Ian Curtis. The band members were seeking to escape from the oppressive brutality of their "disconnected surroundings" and "fractured lives" (*Joy Division*, p. 16). Curtis did accomplish an "escape" of sorts when he hanged himself in May 1980 at the tender age of twenty-two. Curtis, struggling to cope with fame and relationship problems, had become morbidly obsessed by the suicidal overtones of Throbbing Gristle's "Weeping" (1978), which refers explicitly to slashing wrists and swallowing pills:

I don't want to carry on
Except I can't even cease to exist
And that's the worst.

Sounds, with savage irony, characterised Joy Division's debut album, *Unknown Pleasures* (1979), as the last record you would play before you committed suicide. The lyrics of the track, "Shadowplay," draw upon the Platonic concept of *the shadow and the real*, with disturbing impressions of loneliness and alienation. Nothing feels real, like Plato's cave. The shadows represent the fragments of reality that we are able to perceive through our mortal senses, but are not accurate representations of the real world. The song's protagonist endures a fatalistic sense of hopelessness, as he confronts his own inevitable demise:

To the centre of the city where all roads meet, waiting for you
To the depths of the ocean where all hopes sank, searching for you
I was moving through the silence without motion, waiting for you
In a room with a window in the corner, I found truth.

And yet Joy Division were capable of expressing a Gothic doubling of the abstract and the mundane, the imaginative geography of Manchester as both nightmarish and sterile, conveying in the words of Morley "a sense of solitude and atomic aloneness" through music that depicted "catastrophic images of compulsion, wonder, fear" (*Joy Division*, pp. 111, 150). This is the essence of the origins of Gothic Rock as an alternative reality; a medium for exorcising the demons of traumatic suffering and desolate loneliness; and an inexorable decline into the warm, numbing sensations of oblivion as the ultimate mode of survival, refuge, and escape.

Gothic Rock in the twenty-first century has morphed into a broader Goth subculture. It is no longer anchored on sonic distortion, and melancholy lyrics of sorrow, mourning, and death. The black parade of My Chemical Romance and Marilyn Manson might antagonize the likes of Steve Severin and Pete Murphy, but the purists are wrong.

Gothic evolves—it is not static. Gothic diversifies—it is not homogenous. Gothic will always permeate our deepest terrors and anxieties. Gothic will eternally find its home with the *undead*.

11

Stone the Stone-Throwers or Groove Past the Gatekeepers?

OCEAN CANGELOSI

In a world bound by societal norms, Punks and Post-Punks live unshackled. Both find themselves in the crosshairs of Conformity Cops, who target their unconventional styles, sounds, and lifestyles. Neither bows to mutable traditions as if they were the immutable laws of God. They unmask the real villains as those who wield morally inflated customs to crush the freedom and dignity of those marching harmlessly to their own beat.

Their rebellion against custom does not reduce to moral nihilism. As Ill Repute insists, "My morals are good, my values are right . . . / The way I look don't mean shit / It's what's inside that counts" ("Book and its Cover"). Though both defy Piety Pretenders, they adopt different methods of resisting the unrighteous reproach they face for their unapologetic authenticity.

Punk rockers bully their bullies and accost their accusers. Slap their cheek, and they'll strike yours; then they might turn your other cheek and strike it too. Try to stone them to death, and you might end up thrown off a cliff. Punks skillfully serve the Condemnation Clan a taste of its own unrighteous medicine.

In contrast, Post-Punks tune out the Derision Division with self-assured indifference, tuning into tranquility, musing beyond the mindless masses, and rising above reproach with resilience. Post-Punks laugh off the Blame Brigade by playing with things like makeup, soundscapes, and psychedelics, all while choreographing another mesmerizing music video. With Jedi-like focus, they protect their creative flow from the noise of naysayers, channeling energy into artistic achievement rather than reprisals against revilers.

Every misunderstood misfit and marginalized soul must choose their path of resistance: anarchy or artistry. Their lives and happiness may well depend on mastering the misfit's dilemma.

How Punks and Post-Punks Resist Unrighteous Reproach

Fortunately, great misfits before us have harmonized clash and craft. Consider the album *Punk Girls* by Thee Headcoatees, far more than an iconic *all-female* punk band. Emerging from the influential Medway scene in the Nineties—where many garage bands embraced Post-Punk sensibilities—they joined the lineup with Billy Childish's all-male counterpart band, Thee Headcoats. However, Thee Headcoatees soon became legends in their own right by blending Punk's fiery defiance with Post-Punk's too-cool-for-school attitude.

Two tracks—"Punk Girl" and "Sticks and Stones"—show-case the distinct responses to reproach. While "Punk Girl" res-onates with more aggression, enhanced by Kyra's unrivaled scream, both songs thematically focus on women stigmatized for rebelling against conventional roles. "Sticks and Stones" highlights women branded "dumb chicks" and "bimbos" for refusing to become subservient wives. In "Punk Girl," women are derided as "rude, spat at, and booed" for daring to be them-selves. Insults like "silly tart" and "stupid bitch" manifest soci-ety's misplaced disdain for spirits brave enough to be free.

Yet, it's their responses that set the two songs apart. Punk girls scream, "I'll fix your face / I'll scratch your eyes / I'll laugh at you / through your cries." When people put them down, punk girls "cut them down to half their size / and beat them till they realize" that they shouldn't have messed with punk girls. They vigilantly defend their freedom, standing ready to reciprocate any misplaced blame thrown their way. The anthem "Punk Girl" encapsulates the Punk ethos in its unyielding defiance and promise to finish the fight. Punk girls who shout it have had enough and are looking for blood.

In contrast, when Post-Punk girls are called "stupid bimbos" and told to get a life by making "a man a little wife," they counter with cheeky schoolyard chants: "Sticks and stones may break my bones, but names will never hurt me." Rather than getting ensnared in Loserville, they stick out their tongues and continue dancing to their own rhythm in Girlsville.

Post-Punks' self-assurance is rooted in the insight that ignorance often fuels judgment. They don't need to square up to every detractor when the "ghouls and fools" who "make their rules" no longer hold sway over their personal choices. Encapsulating this sentiment is the double entendre "spunk will not desert me," which displays both an undaunted spirit and sexual satisfaction their accusers lack. By reclaiming and confidently deploying language used to put them down, they render it powerless against them in a show of liberation made possible through self-acceptance.

Before anyone rushes to accuse Thee Headcoatees of wrongly perpetuating heteronormative ideals, understand that Post-Punks dismiss critics attempting to dictate their preferences. For Post-Punks, it's not only about besting the Bully Brigade, but also about enjoying the ride.

Flip Tables or Turn the Other Cheek?

As the two songs on the same album show, the virtuous person needn't march to one beat. Even turn-the-other-cheek Jesus occasionally becomes table-flipping Jesus. Ironically, all the conformists who crucify misfits in the name of Jesus forget that they once crucified him as a misfit. Those who face judgment from the church find themselves in esteemed company, while those who judge in the name of Jesus scoff at his command, "Judge not, or you will be judged" (Matthew 7:1). Stone throwers follow not in the footsteps of Jesus but of the Piety Pretenders who sought to stone him to death as a deviant sinner.

Even Jesus couldn't help going full Punk mode on those who slam heaven's door in people's faces, portraying themselves as morally superior while they mistreat the marginalized and vulnerable. According to the Gospels, sanctimonious stone-throwers are the *only* people Jesus curses to hell, despite their firm conviction that they enjoy the moral high ground (Matthew 23). So, "Christians," are you still eager to cast stones at misfits?

The world needs punks like table-flipping Jesus, at least until he returns and sets the captives free. However, this tactic requires taking up one's cross. Confronting the Conformity Clones not only risks entanglement in the system they control, but also diverts focus from personal pursuits and depletes emotional reserves. Virtue shouldn't demand crucifixion just to sidestep slactivism. While taking up our cross is commendable, pursuing our craft remains a virtuous path.

To be sure, Post-Punks are prepared to unleash their Punk spirits in defense of themselves and others. They do not turn a blind eye to injustice or violence. Still, they don't want to spend all of their precious studio time battling the Fuss Force.

So Post-Punks cheekily "turn the other cheek" in some cases. In the context of Jesus's teachings, a slap represented a demeaning gesture employed by the powerful to assert dominance over perceived "inferiors." Rather than advising the insulted to cower and retreat, Jesus encouraged them to boldly offer the other cheek in a show of strength, looking straight in their oppressor's eye and asserting moral superiority. Faced with insults, nonviolent Jesus would also mic-drop wisdom, leaving his adversaries speechless and his followers pondering, much like those deciphering Post-Punk lyrics.

He who is without sin cast the first stone. Should we really nitpick a missed note in another's riff, when our whole album's trash? Post-Punks release their stones, refusing to mirror those who hurl them unjustly.

Forgive them, for they know not what they do. Norm Nannies, with their ghoulish grip, swaddle individuals in their mandates, confusing suffocating customs for divine commands. Jesus insists that those who enforce human precepts as divine law worship him in vain (Matthew 15:9). He, for instance, wore attire akin to today's "casual linen dress," yet many of today's "followers of Christ" vilify men for wearing these "cursed garments." Were Jesus to preach in contemporary churches, he might find himself jailed under anti-drag laws. Fortunately for churches, Jesus understands just how deeply they have been socially conditioned, restricting their freedom of thought and action. All the Bylaw Bullies should feel grateful that compassionate spirits like Jesus and Post-Punks even consider forgiving their transgressions.

The Best Rebellion Is to Have Fun

Punk rock and Post-Punk beat within every heart, unless silenced by conformists. While the world needs its punks, the path to Punk stardom is not without its wounds. There are times to flip tables, but also times to release the stones thrown at us. At times, we bear our cross; other times, we focus on our craft, poised to confront Creepy Conformity Clowns when they reappear. Navigating the misfit's dilemma while marching to our own drum, let Thee Headcoatees remind us to enjoy every defiant beat.

IV

Post-Punk and the Big Scene

12

Morrissey's Post-Punk Daoism

THORSTEN BOTZ-BORNSTEIN

In May 2006, Morrissey posed in *Uncut* magazine as St. Sebastian and as a Christ-like figure enhanced by supernatural light. "I live a life that befits a priest virtually," he said in 1983 ("Morrissey Needs No Introduction," p. 24). He also presented himself as Joan of Arc and Padre Pio.

While many critics have highlighted the singer's troubled connections with Catholicism, what has gone largely overlooked are the Daoist themes in Morrissey's art and overall personality. Better than through a presumed tortuous Catholic anti-Catholicism, the singer's peculiar mixture of the ascetic-spiritual and the agnostic-skeptical can be explained through an exploration of this Chinese philosophy.

Gavin Hopps quotes from Harvey Cox's interpretation of contemporary theology, *The Feast of Fools* (1969), where Cox writes: "Like the jester, Christ defies custom and scorns crowned heads. Like a wandering troubadour he has no place to lay his head. Like the clown in the circus parade, he satirizes existing authority by riding into town replete with regal pageantry when he has no earthly power" (p. 140). Hopps applies this statement to Morrissey, but Cox could equally well have disserted on the wandering and mocking Zhuangzi, whose irony and wit were combined with sacrifice and renunciation, whose intellectual refinement were mixed with carnivalesque absurdity, and who captures much of the subversive virtue that we find employed by the Anglo-Irish troubadour. "Subversive Virtue" is the title of a subchapter in Hopps's book referring to James Francis's book of that title.

Daoism is one of the three major systems of thought in China, along with Confucianism and Buddhism. Traditionally traced to the mythical Laozi (Lao Tzu), it owes most of its initial philosophical expressions to Zhuangzi (Chuang Tzu) who lived in the fourth century B.C.E. The link between Morrissey and Daoism can be conveniently established via Oscar Wilde, whose relationship with Zhuangzi's philosophy has been much commented upon. The young Wilde wrote one of the first reviews of what is now called *The Zhuangzi* when it appeared translated by Herbert Giles in 1890 and would stay under a "Daoist" influence for decades. It's known that Morrissey's worldview and art were shaped by Wilde, whose *Complete Works* Morrissey received from his librarian mother at the age of eight with the words: "It's everything you need to know about life" (*A Light that Never Goes Out*, p. 78). According to Morrissey's own words, every single line immediately affected him. Many of Morrissey's texts, as well as aesthetic elements such as the use of flowers, are inspired by Wilde, who was notorious for decorating his Oxford rooms with lilies.

Daoism and Post-Punk

There's an affinity between Daoism/Buddhism and the subcultural context from which Morrissey emerges. Individualism, anti-authoritarianism, and anarchism are themes central to both Morrissey's Post-Punk heritage and Daoism. Further common values are spontaneity, the rejection of rigidity, and the idea to live for the moment.

Before Punk, the hippie generation had adopted similar values and produced Western versions of Buddhism and Daoism. As these subcultures evolved, Punk submitted them to a peculiar transformation. Punk rejected the flowery, kitschy, New Age version of Eastern principles and practice because, first of all, Punk is not about feel-good. Nor are Buddhism and Daoism, as they talk much about the inadequacy of life, impermanence, death, or the ugliness of the body. So it makes perfect sense to see Morrissey's Post-Punk "non-feel-good" version of rock as compatible with Daoism. In Punk we find many of those "negative" themes combined with "positive" ones such as honesty and unflinching commitment. This combination is also characteristic of those East Asian philosophies.

Further developments are just as important. While original Punk had anti-aesthetic tendencies, the British glam rock scene emphasized aesthetization. Glam rock can most reasonably be seen as the "dandyist" continuation of Punk. Dandyism, which was very influential throughout the whole nineteenth-century in the upper strata of English and French societies, was a challenging fashion movement. Though sometimes ridiculed as superficial and mannerist, its major figures also formulated pertinent—though also mostly highly ironical—social criticism. According to Hawkins, historically, Morrissey stems from a "strong line of British dandies," which includes Brummel, Byron, Wilde, and David Bowie ("You Have Killed Me," p. 309).

Morrissey becomes the Oscar Wilde of Post-Punk. However, in Morrissey's hands, Post-Punk receives a further twist: he avoids using the ostentatious language of glam rock and puts forward principles of negation, renunciation, and nothingness that are also the basics of Daoism.

The self-estranging irony, the incorrect behavior, as well as the conviction that aesthetics is more important than ethics, are emblematic of Zhuangzi, Wilde, and Morrissey. All three act in similar contexts: Wilde's anti-Victorianism mirrors Daoist anti-Confucianism, both of which sparked a sophisticated anti-conformism. Like Zhuangzi, Wilde finds hope not among the virtuous but among those who are "ungrateful, discontented, disobedient, and rebellious" ("The Critic as Artist," p. 234). Both Daoism and Wilde fight the puritan earnestness and pedantism that they face in the form of snobs and the careerists, and "think against prevailing conventions in a way that appears to be systematically perverse, hence 'contrary' to the dominant discourse" ("From Chinese Wisdom to Irish Wit," p. 77).

Morrissey fits into this struggle. First, Morrissey fought the decadent and violent working-class culture of his native "Victorian knife-plunging Manchester" (*Autobiography*, p. 1); and later Thatcher's England, which was no longer Victorian but the world of a prime minister who was "devoid of either irony or humor" and "intolerant of ambiguity and equivocation" (Campbell, *Margaret Thatcher*, p. 64). More broadly speaking, Morrissey combats an individualist, shiny technicolor consumerist culture that lacks humanity.

The Art of Weakness

Paul Woods called Morrissey the "unlikeliest rock'n'roll star" (p. 5) because he avoids all taint of rock'n'roll machismo and plays up the social awkwardness of the misfit and the outsider. Through his "weakness," Morrissey becomes the "antithesis of a 'rockist'." Gavin Hopps titles a section of a chapter of *Morrissey: The Pageant of the Bleeding Heart*, "The Art of Weakness," and a further subsection "The Strength of a Flower." Strength arising from weakness is a typical Daoist theme, most famously employed through the metaphor of the watercourse: water always finds the best line for its course not by forcing itself through obstacles but by following a propensity.

Morrissey undertakes a deconstruction of the stardom system by following the Daoist system of "strong weakness": "What makes me more dangerous to them than anybody else is the fact that I lead a somewhat religious lifestyle," he said in 1985 ("Morrissey Needs No Introduction," p. 58). It is a process of deconstruction because in the end, ordinariness is no longer the contrary of the glamorous, but ordinariness becomes glamorous: Morrissey is not anti-glamorous but glamorous in his ordinariness, that is, strong through weakness. For the sleeves of his albums, which he often designed himself, he preferred to take "images that were the opposite of glamour and to pump enough heart and desire into them to show ordinariness as an instrument of power—or, possibly, glamour" (*Autobiography*, pp. 196–97).

Uselessness

Linked to the art of weakness is the affirmation of uselessness. Normally, to be useless is a weakness, but, as the *Zhuangzi* says, "Of petty uselessness great usefulness is achieved." First, Morrissey develops an ironic anti-work stance. "Jobs reduce people to absolute stupidity as they forget to think about themselves," he says in 1983 ("Morrissey Needs No Introduction," p. 18). In "You've Got Everything Now" and "Heaven Knows I'm Miserable Now" he suggests that getting a job is no guarantee of happiness. A civil service job he quit after two weeks, "horrified by its mundane nature" (*A Light that Never Goes Out*, p. 118), and he holds that he had even been "deemed physiologically and psychologically incapable of delivering letters" (*Autobiography*, p. 122). During a trial run as a hairdresser, he "failed to differentiate between oily hair and an actual wig" (p. 121). Morrissey was useless for anything. However, he was also useless for the pop business. He did not start singing and become a popstar because that was the most useful thing to do. On the contrary, his singing emerges from uselessness and therefore his entire career remains "useless."

The "perfect popstar" (in parallel with Zhuangzi's "perfect man" and Wilde's "perfect gentleman") must be a "useless" anti-popstar. Morrissey's career as a popstar is not useful, because if it were, he would compete and try to become the best in the sense of the most glamorous, most rebellious, and most transgressive. Punk and glam rock, from which he emerges, went in this direction. Instead, Morrissey refuses the strong structures of hierarchies and becomes like water. He steps out of the pop system in the same way in which Wilde stepped out of Victorian England's culture of duty with its "rigid male hierarchy whose ideal was exemplified by the image of the 'gentleman'" ("From Chinese Wisdom to Irish Wit," p. 78).

Aimless Wandering

Kevin Cummins has titled his comprehensive photo documentation of Morrissey *Alone and Palely Loitering* (from the famous poem by Keats). In the *Zhuangzi*, aimless wandering is called *you* (遊) which is a principal Daoist concept and has been translated as aimless roaming, rambling, sauntering, or as "free and easy wandering." While Confucians focus on the "hard" structures of moral and personal duty, the *Zhuangzi* promotes carefree wandering (*xiaoyaoyou* 逍遥游). Most striking is Morrissey's "wandering" voice, that seems to express a state of longing without longing *for* something. His texts are wandering, as they rarely adhere to "harder" rhyme structures but are fluid, often jeopardizing the meaning of the song or ending with melismas. Furthermore, in performances, "there are many hammed impersonations, travestying pronunciations, carnivalesque noises . . ." (*Morrissey*, p. 86). Other elements are more literally related to wandering. Hopps points out that one of the most recurrent themes in Morrissey's lyrics is "the notion of being a 'gypsy,' a wanderer, of 'moving home again,' which strangely coexists with a sense of 'never going anywhere'" (p. 2).

In more abstract terms, wandering mobility is linked to an elusive simultaneity of positions that would normally exclude each other, which is a Daoist strategy, too. The excessive use of the words "no" and "never" in so many of Morrissey's songs does not seem to refer to the simple negation of a "yes." Morrissey does not elevate the "no" to the status of an essence, but, through wandering lyrics and music, the "no" begins to wander, that is, to exist beyond "yes" and "no." Hopps confirms this when writing that "despite the emphatic 'no', overall, Morrissey's affairs have a "curious 'yes' and 'no' character" (p. 57).

Identity

Within the meandering rejections of essences, identities cannot grow either. "Identity is less a fixed essence and more a slippery, shadowy effect that nonchalantly floats across artificial categories" (*Morrissey*, p. 282). For Daoism, the self as an integrated and consistent identity is nonexistent, too. It does not mean that

Daoism sees humans as identity-less, but identity is supposed to constantly emerge from the reality of human life.

In a Daoist fashion, Morrissey overcomes identities as he explained in early interviews:

> I don't recognize such terms as heterosexual, homosexual, bisexual, and I think it's important that there's someone in pop music who's like that. Their words do great damage, they confuse people, and they make people feel unhappy, so I want to do away with them. (1985, "Morrissey Needs No Introduction," p. 12)

> I just want something different. I want to make it easier for people, I'm bored with men and I'm bored with women. All this sexual segregation that goes on, even in rock'n'roll. (1983, "Morrissey Needs No Introduction," p. 17)

Gender does not crystallize itself in the form of hard structures. However, Morrissey also avoids elevating, for example, the "gender fluid" to a new kind of gender. Those who transcend gender dichotomies might call themselves androgyne, gender fluid, pan-gender, or demisexual. The problem is that even these categories are still derived from the initial male-female dichotomy. Morrissey leads the entire project of identification ad absurdum, which is a Daoist technique. He does not create a new gender but rather situations in which gender identity does not matter. It has been noted that on some occasions, his descriptions imply "a gay viewpoint" and on others "a straight viewpoint," but "every instance is fraught with ambiguity" (Power, p. 105). The result is a combination of opposites that do not look for a mere androgynous compromise: "We're going to be a gay band, but not in a Tom Robinson, effeminate kind of way but more in an underlying kind of macho type way" (*Songs that Saved Your Life*, p. 17).

Morrissey might have worn outsized women's shirts or feminine items such as white beads, nail varnish, women's brooches, or have excessively emitted upward whooping falsetto voices. But even then, the aesthetics did not look like a willful attempt to establish a feminine identity. Morrissey seems to have an absolute "non-sex," which he once called a fourth sex: "I feel I'm a kind of prophet for the fourth sex. . . . With every Smith's appearance it comes closer" (*Morrisey in Conversation*, p. 17). Morrissey is playful, but his identity transformations are not a matter of a "chameleon aesthetics" à la David Bowie and of androgyny. Androgyny is just another identity, and even one that matters very much. Morrissey does not negate "this" or "that" identity, nor does he fuse various identities into a new one. He merely *performs* identity within emotional contexts, values, and desires that are changing and thus circumvents identity by becoming entirely "useless" for the identity business. This "useless" non-identity will not emerge as a non-distinct anti-identity either, but rather as a richer identity.

The "no" stance is not achieved through transgression but through playful action based on "uselessness." Most clearly, Morrissey follows this scheme in the song "Sheila Take a Bow" where he sings:

> Take my hand and off we stride
> La la la la la la la la
> You're a girl and I'm a boy
> La la la la la la la la
> Take my hand and off we stride
> La la la la la la la la
> I'm a girl and you're a boy
> La la la la la la la la.

The "la la la" is not *merely* capricious but functions more like a koan-like interjection, temporarily cancelling all language-based rationality and bringing about a gender change that is absolutely irrational. While singing that he is female, Morrissey has not become woman-like but, obviously, he remains the same person. There is no pose, that is, none of those poses that in rock music are often meant to be transgressive and provocative. "Traditional" gender fluidity in rock music is part of a revolution program and therefore, in principle, not different from leather jackets, noise music, white-painted faces, or smashed guitars. The effect that the boy/girl switching has in "Sheila Take a Bow" is simply one of absurdity and of something that cannot be grasped.

The famous Butterfly Parable from the *Zhuangzi* describes a similarly fluid ontological switch: "Once, Zhuang Zhou fell into a dream and then there was a butterfly, a fluttering butterfly, self-content in accord with its intentions. Acting happy with himself and with wishes gladly fulfilled" (Moeller, p. 446). The Butterfly Parable appears in a chapter called "Adjustment of Controversies" (also translated as "The Equalization of Things" or as "The Smoothing out of Differences"), which deals with the topic of "transformation" (*hua*). Zhuangzi does not move from one state of being to another but simply does not know whether he is a butterfly dreaming that he is Zhuangzi or whether Zhuangzi is dreaming that he is a butterfly. Identity, reality, and language are undermined, and as a result, the "butterfly" becomes entirely insubstantial. There is no revolution and no alternative identity; instead, identity simply no longer matters. The whole process appears to be innocent and fluid.

Handicap

Morrissey's hyperbole and sentimentality, his self-presentation as a persecuted being or as a misfit or outsider, should be recognized as an aesthetic strategy in its own right. The Smiths' love songs have been found "ludicrously contrived" and "anguished to the point of absurdity" (*Morrissey in Conversation*, p. 57). Morrissey's obsession with awkwardness manifests itself most clearly through his interest in disability. Wearing an unnecessary hearing aid, the singer expresses solidarity with those who have difficulties moving around smoothly.

In the *Zhuangzi*, disabled persons occupy central positions. We find a hunchback, "Crippled Shu," Shushan Wuzhi ("No-Toes"), or "a person who had no lips, whose legs were bent so that he could only walk on his toes, and who was otherwise deformed" (5:5). Shu is described as follows: "His chin seemed to hide his navel; his shoulders were higher than the crown of his head; the knot of his hair pointed to the sky; his five viscera were all compressed into the upper part of his body, and his two thigh bones were like ribs" (4:7). Talking about ideal forms that are supposed to be pre-existent in some Godly realm is a Platonic paradigm that has left its mark on Western culture. It also pertains to a Confucian conception of "normality" that Zhuangzi criticizes. While Confucius praises the courage of handicapped people, Zhuangzi attempts to "equalize" disability.

Morrissey has a similarly empathetic/cruel look at disability. In "November Spawned a Monster" he addresses the topic most directly when singing:

Poor twisted child
So ugly, so ugly

A frame of useless limbs
What can make good
All the bad that's been done?

The end of the song remains enigmatic as it suggests an absurd and ungraspable transformation similar to the gender transformations that have been described above:

Oh, one fine day
Let it be soon
She won't be rich or beautiful
But she'll be walking your streets
In the clothes that she went out
And chose for herself.

The Wuwei Dandy

Morrissey's aesthetics of renunciation, which is a sort of phleg-matic attitude already known from dandyism, leads to an art of weakness that affirms uselessness. The deadpan gender switches, which announce that here gender identity simply does not matter, can be interpreted as a "non-doing" known in Daoism as *wuwei* (無為). *Wuwei* is a non-directed action that is still moving somewhere. With regard to identity this means that there is neither a plan nor knowledge about identity; but there is not one about identity transgressions, countercultures, or cultural revolutions either. The person who practices *wuwei* has been called "ignorant and without knowledge or desire, and without any particular direction" (Li, p. 89). *Wuwei* emerges playfully whilst acting, and Morrissey is a prime example of this spirit of *wuwei* as he presents negative "non-feel-good" themes in a light and playful fashion that is not dra-matic (as Punk once was) and can easily appear as Daoist.

13
Folk Punk and Global Indigenous Philosophies

Matthew Crippen

Punk is like hardcore porn. It's raw. Also, even if we can't define it, there's no mistaking it. Post-Punk is different. It's an impure form that mixes many elements, so that it's not only hard to define, but also can be difficult to know whether we're hearing it. This is likely even more the case for folk punk, which originated in the late Seventies.

In a sense, all music is impure. Punk is an outgrowth of rock, in turn developed from American blues, which made heavy use of the guitar, itself arising in Spain, probably during the Muslim period there, as an evolution of the Middle-Eastern oud. But folk punk takes it to the next level. It openly draws on contrasting musical styles, such as contemporary metal and old-fashioned acoustic. It also sometimes mixes in local indigenous instruments, singing techniques, and wisdom traditions. This is fitting because few Indigenous cultures have worried much about purity—historically more of a concern for colonial rulers. The same holds for philosophy itself. Until fairly recently, "philosophy" was a catch-all for virtually every enterprise involving serious thinking.

In these senses, folk punk is an analogue to philosophy, both in its general and Indigenous forms. This kinship is strengthened by the fact that many folk punkers and philosophers have engaged in political protest. But whereas older performers risked alienating large numbers of potential customers because of the stances they took, recent musicians (or their producers) have tended to water down political messages and even convert "authenticity" into a brand. Without these merchandising strategies, we'd probably miss out on hearing some decent bands in an increasingly crowded global market, but this raises questions about whether the anti-corporate punk ethos is dying.

Adulterated Punk

Post-Punk—and thus folk punk too—often has a comparatively layered and hence impure sound—at least compared to the power trio of guitar, bass and drums plus vocals that we associate with classic Punk bands like the Sex Pistols.

Songs like The Pogues' "Lorca's Novena" and the Levellers' "Sell Out"—while retaining a relentless Punk drive—are much more textured and polished. The first of these has eerie backing vocals and a sample of dogs howling in the background. There's additionally Spanish guitar, harmonica, keyboards, bell sounds and drums played in an almost military marching style. The lead vocals are sung in the pronounced, proudly unrefined UK accent that's become a mainstay of Punk. The vocals in "Sell Out" are similar. However, this song likewise breaks with standard Punk conventions by including a synthesizer and Celtic-style fiddle, along with electric bass and guitar. Other performers, such as South Africa's National Wake, Siberia's Otyken, Mongolia's The Hu and Taiwan's Nini, not only mix acoustic and electric sounds, but blend Western and non-Western cultural styles of music.

The fact that folk punk aggressively abandons purity fits the history of philosophy, which has merged cultures. Indeed, the further we go back in the Western canon, the less identifiably Western it is. Ancient Greece and Rome traded goods and ideas through North Africa and into the East, with Augustine living in North Africa. The Islamic world preserved Greek literature, and Muslims from regions bordering India deeply influenced Christian theologians, such as Aquinas. One author, Victor Mair, even speculates that the Chinese word *dao* has extremely old roots that spread into ancient languages around the world, including European ones.

So, it's not surprising that medieval and ancient European outlooks often mirror non-Western ones stressing public customs as foundations for human psychology. Such ideas appear in Confucianism, African ubuntu, and Islam, despite their differences in other regards. Islamic Sufism also overlaps Indian Vedic works like the *Bhagavad Gita* because both suggest that enlightenment entails the oceanic surrender of self to the divine. Although Confucians and Daoists disagree on certain things, they share a common vocabulary, and elements from both seeped into Buddhism after it entered China from India.

All three traditions adhere in different ways (along with the *Gita* and Sufism) to the notion that reality—whether social or cosmological—exists as an integrated network and not a collection of separate things.

This last idea is important in the social philosophies that some folk punkers advance, which in turn echoes philosophers such as Henry David Thoreau and Ralph Waldo Emerson, who in fact read the *Gita*, as well as, Buddhist, Confucian, and possibly Daoist texts. While stressing freedom, Emerson and especially Thoreau departed from standard libertarian individualism because they stressed inescapable social interconnectivity, so that we're often responsible for events happening far away from us. The Levellers' song "Sell Out" makes the same point. It opens by saying that freedom is "dead and gone," and goes on to suggest that this relates to things like South American forests being cut down. From Thoreau's interconnectionist perspective, this makes sense: destruction elsewhere takes away others' freedom, and if we were participating in economies leading to this outcome, then we're morally guilty.

Celebrating Impurity

In the late 1970s and early 1980s, National Wake breached South Africa's racial purity rules—which were part of the country's colonialist legacy—since the group was mixed race. This alone was a political statement. And it cost them commercial success until long after the end of the apartheid era.

Musically too, National Wake fuses styles. They have a sparse, driving, electric and Lo-Fi sound in the punk vein. Simultaneously, their most famous song—"International News"—incorporates Afro-style playing. For starters, the guitar work has ska elements, which originate in Black Jamaican culture. Closer to home, it subtly mirrors the bright, repetitive and circular melodies of instruments like the Mbira (a.k.a. thumb piano), which is traditional to sub-Saharan tribes. More recent bands, like Zimbabwe's Evicted, are also mixed race and incorporate the same Mbira-like guitar riffs into their Punk compositions, in fact doing so much more explicitly.

In a similar spirit, the Siberian Indigenous group Otyken employs a mix of electric and acoustic instruments as well as scream-drive singing techniques. This style resembles the throat singing that occurs just across the Bering Strait, among the Inuit, who are ancestrally related to Indigenous Siberians. But the ethnicity of Otyken simultaneously bridges various Turkic, Russian, and East Asian lineages that mix in that part of the world, and also illustrates that Indigenous cultures, by their very nature, are usually wonderfully impure.

A mirroring commonality that's shared by Indigenous communities and folk punkers from around the globe is a tendency to pull on multiple resources, regardless of whether or not they have a longstanding history within local traditions. Otyken plays Asian folk instruments but also electronic keyboards. Analogously, the Great Plains tribes of North America adopted non-native horses into their practical and cultural lives. Because of this, individuals took names like Crazy Horse, and the month of May became the Moon of shedding ponies. The Lakota tribesman Black Elk likewise adopted Catholicism without abandoning his Indigenous beliefs.

The thing is, there's a tendency to want Indigenous people to retain their "traditional" ways, as judged from an outside perspective. People sometimes get offended if Indigenous individuals use plastic beads at a Pow Wow, as if they're supposed to reside in the past, while the rest of us are permitted to live in the contemporary world. Or likewise, some Celtic musicians have ejected electronic keyboardists from open mic nights, claiming that including such instruments breaks tradition. But the fact is that Celtic mainstays like mandolins and fiddles are probably evolutions of instruments that worked their way from Asia through the Middle East and into Italy, so are not purely traditional. Additionally, the Celts themselves invaded the British Isles from mainland Europe. So, Celtic culture is not native to the places it's most associated with.

An analogue of this confused way of thinking in the musical world occurred when folk icon Bob Dylan first introduced electric guitar in his song that appropriately begins with the line, "I ain't gonna work on Maggie's farm no more." Some fans saw this breach of acoustic purity as treasonous. The song might be seen as a proto-punk entry, and it was later covered by the Punk-inspired band Rage Against the Machine.

As if protesting purist tendencies and artificial barriers, the Levellers played in 2012 at the A38 venue. This is a mobile boat stage floating on the Danube, constructed partly with the idea of rejecting borders. There, the Levellers laid down what's possibly the most Punk version of their song "Sell Out" and also one of their best performances of it. Not incidentally, this rendering fused funk and ska into Celtic Punk, bridging boundaries.

Shredded Societies

We tend to associate acoustic sounds with older folk traditions, and folk punkers' lyrics tend to reference the past. These artists often sing about ancient places and heroes. But this is typically counterpointed with electric sounds and occasionally dissonant harmonies and arrhythmic beats, evoking grinding gears and misfiring cylinders—aural metaphors for social breakdown in the contemporary world. We hear this in "International News," with the musical style reinforcing the lyrics, which have to do with news blackouts in Africa that were legally imposed, particularly in relation to violence and military crackdowns.

Another tune that has aural metaphors for social breakdown is Neil Young's "Rockin' in the Free World," from 1991. Two versions of it bookend the album it's on, *Freedom*, one of them acoustic, the other electric, and the combination of the two standing as something close to folk punk. The song takes advantage of the fact that rock music culturally associates with America and freedom. Yet its lyrics describe a society falling apart, and they twist George H. Bush's Thousand Points of Light speech, changing the original reference to a kinder, gentler conservatism to "a kinder, gentler machine gun hand." The song's course, which is the same as its title, is accordingly sarcastic. All of these sentiments are amplified by the screeching guitar work and rough drumming that resembles a broken belt on an engine that is running in an off-time way.

Also from a 1991 album called *Levelling the Land*, "Sell Out" repeats this pattern, with its bridge having the rhythm of a broken lawn mower, especially in the A38 venue version. The lyrics speak about not believing in modern ways and policies that have "failed the test of time" and of wishing to "walk in ancient places." Reinforcing this, the band's name is itself a reference to a seventeenth-century political movement that aimed at extending the suffrage and promoting equality and tolerance.

The lyrics of "Sell Out" further suggest that people are tranquilized by mass media, echoing Thoreau who said the same of newspapers and other popular forms of communication. In a way, this is the reverse of the problem highlighted in "International News." Yet the result is largely the same since business interests end up censoring what we're exposed to, as the filmmaker Andrei Tarkovsky discovered upon defecting from the USSR to the West in the 1980s, only to still have his artistic freedom limited by economic factors. *Levelling the Land* has another folk punk song, "The Game." It suggests that political leaders treat international conflict and war with the gravity merely of card games. This point is buttressed by a slower ballad on the album—"Another Man's Cause"—that talks about the Falklands War and soldiers dying for purposes that have nothing to do with them.

The Pogues' "Lorca's Novena," released one year earlier in 1990, is about the assassination of the poet Federico García Lorca by right-wing nationalist forces at the beginning of the Spanish Civil War, likely because he was socialist and gay. Recorded near the end of Margaret Thatcher's era, this period was not kind to leftists and saw public services dismantled. The AIDs epidemic, which disproportionately affected gay men, was at its height. Thatcher's administration introduced legislation (Clause 28) that limited the extent to which teachers could discuss homosexuality, also deploying ads suggesting Labour politicians, who were more supportive of the gay community, were trying to pervert children. The Falklands War was prosecuted under Thatcher's watch, and was a late stage of colonialist conflict.

A commonality between all these songs is that they deal with societies in crisis. The case of South Africa is of course most serious. The albums from the 1990s are nonetheless addressing consequences that follow from the rapid rise of neoliberal and neoconservative political philosophies, which often amount to the same thing. Among other outcomes, these political programs increased wealth disparity in industrialized countries and further entrenched plutocracy—or as "Sell Out" puts it, fueled a situation where "the power of the rich is held by few."

Saving Place

In addition to stripping ethnic identity, global colonial and neo-colonial orders have contributed to what some have called "placelessness," a concern highlighted in Otyken's name, meaning "sacred land" and also in the album title, *Levelling the Land*.

As Afro-oriented scholars Kenneth Amaeshi and Uwafiokun Idemudia observe, globalization trivializes place and promotes what they call "placelessness." So in the same way that "homes" have become "houses" to be flipped on the market, place becomes an exchangeable good. As Martin Heidegger elaborated decades ago, economic and technological modern arrangements strip the uniqueness out of things, converting them into undifferentiated commodities to be stockpiled, as when trees become a woodlot, measured in BTUs or as exportable units of trade. (It's no small irony that Heidegger supported the Nazi regime, which imposed conformity and used industrial systems to liquidate people).

On the face of it, many folk punkers are reacting against the erasure of place. But just how this gets expressed depends on national identity. The Levellers are predominantly anti-patriotic, objecting to UK meddling in other countries. The same in some ways holds for National Wake in that its members rejected entrenched Afrikaner values that enforced apartheid.

The ethno-patriotism of Otyken, The Hu and Nini is also anti-colonial. It is because it is an affirmation of local culture and thus a rejection of imperialist interference (or something close to it) under which the peoples of Northern, Central and Eastern Asia have historically suffered. Otyken shoots many of their music videos in wild-looking and sometimes snow-covered outdoor areas. They dress in what appear to be traditional Siberian outfits. They play instruments like the komuz and igil. They additionally paint their faces. The accordingly seem to celebrate both their land and culture.

These patterns repeat in The Hu's music videos. One of them, "Wolf Totem," is set in Mongolian grasslands with tents in the background and motorcycles in place of the horses that would have been used in the past. According to the band's website, the group employs instruments like the morin *khuur* (aka the horsehead fiddle), the *tovshuur* (aka the Mongolian guitar) and the *tumur khuur* (aka the jaw harp) as well as techniques like throat singing. The vocal rhythms of the song are like galloping horses—driving, heavy, and repetitive—backed by drone harmonies. The lyrics catalogue a range of mighty animals and make mention of Genghis Khan, who is more of a folk hero in Mongolia than the villain that the West portrays him as.

Though from Taiwan, Nini's ethno-patriotism is broader than that country. Her videos for "Homeland" and "LongMa" have her playing Chinese folk instruments in ways reminiscent of Punk and metal, even though her sound is largely acoustic. Her costuming mixes traditional Chinese elements with contemporary rock fashion. The visuals and lyrics for her videos are directed toward Chinese culture generally, though some scenes are of Taiwan landscapes specifically. This reiterates connections between culture and place, with the title "Homeland" reinforcing this.

A broader theme that connects the Levellers and their Asian counterparts is that all of them focus quite a bit on the past. A longma is a mythical horse with dragon scales and wings that associates with legendary Chinese rulers of bygone times. We've already seen that the Levellers dream of ancient places and also sing of belonging to ancient races. In these regards, these musicians resemble thinkers like Thoreau as well as older ones like Confucius. An obvious part of what motivated these philosophers to their views was their deep dissatisfaction with the present. But they were a little unusual in that they overtly looked to their predecessors for answers—Thoreau especially to ancient Asians and Confucius to earlier Sage Kings. A second parallel is that Thoreau identifies deeply with the land, and Chinese philosophy is often said to be a product of patient thinking that occurs in bucolic settings.

Sell Out?

Folk punk—along with the broader Punk movement—is generally seen as resisting commodification. This doesn't mean musicians in this oeuvre don't want to sell albums. Instead, it means that their artistic choices do not revolve around maximizing sales. When the Levellers and Pogues criticized Thatcher, patriotism and homophobia in the early 1990s, they immediately cut themselves off from a significant demographic. National Wake's predicament was more extreme. They split up after just one album, which was withdrawn because of government pressure, after selling only 700 copies, according to some accounts.

Thoreau likewise objected to commodification, especially of place, complaining in more than one of his writings that land is artificially carved up and parceled out. Thoreau also had near-total disrespect for the establishment, and like Friedrich Nietzsche, he might be regarded as a punk philosopher. And because he fused new and ancient ideas, he might be a folk punker. His influences likely included Indigenous American philosophies, which emphasize togetherness and place-based identity. These issues get repeated in the eco-themed justice orientation of folk punk and also songs about the land.

At the same time, Thoreau was cynical of pop movements. He complained that news media—the mass entertainment of his day—tranquilizes us, claims echoed by National Wake and The Levellers. He also said that we think we're solving a problem by merely petitioning it, and singing about a problem doesn't seem that different. It's not that we shouldn't have protest music. But thinkers like Herbert Marcuse observe that it's hard not to buy back into an establishment that has a way of reabsorbing everything. Yoga entered the West as a protest movement but soon became a part-time job for students, a hobby for yuppies and a venue for sexual cruising. Soon after, we got retreats, Lululemon and a multibillion-dollar industry.

Otyken appears to be an analogue to the situation that Marcuse describes. Unlike earlier folk punkers, they clearly have costume designers and prop makers constructing instruments (for instance with skull resonators) that are only for videos, along with makeup artists and more. In fact, the set up with this group is close to girl and boy bands in that the enterprise is operated by a producer who writes the music and makes image decisions, as well as deciding on the band's specific membership. This is a way to cash in on youthful beauty and New Age mysticism and franchise identity. Otyken's music videos display the band's names in Western characters on their drums and at the beginning of videos as a marketing strategy, even though this is not the linguistic script of Siberia. Lyrically, Otyken doesn't sing about anything particularly political, just about the land, wind, and things like this, as if to appeal to a maximum market base. Nini is similar to the extent that her lyrics, by not being Taiwan-specific, keep her salable to the larger Chinese market.

Nothing forces Otyken's producer and members to adopt these self-commodifying approaches, even if they don't want to take the blatant political risks that National Wake did in South Africa in the late 1970s or Pussy Riot has more recently in Russia. To be fair, it's a saturated market, and without bands and producers using the techniques at their disposal, we'd likely not get to know what's, after all, decent music. At the same time, we have to ask whether today's commodifying climate makes genuine Punk increasingly rare.*

* Special thanks to Ayaulyn Chinaliyeva for her outstanding assistance on this chapter.

14
Icons Falling from Spires

CHELSI BARNARD

Post-Punk emerged in the wake of Punk Rock, departing from the traditional elements and raw simplicity of Punk to adopt a broader, more experimental, artistic, and avant-garde voice. One of the first pioneers of the movement was Susan Ballion, the lead singer of Siouxsie and the Banshees. As a cis-gendered, hetero-sexual white female, Siouxsie explored oppression and expressed dissent by borrowing mystical power symbols from oppressed cultures and subverting gender binary narratives.

Throughout history, cis-hetero male whiteness has been constructed as the social norm, leading to the deprivation of cultural symbology for marginalized people. White women have historically grappled with power by engaging in cultural appropriation, and this tendency shows how patriarchy has deprived white women of access to empowering symbology, thereby leading them to be complicit in the oppression of other groups. Furthermore, white supremacy has left Caucasian descendants void of cultural heritage and robbed them of any cultural hallmarks not indirectly tied to fascism in some form. Women like Siouxsie Sioux used cultural appropriation and subversion during the Post-Punk movement to break free from patriarchal constraints and assert their power.

Grappling with Patriarchal Power Structures

As Punk became more mainstream, with bands like The Sex Pistols and The Clash achieving commercial success, some experimental and artistic bands felt overshadowed by the more popular, less innovative Punk bands selling out to the establishment and giving up on societal change. Siouxsie and the

Banshees wanted to maintain their artistic integrity and continue to push the boundaries of music from new perspectives rather than conform to the commercial pressures of a male-run corporate music industry.

At the same time, the hippie movement's failure to effect significant social change left many punks feeling that activism had been too passive and naive in their attempts to change society with tangible action. Whereas hippies had emerged from the countercultural and anti-war movements of the 1960s, the punk movement emerged in the late 1970s as a reaction against mainstream culture's corporate commercialization and capitalist conformity.

French theorist Luce Irigaray argues that the very language and embodiment of power are vastly different for women than for men.

> The problem for women is not just that they are "other"—it is that they are not even recognized as being another. They are relegated to the inferior position of the same, which is why their difference goes unnoticed, unseen, and unthought. Women's struggle for equality is not just about gaining access to the same positions and roles as men—it is about challenging the very definition of the same and insisting on the importance of sexual difference in all areas of life. (*This Sex which Is Not One*, p. 23)

Ballion's rebellious, revolutionary, and subversive symbology set the stage for the band's indignation and animosity towards the status quo as a disruptive feminine critique.

Subverting Gender Narratives

Although her peers were predominantly male, Siouxsie Sioux's strong and distinctive voice often featured dramatic inflections, growls, whispers, and wails, giving her performances distinctive emotional intensity. Her unpredictable vocal phrasing with unexpected pauses, volume changes, and melody shifts keep the listener engaged and on edge. Shifting from aggressive and confrontational to introspective and vulnerable in a single song and using vibrato to add depth and emotion made her one of the most highly expressive vocalists of the era. Vocal stylings and antics usually only expected from a male singer were now embodied with intensive and unapologetic femininity.

Luce Irigaray states that when patriarchal tradition dominates language and linguistic structures, women have to challenge gendered hierarchies to create a language that breaks free from the constraints of the dominant discourse.

Women have had to invent a language of their own, a language that breaks free from the discursive constraints of the symbolic order, to articulate their experiences and perspectives. This language is not just a means of communication, but a way of challenging the very foundations of the dominant discourse and creating new ways of being in the world. (p. 22)

Irigaray suggests that women's experiences and perspectives have been marginalized within traditional Western philosophy because they do not fit neatly into the binary oppositions such as male/ female, mind/body, and reason/emotion historically associated with male privilege. By creating a new language, Irigaray argues that women can not only communicate their experiences more accurately but will create new ways of being in the world that are not constrained by gender norms. In this sense, language and linguistic expression are not just a means of communication but a tool for resistance and societal transformation.

Rage is not often associated with femininity because traditional Judeo-Christian gender roles and stereotypes have historically portrayed women as passive, nurturing, and emotional beings. In contrast, men are portrayed as strong, aggressive, and rational. This gendered binary has contributed to cultural bias against women expressing anger, as it is seen as unfeminine and goes against societal mores. Any woman who expresses anger may be viewed as hysterical, irrational, or out of control and often faces negative social and professional consequences. Many activists have called for the reclamation of women's anger as a powerful tool for social change and resistance against systems of oppression.

In her essay "The Uses of Anger: Women Responding to Racism," feminist theorist Audre Lorde argues that women are often discouraged from expressing their anger, especially in response to oppression or injustice. She contends that this suppression of anger is a form of oppression and that women should not be afraid to express their anger to challenge the status quo, which she suggests can be channeled into productive action.

Every woman has a well-stocked arsenal of anger potentially useful against those oppressions, personal and institutional, which brought that anger into being. Focused with precision, it can become a powerful source of energy serving progress and change. ("The Uses of Anger," pp, 124–133)

Siouxsie's use of provocative and controversial lyrics in themes in the early years of the band can be argued as an attempt to challenge conventional ideas about gender, sexuality, and power. The band's 1978 single, "Love in a Void," suggests an obsession with violent sex, with lyrics such as "We love to play, play with pain / I love you driving me insane." This language and imagery were uncommon in popular music then and were seen as shocking and taboo. The song "Jigsaw Feeling" from the band's 1979 album "Join Hands" describes a woman's dissociative experiences during instances of sexual violence. The song's lyrics describe a woman who is disconnected from her own body and emotions and feels fragmented and powerless due to the violence she has experienced. The song's controversial nature contributed to its significance, as it helped to bring attention to the issues of sexual violence that largely affect women and to challenge the silence and stigma often surrounding it.

The band's song, "Red Light," from the 1980 album *Kaleidoscope*, provided a critical perspective on the issue of prostitution and the exploitation and violence that often accompany it. At the time of its release, the topic of prostitution was highly stigmatized and often went unacknowledged in popular culture. The lyrics describe a woman's experience as a sex worker in vivid detail, highlighting the pain, degradation, and violence that are often part of the reality sex workers experience. By giving voice to the experiences of survivors and acknowledging the trauma and pain of sexual violence, the band created a powerful and empowering message that resonated with many listeners.

Oppressed Cultures Appropriated as Symbols of Rebellion

Known for her unique makeup style, Ballion drew inspiration from various cultural sources, including Native American and traditional Egyptian styles. Cultural appropriation involves taking elements of another culture without respect for its meaning, significance, or context and often exploiting or commodifying it for personal gain to project a particular image. This concept can be particularly damaging when it involves sacred or religious symbols, artifacts, or practices. Appropriation reduces complex and diverse traditions to superficial representations and reinforces harmful views while perpetuating misunderstandings about other cultures, leading to further discrimination and harm.

Feminist theorist Linda Martín Alcoff states:

> The problem with cultural appropriation is not that it is 'appropriation' per se, but rather that it involves the taking of what is not freely given,

the taking of something that does not belong to one, the taking of something that belongs to others in virtue of their membership in a culture, community, or group. In other words, the problem is not one of copying or borrowing per se but of theft. Cultural appropriation can involve the usurpation of symbols, artifacts, genres, rituals, or techniques, as well as ideas, beliefs, values, and practices. It can involve the theft of meaning, the degradation of symbolic power, the erasure of history and memory, and the imposition of false consciousness. It can contribute to the erasure of marginalized cultures and peoples, and to the maintenance of structures of domination. ("The Problem of Speaking for Others," p. 138)

The history of oppressed people's movements and symbols co-opted by white people to further their causes has always been a complex and ongoing issue. There are many examples throughout history of whites appropriating the language, symbols, and strategies of oppressed groups to gain power or status without actually challenging the systemic oppression faced by said groups.

The band name "Siouxsie and the Banshees" includes a derogatory slang term used by white colonizers to describe indigenous peoples in North America. The word 'banshee' came from the native observance of death. Some indigenous cultures used wailing as a collective and public practice to bond community members together when mourning the loss of a loved one. Most of these practices were often suppressed or discouraged by European colonizers, who saw them as evidence of savagery or barbarism.

According to Siouxsie, the reference was a tribute to Irish mythology, with banshee representing a female spirit who wailed to warn of impending death. Ballion chose the first half of the name as a tribute to the Sioux tribe, which she had long admired for their strength and resistance against oppression. In a 2007 interview with *The Guardian*, Siouxsie said, "I didn't know about cultural appropriation then, and the fact that the word could be used in a derogatory sense. But I did know that it had a strength and a resonance that I liked. It had a spirit about it that I found very attractive."

Siouxsie Sioux oversimplified and dehumanized diverse Asian cultures and identities in the song "Hong Kong Garden," released as a single in 1978. The lyrics of the song describe a Chinese garden as a place of exoticism and mysticism, with lines such as "Slanted eyes meet a new sunrise, a race of bodies small in size" and "Chinks in fancy dress, who could ask for more?" are depictions of Chinese people. In a 1991 interview with *Melody Maker*, Siouxsie stated that "Hong Kong Garden" was "naive and ignorant" and regretted its orientalist stereotypes. She acknowledged that some of her work had been contentious and offensive to specific audiences.

Feminist theorist bell hooks argues that white women have the privilege of borrowing from cultures not their own with minor consequences. In contrast, other women do not have the same freedom to move in and out of cultural territories without taking significant risks to their lives and livelihoods.

> White women have the privilege of being able to borrow, as well as to create fictions and images, from cultures not their own. In a racist society, whites are able to freely move into and out of the cultural territories of others, appropriating their experience and history. This is a privilege that black women, and other women of color, do not share. ("Talking Back," pp. 9–25)

In hooks's view, cultural appropriation perpetuates systems of oppression and marginalization while surrendering the importance of intersectionality and solidarity across different groups of women.

> The white female's appropriation of black style—once again to enhance her own beauty, to improve her own appearance—is still a sign of her power. It still does not signify that she has surrendered that power in order to become an all . . . She borrows from [other] women, but she does not join with them in the struggle against sexist oppression. (*Ain't I a Woman?*, p. 113)

Many Post-Punks were angry with their governments because they saw them as an institution complicit in maintaining the status quo, perpetuating inequalities, and suppressing dissent. Post-Punk lyrics often tackled themes such as state surveillance, police brutality, government corruption, and the erosion of civil liberties. The high unemployment rates and social unrest fueled the anger of many Post-Punks. The Thatcher and Reagan administrations, in particular, were seen as hostile to working-class and minority communities, and Post-Punk musicians responded with fierce criticism and opposition through their stage presence and lyrical expression.

Feminist theorist Angela Davis states:

> The roots of sexism and homophobia are found in the same economic and political institutions that serve as the foundation of racism in this country and, more often than not, the same extremist circles that inflict violence on people of color are responsible for the eruptions of

violence inspired by sexist and homophobic biases. Our political activism must clearly manifest our understanding of these connections. (*Women, Culture, and Politics*)

Davis states that white women cannot move forward until they realize that their struggle is tied to racial, economic, and social inequalities. "We must begin to create a revolutionary, multiracial women's movement that seriously addresses the main issues affecting poor and working-class women."

Examples of how the band addressed various political and societal issues are evident in the track "Red Over White," released in 1980 during the height of the Cold War and metaphorically explored the destructive power dynamics and political tensions between nations. While the song "Isreal" is primarily focused on the Israeli-Palestinian conflict, it encompasses broader themes of political conflict, social injustice, and the abuse of power. Moreover, while the song "Cities in Dust" does not directly address government issues, this song metaphorically captures the destruction and decay caused by political and societal upheaval. It reflects the band's general discontent with the state of the world.

A Lack of Empowering Symbology Not Associated with White Supremacy

White supremacy is a social and political system based on the belief that white people are superior to people of other races, cultures, and ethnicities. It is used to justify and perpetuate systemic violence, racism, discrimination, and inequality, giving white people more power and influence in society than people of color. Despite the many different cultures and subcultures falling under the umbrella term of "white" or European, each has unique traditions, languages, and histories. Due to violent incidents and groups throughout history, celebrating white culture can be perceived as an attempt to maintain or reinforce this power imbalance. The misuse of pre-Roman European symbols by white supremacist groups to promote their ideologies of racism, nationalism, and authoritarianism has led to a widespread association with fascism. White supremacists appropriated Celtic and Norse symbols to invent an idealized Aryan heritage.

One of the more agitating songs the band released was "Metal Postcard," originally released on the bands debut album *The Scream* in 1978, containing surreal and disturbing imagery, which some listeners found unsettling. The song's lyrics describe a postcard that depicts an eerie atmosphere, stating, "A cracking sound from the wall / A metal taste and it's in your mouth" created a sense of unease and discomfort. The song's lyrics include references to "crackling" and a "swastika," among other images.

These references suggest a connection to fascist iconography, particularly the use of metal and industrial imagery in Nazi propaganda. Critics found the song's disturbing imagery excessive and gratuitous. At the same time, fans regarded it as a groundbreaking and innovative work with a sense of disorientation and uncertainty that helped create a haunting and evocative portrait of the human psyche.

In recent years, many have criticized Siouxsie for wearing a swastika armband during one particular performance in London in 1976. What might now be seen as support or association with nazi culture was, at the time, used as provocative and confrontational imagery to challenge the status quo. In an interview with The Independent in 2005, Siouxsie explained that she wore the swastika as a way of reclaiming the symbol from its association with the Nazi regime and using it as a symbol of rebellion and provocation. Siouxsie explained that the armband was a modified version of a British Union Jack flag, which she had sewn onto her shirt as a punk fashion statement. She later replaced it with a swastika to shock and provoke but never intended it to endorse Nazi ideology. She also noted that she was inspired by the Situationist International, an avant-garde movement that sought to subvert capitalist society and challenge traditional power structures.

In a 1977 interview with *Sounds* magazine, Siouxsie explained that the swastika armband was meant to be a subversive gesture to challenge the status quo and confront the complacency of mainstream society. She said, "It was us taking the piss out of everything, especially the British punk scene. You know, all these people who are so forward and so liberal and so aware of everything, and they all wear a Union Jack, they all wear a swastika . . . It was in response to all of that."

Radical labor activist Lucy Parsons advocated for workers' rights and overthrowing capitalist oppression. She argues that in the revolutionary struggle against oppressive power systems, workers should use strong language and controversial symbols to challenge and subvert oppression. She states that those in power often use symbols of patriotism and nationalism to maintain their dominance over people, and the oppressed class has a responsibility to use these symbols subversively as a powerful tool for activities in their struggle for justice and equality.

In every age, it has been the tyrant, the oppressor, and the exploiter who has wrapped himself in the cloak of patriotism, or religion, or both to deceive and overawe the people . . . We are aware that many object to the severity of our language, but is there not cause for severity? . . . I appeal to the sense of justice and to the generous instincts of my readers to vindicate the position which could not be withheld from me, as a woman and a lover of my country, when I saw its very foundations being undermined by slavery, ignorance, and financial ruin. ("The Principles of Anarchism")

Parsons argues that when oppressed peoples highlight the power of new ideas and growing unrest amongst their peers, it threatens the power structure with the possibility of change and motivates others to take collective action to continue to spread ideas of freedom and resistance in all their forms. "More and more, as ideas and methods of freedom spread, more and more people begin to question the old ways of oppression and to ask for something better. It is the spreading of these new ideas and the growing unrest of the workers that makes the powers that be tremble."

Lack of Empowering Symbology for White Women

Patriarchy has deprived women of access to powerful symbology by positioning men as society's dominant cultural and social group. This power dynamic has led to the historical exclusion of women from positions of power and influence, as well as from access to empowering knowledge and practices previously passed down through female lineages. As a result, white women have been deprived of cultural symbology from their heritage and from empowered femininity that could have been used for their liberation.

Monotheistic religions contributed to the marginalization of female spirituality and the elevation of male religious figures, who were seen as more worthy of interpreting divine messages. Religions viewed women's bodies and eroticism as sinful or unclean, leading to the policing and controlling women's sexuality and the exclusion of women from specific religious practices. The development of patriarchal norms limited women's access to spiritual and religious conclaves of the pagan past, preventing them from continuing to foster intimate connections to each other, the natural world, the rhythms of the earth, and their roles as mothers and women. Whereas women were once seen as the guardians of spiritual practices in many ancient cultures, and their leadership was highly valued, they are now largely deprived of symbols and practices tied to their unique experiences.

The Divine Feminine has a long and complex history that dates back to ancient civilizations. In many ancient cultures, such as those in Mesopotamia, Egypt, and Greece, numerous goddesses were worshipped alongside male gods. In many indigenous and pagan traditions, women were priestesses, healers, and leaders. Feminist author Merlin Stone states that the historical and archaeological evidence for prehistoric goddess-worshipping cultures emphasized the importance of honoring the divine feminine.

> It is difficult to grasp the immensity and significance of the extreme reverence paid to the Goddess over a period of (at least) seven thousand years and over miles of land cutting across national boundaries and vast expanses of sea. Yet it is vital to do just that to fully comprehend the longevity as well as the widespread power and influence this religion once held. (*When God Was a Woman*)

Stone states that the suppression of women's rights began with the suppression of women's rites, saying that

> In most archaeological texts the female religion is referred to as a "fertility cult," perhaps revealing the attitudes toward sexuality held by the various contemporary religions that may have influenced the writers. But archaeological and mythological evidence of the veneration of the female deity as creator and lawmaker of the universe, prophetess, provider of human destinies, inventor, healer, hunter, and valiant leader in battle suggests that the title "fertility cult" may be a gross oversimplification of a complex theological structure.

The idea that women are more likely to create and build rather than destroy shows their potential to be more competent and compassionate leaders. Still, it does not mean they're only relegated to meekness.

> The Great Goddess—the Divine Ancestress—had been worshiped from the beginnings of the Neolithic periods of 7000 BC until the closing of the last Goddess temples, about AD 500. Some authorities would extend Goddess worship as far into the past as the Upper Paleolithic Age of about 25,000 BC. It is only as many of the tenets of the Judeo-Christian theologies are seen in the light of their political origins, and the subsequent absorption of those tenets into secular life understood, that as women we will be able to view ourselves as

mature, self-determining human beings. With this understanding we may be able to regard ourselves not as permanent helpers but as doers, not as decorative and convenient assistants to men but as responsible and competent individuals in our own right. The image of Eve is not our image of woman.

American feminist Robin Morgan highlighted the interconnectedness of women's experiences and the need for collective action by stating, "The "Othering" of women is the oldest oppression known to our species and it's the model, the template, for all other oppressions" ("The Anatomy of Freedom," p. 232).

The European witch hunts of the sixteenth and seventeenth centuries were a tragic period that resulted in the deaths of tens of thousands of people, the majority of whom were women. One major factor was the patriarchal society of the time, which saw women as inferior to men and prone to moral corruption. Women who defied traditional gender roles or expressed unconventional ideas were seen as a threat to the social order, and this fear was exacerbated by religious anxieties related to the Protestant Reformation. Many women accused of witchcraft during the witch hunts were healers, midwives, or herbalists, and their practices were often based on traditional knowledge passed down through generations of women. These practices were seen as a threat to the patriarchal medical establishment and the religious authorities of the time, who sought to enforce a strict orthodoxy and limit the role of women in spiritual and healing practices.

Women were more likely to be poor, illiterate, and socially isolated. Torture and other forms of violence often resulted in false confessions, which in turn led to the execution of innocent people. Women accused of witchcraft faced social stigma and ostracism, even if they were acquitted, and the fear of being accused often led women to self-censor and conform to traditional gender roles. The witch hunts thus limited women's opportunities for social, political, and economic empowerment.

French feminist and theorist Hélène Cixous states that men see sexuality differently than women due to a binary cultural upbringing. Whereas men view the use of sexuality for opposition, power, invasion, and colonization, women's sexuality and the power of the womb have continuously operated in the darkness and secret. Women have used sexuality to create, build, give, and enrich their surroundings. Some women tend to have shame associated with feminine empowerment and often turn against their cohorts to gain influence with the men in power around them. "Men have committed the greatest crime against women. Insidiously, violently, they have led them to hate women, to be their enemies, to mobilize their immense strength against themselves, to be the executants of their virile needs" ("The Laugh of the Medusa," pp. 875–893).

The archetype of the Greek goddess Medusa is an iconic symbol associated with female power, danger, and mystery. After being sexually assaulted in Athena's Temple by Poseidon, Medusa is portrayed as an angry woman scorned rather than a victim of sexual violence. *Medusa* is an allegory representing themes of male versus female power structures, desires, and the fear of feminine rage. Cixous explains that men have "riveted us between two horrifying myths: between the Medusa and the abyss." If women would question these myths, if they would "look at the Medusa straight on," they would find out "she's not deadly. She's beautiful and she's laughing."

Ballion uses the symbolism of witchcraft, feminine rage, and darkness by reclaiming it from negative connotations in popular culture. To her, this positive force represents women's strength, independence, fierceness, and resilience. By embracing the "dark side" of femininity, she challenges the notion that women must be submissive, docile, and subservient. Instead, she refuses to be constrained by societal norms.

However complicated the history of white women grasping for symbology to further their empowerment, the Post-Punk era was a formidable time in progressing class, race, gender, and culture. The continual flux of activism and expression through music built momentum for others to break the chains of patriarchal structures and power imbalance. Susan Ballion explored her oppression and expressed her dissent by subverting traditional gender narratives and adopting mystical power symbols from indigenous and oppressed societies. This appropriation of cultural elements, however powerful they are for cis-hetero-white women in furthering their agenda, has proven harmful when it involves exploiting or commodifying oppressed people. To create a more just and equitable society, it's crucial to approach other cultures with respect and humility and to seek to learn from and engage with them in collaborative, respectful, and mutually beneficial ways.

As Audre Lorde states, "The master's tools will never dismantle the master's house. They may allow us to temporarily beat him at his own game, but they will never enable us to bring about genuine change."

V

Post-Punk Aesthetics

15
Post-Punk and the Aesthetics of Atmosphere

S. Evan Kreider

In many ways, Post-Punk was simply a natural evolution of Punk, but in other ways, it was a radical departure. Whereas Punk was largely known for its raw emotional expression and the occasional political statement, Post-Punk turned to a more subtle emotional expression and the creation of sonic landscapes.

Through the utilization of composition and performance, supplemented with distinctive production and engineering, Post-Punk generates an expansive sense of place and the psychological disposition to accompany it.

Once Post-Punk is examined through the lens of philosophical aesthetics, especially the work of Susanne Langer, it finds its distinct style as a genre that creates a virtual atmosphere through the linking of (as Langer would say) feeling and form.

Symbolization and Illusion

In Langer's view, the arts function as a kind of symbolization. The use of symbols is what distinguishes humans from other animals, and we humans use symbols in a wide variety of contexts, such as language, mathematics, and the arts. Whereas symbolization in, for example, ordinary language is used to communicate meaning in a direct and literal way, artistic symbolization functions differently, as a symbolic expression of feeling. In the spirit of "Show, don't tell," art presents something for the audience to experience, rather than to understand in an intellectual manner. The feelings expressed by art needn't be everyday emotions such as happiness or sadness but can also be more generalized aesthetic feelings that the audience may experience in a more abstract manner.

There's always an element of the virtual in the arts. Using various formal elements, they create more than what can be reduced to their material structure, presenting the illusion of something greater than the sum of their material parts for the sensory experience of the audience. According to Langer, each type of art has a primary virtual aspect. For example, a painting creates virtual space, through formal elements such as perspective and shading, perhaps something as simple as the paint placed on the two-dimensional canvas in such a way as to create the appearance of a three-dimensional space such as a room or landscape.

The primary illusion of music is time: through the illusory movement of its formal elements (melody, harmony, rhythm, tempo), music gives the virtual impression of temporal passage and progression. Langer does not claim that each type of art is limited only to its primary illusion: a painting could also express the passage of time, and music can also give the impression of space.

As a genre of music, Post-Punk would certainly accomplish what Langer claims: the expression of feelings through various auditory forms, involving the illusion of time. However, various genres of music would naturally do this in varying ways, resulting in different musical experiences. Post-Punk's specific brand of illusory expression is that of atmosphere, in the sense of a creating both a particular kind of musical environment and distinctive feeling associated with that environment. It does this through traditional music forms such as harmony and rhythm, but also through more modern formal elements that result from specific engineering techniques such as the use of effects. It also creates virtual atmosphere through its lyrics, which provide the occasion for the listener to experience the virtual atmosphere both auditorily as well as conceptually. To see how Post-Punk accomplishes all this, it is essential to analyze specific tunes by representative bands such as the Cure, Joy Division, Siouxsie and the Banshees, and the Couteau Twins.

Form and Feeling

Our first example of Post-Punk formalism is "Plainsong," the opening song on the Cure's *Disintegration*. The song immediately makes use of the form of dynamics, starting with a few seconds of pianissimo (very quiet) chimes, before the ensemble begins fortissimo (very loud), immediately confronting the listener with a religious-like atmosphere. This is accomplished with very church-like orchestration, with synthesizers that are reminiscent of pipe organs and stringed instruments, as well as a percussion section that includes large cymbals and timpani. The compositional form reinforces this atmosphere, especially the chord progression. "Plainsong" spends most of its time alternating between two chords, which in theory terms would be called the I and the IV chord: the I (one) chord is the tonic (home) chord, the resting place of the key signature (think "do" in "do-re-mi-fa-so-la-ti-do"), and the IV (four) chord provides motion away from and then back to the home chord. This movement, especially from the IV back to the I, is reminiscent of what some music theorists call the "Amen cadence," because of its use at the end of many Christian hymns ("Ahhhhh . . . mennnnnn . . ."), and it adds a grand, religious atmosphere to "Plainsong" as well. When the chords do change at the end of each verse, they move up through what is known as the "deceptive cadence," because it seems to move toward the home chord but moves to an even higher chord instead. This creates a feeling of suspension, which in this case adds to the overall atmospheric effect.

"Disorder," the first track on Joy Division's *Unknown Pleasures*, creates an atmosphere of disorder (naturally) through formal elements such as the compositional contrast among the drums, bass, and guitar. The instrumental break immediately following the first verse is especially effective at this. The drums continue in metronome-like fashion, while the guitar plays more freely, almost without following the tempo of the song at all. In addition, the bass contrasts with the guitar by occasionally playing outside of the key signature of the piece, mostly notably in the descending pattern played a few times between verses that ends on the open E string (the lowest note on a bass in standard tuning), which is sharply in contrast to the E-flat in the key signature and chords of most of the song.

Even more supportive of this disorderly effect is the end of the song. While Ian Curtis repeatedly sings "I've got the spirit but lose the feeling," the bass lines drifts even further off-key, the guitar descends into chaotic noise, and an atonal special effect (perhaps a synthesizer of some sort) provides an atmospheric exclamation, just before the song as a whole song suddenly grinds to a halt.

Siouxsie and the Banshee's standalone single "Israel" also makes good use of chord changes and instrumentation to create its own atmospheric effect, in this case a dream-like soundscape that suggests far-away places and ancient times. The bassline outlines the chord changes, which do not follow more common Western cadences, suggesting something foreign and unfamiliar. Two guitars complement each other, one playing downward arpeggios (chord notes played separately) and the other punctuating each line with a strummed, distorted chord. Perhaps most interestingly is the vocal melody, occasionally but purposely sung ever-so-slightly off-tune, the effect of which is even more pronounced when sung against the vocal harmony lines. This suggests a microtonal approach to melody that is often downplayed in traditional Western music, and more reminiscent of non-Western tonalities such as those found in classical Indian music played on instruments such as the sitar (of which the Beatles made good use on occasion). Once again, this suggests something far from ordinary experience, creating an atmosphere of the unfamiliar.

For our final example of this section, take "Wax and Wane," the second song on the Cocteau Twin's *Garlands*. Considering their approach to lyrics (which we'll address later), it's not easy to determine what any given Cocteau Twins song is "about" exactly. The title and some snippets of discernable lyrics suggest time, change, and perhaps strife and recovery. Assuming that's a reasonable interpretation, then the musical forms create the perfect atmosphere for the ideas. The bassline moves frenetically through the chords, which themselves move in a close linear fashion to one another, suggesting the inexorable movement of time (which, as we recall, Langer thought was the primary illusion of music). In contrast, the guitar mostly plays simple, repeating melodic phrases, suggesting a stasis behind the movement, providing the context against which the bassline's motion expresses the passage of time. Of course, Elizabeth Fraser's vocals complete the tune. Throughout the verses, she largely lingers over two neighboring notes, then suddenly contrasts it with a melody of multiple descending notes during the song's chorus, once again creating an atmosphere of statis and change, waxing and waning.

The Effect of Effects

While Punk was typically recorded in a very raw manner to evoke the feel of listening to the band play right in the audience's face, Post-Punk often made very good use of special effects to help create its atmosphere. One of the most common effects used was some variation of echo or reverberation ("reverb" for short). This made many Post-Punk songs sound as though they were played in very large spaces such as large concert halls, natural caverns, or cliff-surrounded valleys. Furthermore, the relative volume balance between the original ("dry" signal) and the reverb effect could create the experience of the singer or instrument's placement closer or further away from the listener. Every song mentioned above makes good use of reverb to one extent or another, and there are many other examples as well.

The Cure's "Three Imaginary Boys" (from the album of the same name) makes excellent use of echo on Robert Smith's voice, giving the song a dreamy atmosphere, and as the song progresses, the echo is mixed louder relative to the dry voice, giving the effect of the vocals moving far away from the audience. Joy Division's "Dead Souls" and aptly named "Atmosphere" (two singles recorded during the same session) both use reverb to good effect on all the instruments, but especially the vocals and the drums, the latter of which contributes greatly to the hall-like atmosphere of the songs. Siouxsie and the Banshee's "Christine" (from *Kaleidoscope*) follows Joy Division's suit with appropriately placed reverb on the vocals and especially the drums to produce a psychedelic, kaleidoscopic sensation for the audience that creates a fitting centerpiece for the album's title and overall theme. The Cocteau Twin's "Blood Bitch" (the first song from *Garlands*) sets the mood and atmosphere of the entire album with copious use of reverb, especially on the guitar.

Delay is closely related to echo and reverb; in fact, certain uses of delay create just those effects. However, delay can be used in an independent way that creates a more obvious repetition of the notes played, not unlike when a song such as "Row Your Boat" is sung as a round. Apropos of Langer's idea of music as virtual time, delay quite literally involves creating various effects of time, as the number of repeats and the length of time between them, which can be adjusted to suit. Robert Smith uses delay towards the end of "A Forest" (from *Seventeen Seconds*): though the guitar part starts the song without noticeable delay, subtle amounts are added as the tune progresses, with the most obvious amount near the very end of the song, creating an increasingly moody atmosphere for its conclusion.

Delay features very prominently on the vocals of Joy Division's "She's Lost Control" (from *Unknown Pleasures*), with the delay speed modified on the fly to create a surreal warbling effect. The final word of each line in the verses of Siouxsie and the Banshee's "Love in a Void" uses a pronounced and rapid "slapback" style of delay to punctuate each line (though this effect seems to have been removed from recent remixes, sadly). The guitar uses tightly grouped delay repeats throughout the title track on the Cocteau Twins' "Garlands," creating a chaotic cacophony with an almost sinister atmosphere.

There are several modulation effects such as chorus, flanger, and phaser that work by creating very short delays which are then modulated and otherwise modified. This can create a variety of sounds, from a subtle thickening to a wider vibrato or even a pronounced underwater-like trilling. Though used less frequently on vocals and drums, modulation effects were a staple of Post-Punk guitar and bass sounds. The bass that introduces the Cure's "Holy Hour" (from *Faith*) uses a pronounced flanger sound that, per the title of both the song and the album, creates an atmosphere of reverence.

Peter Hook was famous for his use of modulation effects on his signature bass sound in both Joy Division and New Order: the bass that features prominently at the beginning of "Twenty-Four Hours" (from Joy Division's *Closer*) powerfully grabs the listener's attention before the rest of the band comes crashing in. The aforementioned "Israel" by Siouxsie and the Banshees uses chorus on the guitar and the bass, a wide, thick version of it that contributes to the distinct atmosphere described above. Both the bass and the guitar in the Cocteau Twins' "Violaine" (the opening track from *Milk and Kisses*) use a clear, bright chorus sound that creates a shimmering, airy feeling that provides the appropriate atmosphere for the fairy-like voice and lyrics of Elizabeth Fraser's vocals.

The Poetry and Music of Lyrics

Compared to purely instrumental tunes, songs with lyrics present an extra challenge for philosophical aesthetics. On the one hand, lyrics can simply stand on their own as poetry; on the other hand, they serve a musical end as well, much like any other instrument. In truth, they are a bit of both. According to Langer, lyric poetry serves as a kind of virtual memory. This certainly seems apt for Post-Punk, the lyrics of which often have a wistful, memory-like quality to them, as though the singer is relating experiences of times past. This in turn contributes even more to the atmosphere and emotion of the song, as evidenced by the following examples.

"Holy Hour" (The Cure)

I kneel and wait in silence
As one by one the people slip away
Into the night
The quiet and empty bodies

Kiss the ground before they pray
Kiss the ground and slip away
I sit and listen dreamlessly
A promise of salvation makes me stay
Then look at your face
And feel my heart pushed in
As all around the children play
The games they tired of yesterday

After the introduction by the modulated bassline, the vocals deliver lyrics that create a dreamy atmosphere (ironic, given the reference to dreamlessness). Mention of yesterday suggests times past, as do the references to the people slipping away. Silence and quiet, along with sitting and listening, evoke a contemplative mood. The title, along with the references to praying and salvation, give the song a sense of the sacred.

"Dead Souls" (Joy Division)

Someone take these dreams away
That point me to another day
A duel of personalities
That stretch all true realities
That keep calling me ...
Where figures from the past stand tall
And mocking voices ring the halls
Imperialistic house of prayer
Conquistadors who took their share
That keep calling me . . .

Ian Curtis's lyrics fit the music perfectly. The spacious reverb that suggests a large hall is complemented by lyrics that paint a similar scene, tall figures in halls and houses of prayer. Mentions of the past, another day, dreams, and realities could almost have come from Langer herself, suggesting the passage of time and the recollection of vivid memories. The repetition of "they keep calling me" throughout the song creates an ambiguous feeling of fearful longing. The title, though not explicitly mentioned in the lyrics, frames the atmosphere, suggesting something of a museum or mausoleum, silent except for the mocking voices (as well as referring to the novel by Gogol, of course).

"Spellbound" (Siouxsie and the Banshees)

From the cradle bars
Comes a beckoning voice
It sends you spinning

You have no choice
You hear laughter
Cracking through the walls
It sends you spinning
You have no choice ...
Following the footsteps
Of a rag doll dance
We are entranced
Spellbound.

Much like "Christine" and "Israel," "Spellbound" creates a moody, mystical atmosphere. The lyrical mentions of "spinning" and "dancing" describe the virtual motion of the instruments as they themselves imply turning and twirling movements. The "beckoning voice" adds to the magical atmosphere, in which the "entranced" listener "has no choice" but to be drawn into the otherworldly mood. The reference to laughter and beckoning further ensnares the audience into the overall enchanting effect.

"Cherry-Coloured Funk" (Cocteau Twins)

Beetles and eggs and blues and pour a little everything else . . .
You steam a lens stable eyes and glass
Not get pissed off through my bird lips as good news
Still being cried and laughed at before
Should I be sewn in hugged I can by not saying
Still being cried and laughed at from light to blue
And should I be hugged and tugged down through this tiger's
    masque.

Elizabeth Fraser's lyrics form a fitting conclusion for our discussion. In various statements and interviews, Fraser has indicated that her lyrics are highly atypical in that they are not meant to have the more straightforward and literal meaning that many lyrics do. Instead, she chooses her lyrics based on private associations or simply their sound alone, even using words and phrases in languages foreign to her the meaning of which she herself did not know. For the listener, not privy to her private associations, the lyrics are experienced as pure, abstract sound, as though simply another instrument. In this way, they contribute to the mysterious atmosphere of their songs, and allow the listener to form their own meanings and associations, experiencing their own personal feelings and reactions that are highly subjective but no less valid as a consequence.

The Enduring Aesthetic of Post-Punk

Susanne Langer's work on aesthetics has had a lasting effect on philosophy. Her ideas of symbolization, form, expression, feeling, and the virtual dimension of art have set the context for much of the scholarship for the last several decades. Even better, her philosophy provides an accessible way for the interested layperson to reflect on the nature and function of art.

Langer's thoughts on music have had an enduring effect on the relevant academic discourse, and in the case of Post-Punk specifically, serve as a fascinating framework for fans of the genre, which itself endures since its inception almost fifty years ago, thanks to the atmospheric effects it creates which still entrance listeners even today.

16

Recipe for a Post-Punk Song

CANDACE MIRANDA AND WALTER BARTA

How do you produce a Post-Punk song? Post-Punk, as a musical genre, which notably developed after the Punk Rock period of the 1960s, utilized an artistic process, like any other musical genre, which included various artistic techniques.

So, in order to better identify how Post-Punk music is composed, we first have to consider not only how music, specifically, is made but also art more generally. We have to consider in general the philosophy of art, also known as aesthetics, and the concrete things it has to say about the production of art forms, as well as the particular artistic philosophies that Post-Punk employs.

Post-Punk artists especially engaged in a form of aesthetic eclecticism, a philosophy of aesthetics that defines art as more than one thing and applies that methodologically towards the creation of new art that combines more than one genre, style, or mode. Post-Punk is an excellent exemplification of eclecticism, as it can be seen as an experimental genre that attempts to imitate but also innovate upon the stereotypical conventions of the Rock and Punk genres that preceded it.

Post-Punk as Imitation

In one of the first written volumes in aesthetic philosophy, *Poetics,* Aristotle (384–322 B.C.E.) identifies at least two different modes of artistic creation: imitation and invention.

As Aristotle pointed out, a large amount of the artistic process is imitation, the process of repeating the patterns of past works in the patterns of future works. According to Aristotle, nobody is totally original; everybody is a bit derivative, and that's a good thing, because it is how the artistic process works. Imitation is after all, as they say, the best form of compliment.

Post-Punk artists were no strangers to imitation, often using the melodies, rhythms, and tones of older bands as the model for new songs. The major artistic influence on the Post-Punk genre was (obviously) Punk. Even the moniker "Post-Punk" explicitly states its imitative inheritance of the Punk genre. Most Post-Punk bands started as imitative bands with slight variations on the popular music of the time, many with their earliest beginnings as garage Punk bands influenced by attending the Sex Pistols' 1976 show at the Lesser Free Trade Hall. As Barney Hoskyns, a British music critic, recalls,

> The Sex Pistols show in Manchester clearly was hugely important for the music scene there. Pretty much everyone who was there went on to form the kind of key Manchester Punk and Post-Punk bands.

Even the poster boys of Post-Punk, Joy Division, got their humble beginnings when Ian Curtis and other soon-to-be bandmates attended the Leicester Square show, and after the inspiration of the Sex Pistols, began their journey towards Post-Punk with their little-known Punk band Warsaw. In this we can see how the imitative process was a driving force in the evolution of even some of the most visionary Post-Punk bands.

When imitation is repeated through many instances of art-works, those instances with common pattern become a genre or style. In Aristotle's day, these genres included Epic Poems, Tragic Plays and Comic Plays. In the modern context, these genres might include Punk, Post-Punk, and others— their pre-decessor and successor genres, those they imitated and those that imitate them. This process of imitation across many art-works is how a genre like Post-Punk comes to be its own genre, rather than just an instance of slightly variant Punk (perhaps what it might have been had Post-Punk not caught on enough).

In regard to imitative legacy, with the rise of Post-Punk revival today in bands such as Radiohead and Smashing Pumpkins and even more recently The Raconteurs, Franz Ferdinand, The Strokes, and The White Stripes, it is easy to see the ways in which these bands imitate the Post-Punk bands that preceded them while adding their own twists. Some music writers even dub this emulation a Post-Punk revival. For example, although they add their own touches, you may be able to hear a Post-Punk likeness of sound in songs like Franz Ferdinand's "Take Me Out" and The White Stripes' "Icky Thump" with The Talking Heads' "Psycho Killer" and Gang of Four's "Naturals Not in It." If not made aware of when the more recent of the bands mentioned came to be, we might even suppose bands like Franz Ferdinand and The White Stripes to have belonged alongside those in 1978–1984, the era of Post-Punk, with their similar bass lines, tempos, and monotone, staccato-like vocals.

Furthermore, a Post-Punk element might even be imitated by music outside of what we consider the obvious Punk-inspired genres. To point to one interesting example, it has been speculated by some that The Talking Heads have had the bassline of their famous song "Psycho Killer" imitated outside of the Post-Punk revival today in Selena Gomez's chart hitting pop song, "Bad Liar." Other such popular imitations or compliments within today's musical zeitgeist include Siouxsie Sioux's song "Happy House" being sampled in the intro of The Weeknd's 2011 song "House of Balloons" and Section 25's song titled "Hit" paid tribute to in Kanye West's song "FML."

Ironically, as a philosopher in the Athenian tradition, Aristotle himself partook in the activity of imitation, drawing upon the aesthetic theory of Dionysius of Halicarnassus, who is the first philosopher recorded to have invented the concept of imitation. Of course, Dionysius may have been imitating someone himself, ad infinitum. And all of Western philosophy has been imitating Greek philosophy, including Aristotle, ever since. But Aristotle was still correct (if derivative) in his diagnosis: looking through artistic history, we find a long sequence of imitative legacy.

But then, if the artistic process is largely imitative, what accounts for the creativity, imagination, and originality of Post-Punk and other genres?

Post-Punk as Combination

Aristotle identified invention as another part of the artistic development—the process of introducing a new pattern in a new work that has not appeared in prior works. For instance, someone might coin a new word or phrase, play a new guitar riff, or invent a new technology that has genuinely never been used before.

Post-Punk was a genre that utilized invention. Post-Punk artists were known for creating new patterns for future sounds and ways of music production. As the writers for *Amplified* put it in their Post-Punk music documentary, "thanks to their thrillingly unique sound and intensely charismatic lead singer," Joy Division "sounded quite unlike anything that had gone before." It's because of their new sound that the notable pioneers of Post-Punk, Joy Division, are a great example of Aristotle's mode of invention when speaking of artistic creation. Joy Division provided a sound unlike that of the time— breaking the molds of Punk rock's loud guitar riffs and aggressive lyrics. Everything about them was different, even their front man, Ian Curtis, acted unlike most "rockstars" of the time. He often moved or danced in a stoic, stiff manner while singing his poetic, monotone, near-depressed lyrics like "Love will tear us apart again."

Unlike the artists of Punk, Post-Punk artists accepted technological invention. For instance, Post-Punk music experimented with the use of synthesizers, an electronic musical instrument that creates wave-like sounds. Post-Punk bands utilized the synthesizer, unlike genres before them, to create a sort of Punk, futuristic, technological sound. As music producer Daniel Miller put it, it is because of this newfound acceptance, bands like "Human League or anybody that was disillusioned with the music of the time felt that synthesizers were a logical place to go next." Eventually, after Ian Curtis's death, Joy Division became New Order, and they also adopted the use of synthesizers in their new music, emphasizing the "new" invention element.

Invention also seems to be what sets many famous bands apart from more obscure ones. For example, in their infantile beginnings as Warsaw, Ian Curtis and his band-mates didn't achieve nearly the same level of popularity that they did in their later rebirth as the Post-Punk band Joy Division. This difference in success has been attributed to the fact that Warsaw sounded too much like every other Sex Pistols– inspired Punk band.

This was also the case for many other mediocre Punk bands until they began to develop their own musical styles. Siouxsie and the Banshees, who followed a similar path to Joy Division, were initially not particularly popular, as they mimicked a sound easily found throughout most of London's Punk "garage" bands, until they later changed things up, found a niche within the Post-Punk genre, and gained massive appeal for their "new" sound.

However it's hard to find something genuinely "new" because most artforms are repetitions of older artforms. You might invent a new melody but with the same chromatic scale of notes. You might invent new lyrics but with the same English words. You might write a new Punk song, but, after all, it's just another Punk song—the same vocals, the same guitar, the same bass, and the same drum set as any other wannabe band. So, in that sense, is anything truly new?

Modern artists and art theorists have pointed out that the answer to how invention works may counterintuitively lie in the process of imitation itself but applied repeatedly through combination and recombination. The aesthetic process that embraces this technique of combination has been called by theorists of aesthetics, artistic eclecticism. Artistic eclecticism asks the basic question: what happens when you incorporate influences from multiple different sources in a single new work of art? You get elements from many different old artforms but in a completely new combinatory creation.

Combination is thus a form of imitation in the sense that it collects many different artistic sources for its inspiration. Arguably though, combination is also a form of invention in the sense that it combines the different inspirations into a new product that is a genuinely new combination. It is akin to the concept of recipe creation. All foods that exist singularly have existed for centuries, but every new combination of said food items becomes a different dish. For example, both Bolognese and nduja contain similar ingredients, a base of ground meat, tomatoes and garlic, however they are completely different flavors.

In many ways, Post-Punk metaphorically utilizes different ingredients integrated with Punk in order to form its own musical flavor. In the time Post-Punk was making its premiere, according to Jon King, the front man of Gang of Four, "there was something else going on in the sense that people were trying out . . . proto-mashups" (BBC Four). For example, Gang of Four often experimented with what Andy Gill, the band's guitarist, referred to as a sort of "Punk funk" and the all-girl band, The Slits, also played with this idea of mixing genres with their fusion of Punk and reggae as well as opposing everything that the average rockstar did in order to make their difference known.

The art historian and theorist Johann Joachim Winckelmann (1717–1768) first proposed the notion of eclecticism in his study of the artistic styles of the Renaissance. During this time, artists began imitating not just the techniques of Ancient Rome but also the techniques of Ancient Greece, bringing together elements from each. Furthermore, because of the burgeoning artistic community of the Renaissance, artists began to noticeably imitate each other. The Michelangelos, Raphaels, and Caravaggios would view each other's artworks, observe what they liked, and then repeat those patterns in their own work, combining elements creatively.

Just as the painters of the Renaissance pocketed techniques from their fellow artists, the musicians of Post-Punk did the same—drawing inspiration from different centuries as well as artists of different mediums. Many Post-Punk bands notably drew upon other musical genres such as funk and jazz. For example, according to the BBC Four documentary *Punk Britannia Part III: Post-Punk*, "on July 12, 1979, PiL, Public Image Limited, appeared live on the top of the pops performing a fusion of dub, disco, and Tchaikovsky" with their song "Death Disco." As PiL's frontman, John "Johnny Rotten" Lydon, puts it himself, similarly to the Renaissance painters, he "paints pictures with words and sounds," and those paintings draw from a desire to create an accurate depiction of the progression of life—"Earth, life, death, and all of it."

A more eclectic philosophy of the artistic process also allows many artists to explore drawing on a mixture of inspirations that are outside of music itself as well, such as literature, movies, and the avant-garde art scene. This can be seen within songs such as "Charlotte Sometimes" by The Cure, which was inspired by the book of its namesake by Penelope Farmer. "Killing an Arab" by The Cure references Albert Camus's novel *The Stranger*. And the song "Punk is Dead" by Crass draws from a more general awareness of the Punk scene as an artistic movement with specific genre features and an eclectic influence in the wider British and world culture.

The artist and thinker Joshua Reynolds (1723–1792) took the concept of eclecticism to suggest a notion of "common property," what in modern parlance is often referred to as public domain, those renowned artistic achievements that have entered the community culture to be used and referenced by others as a form of common knowledge. This notion of "common property" enriches the community to the extent that everyone can learn from, imitate, and benefit from the historical artistic endowment.

It is thanks to this concept of "common property" or public domain that many notable Post-Punk songs continue to live on. There's no shortage of covers played by bands and solo musicians alike on social media platforms such as YouTube, TikTok, and the like. There's also a plethora of more well-known artists who have paid tribute to Post-Punk tracks like Velvet

Underground's cover of "Sister Ray" by Joy Division and Keane's rendition of The Cult's "She Sells Sanctuary." And, as we've seen, Post-Punk songs are also not solely limited to being sampled or covered by other modern bands within the Punk rock or indie community but also more mainstream artists in other genres like R&B and pop—Kanye West, Selena Gomez, Rittz, Mike Posner, and The Weeknd, to name a few.

Artistic eclecticism, by embracing genre-blending combination, continues to create new sounds.

How to Make a Post-Punk Song

So, with all of these considerations in mind—imitation, invention, eclecticism, and common property—let's return to our original question: how does one creatively produce a new Post-Punk song? Some of the integral elements that make up a Post-Punk song are lyrics akin to poetry, angular musical sounds, pairings like Punk plus funk, and integration of mediums like fashion and other visual arts—just to name a few ingredients of Post-Punk's mashup. It is far from the cliché of sex, drugs, and rock'n'roll.

First, as a base, to create a Post-Punk song you may want to mix genres that have not been mixed before while also utilizing the do-it-yourself demeanor of Punk. PiL's bassist Jah Wobble was notable for doing just this. As Barry Adamson of the band Magazine tells it, Wobble was "doing this other thing altogether which no one had sort of heard outside of reggae." The Slits also adopted this new and intriguing combination of Punk and reggae. You might take familiar Punk or Post-Punk riffs, chords, and baselines, but add flourishes from other genres until you have come up with a unique offbeat sound. Thus, you have created the musical foundation of a "proto-mashup": a Punk-plus-something genre.

Second, you can begin to create lyrics that combine the feisty anarchic energy of Punk with the more somber and downtempo emotions of other poetical genres. This lyrical combination entices the former Punks along with a more cerebral, intellectual, philosophical audience, mixing poetry with opinions about the social climate. Joy Division, did this very well with verses like,

Someone take these dreams away
That point to another day.
A duel of personalities
That stretch all true realities. (Joy Division, "Dead Souls")

As British musician and journalist John Robb said of lyrics like these, "They show you can talk about very dark, very intellectual kind of subjects in a very poetic kind of way, but make it into great rock'n'roll at the same time. It can work as a great rock'n'roll song, but it can work as a great piece of poetry as well." Some other examples of Post-Punk poeticism include The Slit's title track "New Town" which spoke of "all the 'new towns' appearing all over England." The Post-Punk, reggae sound combined with the song's ominous bassline spoke of peoples' "addictions in the city," as Tessa Pollitt of The Slits describes it. Another poetic and fittingly philosophical example of Post-Punk's integration of the two subjects is the band named The Fall after philosopher Albert Camus's novel of the same name. Mark E. Smith, lead singer of The Fall, was known for music that was categorized by some as a sort of "existentialist street poetry" (BBC Four). Now, after these considerations, your Post-Punk song has been created with its subversive lyrics and unique mixed musical qualities.

Third, publish your music through a music label that is willing to try unusual new experimental sounds. For instance, the label Rough Trade, formed by Geoff Travis in 1978, was open to any new form of genre mixing whether it be extremely Post-Punk or just Post-Punk-esque and especially the music that was censored by mainstream media at the time. They were opposed to what Travis referred to as "shawattywatty Punk" or "children's TV Punk." Thanks to music labels like this, a lot of Post-Punk bands could be heard or at least available for the public to purchase. Rough Trade was particularly very important, because they were open to different style combinations. If you get the first five records that they did, for instance, you'll find synthesizer music, guitar music, women, men, mixed. As Ana de Silva of The Raincoats said of them, "they were distributing reggae as well. It just felt very, very open" (BBC Four). Once you find a label that is willing, you are on the road to publication.

Fourth, consider presenting your music alongside a physical form of art. Because Punk was known for its DIY culture, they also presented their music alongside other mediums of art. For example, they included political posters with their LPs in order to reiterate messages they expressed through their music, and participated in the avant-garde art scene. Some of these Post-Punk visuals continue to live on today as they are replicated on canvas, posters, and other purchasable items like band tees. They are purchased by many modern generations of people today even if the band is unknown to the purchaser, because the message tends to align with a subversive culture, and at the bare minimum it may just be visually pleasing to some. Most notably Joy Division's album artwork, made iconic for its stark black and white data graph by artist Peter Seville, can be seen in store front windows like Urban Outfitters to be purchased as wall décor or as a fashion statement to be worn.

Another example of Post-Punk visual art-turned-fashion is fashion designer Jun Takahashi's clothing line named Undercover. It has been known to copy the album covers and designs of Post-Punk bands like The Jesus and Mary Chain, Television, and The Talking Heads to name a few. Another iconic example of mixed-media Post-Punk art was PiL's record album titled *Metal Box,* which was quite literally packaged in a metal tin, unlike most other Post-Punk bands' records that were packaged in either cardboard or stapled, folded pieces of paper.

According to Scottish music critic, Bobby Gillespie, PiL's *Metal Box* is akin to that of a work of pure art as a metal box encapsulated not only the record in a literal sense, but the album "sounds like Britain felt like to live in back in 1979 . . . it's damp. It's dark, and it's slightly depressed" (BBC Four). This concept of packaging art alongside a record was something not particularly nouveau in terms of how music was sold. Rather, it was something that was borrowed from genres that preceded Post-Punk, but with more license for creative, eclectic combinations.

So, there you have it, the recipe for a Post-Punk song. Through eclecticism, a clever means of imitation and invention, via the collection and combination of many different sources, Post-Punk produces its unique and yet familiar music. Post- Punk can be seen as a special example of these artistic notions in that it sets itself apart from its predecessors but in a manner that explicitly acknowledges its debt to the artistic and philosophical heritage from which it is drawing.

17
Post-Punk Wonder

Jeremy Bendik-Keymer

Written from Cleveland, Ohio,
in violation of the Treaty of Greenville, 1795,
once land of many older nations

Plug In

Nukes, the Cold War, suits, hippies, the Me-generation idiots. That was then. Global warming, mass extinction, Covid, authoritarian neo-imperialism, solo-gunman mass killings, system gaming slicksters, performative self-management and depression. This is now. Living with anxiety is no easy thing.

Can it ever be? Yes. But you got to get comfortable living with unease. Post-Punk wonder shows how. Through sonic trial, we have to confront the disease—the inauthenticity of modern imperial-colonial, capitalist, industrial societies. Let me relay here.

"This isn't real," said Michael Gira of Swans in 1983. We're in New York City during the May festival called *Speed Trials*. How can we find things that are so real that they *make sense to us in our bodies and souls*? What does it take to shake off the dread and the suffocation?

In the early nineteenth century, the romantics knew: once we walked in waves. But the scene is on the corner where the concrete is patterned with spit, shit, and gasoline. There's no wind rising through the wood on upturned leaves, colliding branches, no forests of air like oceans. *There's static on the radio*, and we turn the volume up and down like shore-born surf on rocks, a gale warning. These are preparations for distortion's beauty: also our nature seen.

The band plugs in—an amp's pop and buzz shrieks high. Can we be authentically vulnerable in our anxiety and find possibility deep inside it?

The Sonic Lineage

We're riding a very specific flow from the Noise scene of the late 1970s and early 1980s in New York City. Some called this tradition "Noise Punk," contrasting it with the "Post-Punk" of what emerged from Wire, Warsaw, Joy Division, Factus 50, New Order, or Siouxsie and the Banshees. But I land it squarely as a particular, New York–based form of what comes in the wake of punk, a deepening of certain themes and of several sonic possibilities.

This sonic lineage actually included The Fall in its origin festivals, and we can hear the interest in laying down non-linear drumming that we find in Joy Division's "Atrocity Exhibition" (1980) as well as the long-form, building, screeching, sonic discomfort of the last half of "Voodoo Dolly" on the Banshees' *JuJu* (1981). Swans lays down carny style chants just like Mark Smith of The Fall, and Sonic Youth's first albums carry the layering, lacerating, lyricism, and flamboyance of the ornate aesthetic associated with Post-Punk. Yet the action is strangely, powerfully more positive, more activist. This isn't disaffection; it's being affected in and beyond the imperial and exploitative system by the possibility of finding sense and meaning that cuts and works against and despite that system. It is an opening, a direction beyond nihilism and toward authenticity and creativity *without* avoiding, and *only by confronting* alienation, dread, and disharmony.

I've in mind a festival in the Village in May 1983 staging The Fall, the once hardcore Beastie Boys, Live Skull, Sonic Youth, Lydia Lunch, Carbon, the Swans, Toy Killers. We can start with Swans, influenced by Antonin Artaud's Theater of Cruelty and follow Sonic Youth's gesture extended over decades, especially in their first EP *Confusion Is Sex* (1983), *Sister* (1987), *Daydream Nation* (1988), and *Washing Machine* (1994), then echoed in the nostalgic *NYC Ghosts & Flowers* (2000) of the new millennium. Also relevant is the emergence of space-rock in the late Eighties, including My Bloody Valentine/MBV and such strange mid-to-late 90s offshoots as Bristol's Flying Saucer Attack and Crescent or Auckland's Thela (circa 1996) and White Winged Moth (1995-2000)—or the completely different feel of Windy and Carl from Dearborn, Michigan, becoming ambient, for instance in *Antarctica* (1997) or *Depths* (1998).

Finally, there are after-pulses in Deerhunter's *Monomania* tour in 2013 when they extended Ramones-like songs such as "Punk" into twenty-plus minute long exercises in feedback, a veritable urban theology as Bradly Cox explained when discussing his own queer, anxiety disorder and how music addressed it.

That's the decades-long *distortion vector* that I've been tuning into for its existential relevance. It's still with us today in Feeble Little Horse's *Hayday* (2022) and *Girl with Fish* (2023).

The Philosophical Tradition and the Simple Intuition

I take this sonic lineage's philosophical origin to be solidly romantic, Germanic to be precise, a cultural unconscious surfacing more than a hundred and fifty years after the fact. We can go back to one of the strangest of German idealists, F.W.J. Schelling, whose *Philosophical Investigations into the Essence of Human Freedom* incorporates irrationality, mystery, and evil as potent parts of the whole of things (Thomas, *Freedom and Ground*). This same Schelling also stirred the existentialist Søren Kierkegaard (1813–1855) to make anxiety central to his work thereby influencing Martin Heidegger (1889–1976) three quarters of a century later and, through Heidegger, French philosophy from the 1960s through the 1990s (Jean-Luc Nancy, *The Birth to Presence*).

What Schelling had at the center of his work was a potent philosophy of imagination in which the receptivity of consciousness to fundamental intuitions opening the space of possibilities for the free play of the imagination was primary to having an excitable, human mind. Some such theory of mind involving the gradual piecing together of the meaning and sense of things through a freely moving openness of association and intuition is also important for *wonder*.

From such an origin, let's follow out a simple intuition with its associated idea: *Post-Punk distortion was a particularly urban, sonic way to take negative anxiety and to find the positive anxiety within it.* We hear it in Sonic Youth's "Cotton Crown" (1987):

You're gonna take control of the chemistry.
You're gonna manifest the mystery.
You've got a magic wheel in your memory.
I'm wasted in time, and I'm looking everywhere.
I don't care where.

What I think Post-Punk Wonder did was to take a social situation that was particularly oppressive with negative anxieties and help people *carry* them by surfacing the underlying excitement around sense and meaning that makes things matter at all. This underlying condition of excitement is what Martha Nussbaum (*Upheavals of Thought*) calls after Lucretius the "original joy" of the mind: its striving to make sense of things because things strike us as mattering *and* unclear. The surfacing helped Post-Punkers find possibility in a society that often seemed impossible. The surfacing was the "fuck you" that became a "fuck yeah" of Post-Punk sound: the beauty in Post-Punk's sonic and manifest "mystery" *losing* control of the "chemistry" to find an open space for our lives to grow and to be real.

The Vortex of Positive Anxiety

To understand these points and their philosophy, it helps to keep the distortion vector I've just indicated in mind. For instance, on some of their earliest (pre-Jarboe) work, "Weakling" during the *Speed Trials* (1983), Swans builds a repetitive, intensifying experience of heavy, pared down yet splashy, angst, incanting the insecurity and internalized trauma of a fictional character. The sound-experience is like an exorcism or a dislocated act from exposure therapy.

Or during the same year, Sonic Youth's mantra, "Nature Scene" from *Confusion Is Sex* deconstructs the guitar solo so that it is a mess of jangly dissonance and scratch. This cycles between Kim Gordan's pre-RiotGirrl call as she remembers sex workers and the spatialized class exploitation of New York City's street corners. Five years later, SY's anthem "Cotton Crown" oscillates between almost sarcastic irony about dope-headed, quasi-religious, urbanite, alternative groovers and the gorgeous *harmonics* of fuzzed out, screeching guitars sending up a vortex of spirit from the ground into the sky of the city. These multi-layered experiments *tarry with the negative* in life in a dogged or spirited intent to make something meaningful despite it.

We can call this sound art the "vortex of positive anxiety." As Kierkegaard (*The Concept of Anxiety*) first established for a generation that came almost a century after him, the human condition is one of fundamental anxiety. This means that we are groundless *but seeking grounds*. We exist *needing to make sense of the world*. This was a point that Kant first established. But it was Schelling's dark moods, his philosophy of mind that saw in the fundamental receptivity of the mind a pulsing, unconscious sense-making even in the irrational, that put the point in reach for Kierkegaard, although he tended to disown Schelling. Hearing Gira moaning, intoning in the legendary live version of "Blind Love" from Swans' 1987 European tour, you can get a sense of this groundlessness until you find sense and meaning in this life. You have to stage dive with your soul to hear this eighteen-minute-long song.

Post-Punk took the vortex and made something absolutely gorgeous with it. "Absolutely," the term from German

Romanticism exactly: to resolve our searching into an infinity as we *become comfortable with unease and refuse to avoid our anxieties*. This is the way to hear "Dirty Boots" from Sonic Youth's breakthrough into the mainstream, *Goo*, "the year that punk broke" (1990)—and became something else entirely. The informal, Post-Punk tradition of distortion took the vortex of anxiety and realized that we can *ride* it like a leap into the dissolution and recombination of forms: into positive anxiety. "Dirty Boots" does not know what to make of this yet, still nostalgic for something between irony and sincerity. But the sincerity, the authenticity are breaking through with the positive anxiety.

So, we see the turn into what came to be known also as "space rock" even (guitar based) "ambient" music: by the time we come upon Flying Saucer Attack's "To the Shore" (1995), Thela's "Untitled #2" (1996), or Windy and Carl's "Sirens" (1998) the lead off to their *Depths*, we have focused in on a space *in our minds* where we can hold dissonance and find beauty in it, find the possibility of making sense and meaning by hearing and then seeing the world differently according to the productive power of the imagination to recombine forms and to strip negative anxiety from them, to make something beyond purposelessness.

Anxiety is often thought of as negative, as a kind of groundless worry that something is really, really off in your world, but you don't know what. Heidegger (*Being and Time*) described it in the early twentieth century as the presence in our norms of a troubling oscillation around what makes sense so that, sometimes without realizing it, we are adrift and at a loss about how to make life make sense, this disturbing us in countless ways many of which are not experienced but simply enacted. Both Kierkegaard and Heidegger had Christian baggage that was unworked through and perhaps a good dose of narcissism that troubled their souls, though, for the fact is that anxiety cannot be fundamentally negative.

Here's why: For there to be worry, dizziness, unease, or dislocation over what makes sense, *we have to first find the world and our lives in it as a source of sense and meaning*. No meaningfulness, no worry. No sense, no dizziness when sense slips. No understanding, no unease when things go up into the air. No home, no dislocation when cast outside one's habitual modes of existence. But for there to be meaningfulness, sense, understanding, and even home, there must *the possibility of each of these emerging*. And what is that possibility most simply? It is *the pregnancy of things making sense*, the open field of the mind's aptitude for this rich, meaningful life. Perhaps you've seen it in children wondering over everything, excited? At least unless someone has disabused them of their mind's original joy? That pregnancy is *the possibility of possibilities*; it is pure anxiety, and it is *positive*. The positive comes first, or the negative could not be.

A Tougher, More Enduring Wonder

In English, "wonder" often sounds rosy and naive. This is due to its roots in Hume's interpretation of wonder at the end of the eighteenth century. For the neo-Humean, largely anglophone tradition of thinking about wonder, wonder is an *emotion* that is *rare, epiphanic, pleasant*, and akin to *delightful surprise* (Sophia Vasalou, *Wonder*). But this is a largely unfocused experience of wonder. It is not possible without the underlying positive anxiety of the mind, and yet attention to that positive anxiety shows that both wonder and *wondering* (the act) can be more extensive and more pervasive than the neo-Humean tradition makes them out to be. Rather, following Kant in the *Critique of Judgment* and beyond through the German Idealists such as Schelling, *wonder can become a cast of mind*, and it is *found in the mind by degrees whenever the mind is healthy* (Bendik-Keymer, *Nussbaum's Politics of Wonder*).

For the alternative, Germanic tradition of wonder, *wonder is the mind's positive anxiety when considering the sense and meaning of things*, trying to figure them out. This alternative tradition of wonder understands wonder as a *facet of the mind*, a kind of mental excitement and buzzing, not necessarily emotional in any given way, but potentially *ongoing* (e.g., in meditative or creative flow), *ordinary* (as an everyday openness), often *difficult* (as going through cognitive dissonance is). Such wondering is on a continuum that includes even *awe* at the limit, but which can more commonly be found in a kind of contemplative *beginner's mind* that is not so much surprised as apprised of the ungrounded, pregnant rising of sense and meaning in things. Here, we find wonder as the background condition of the mind's openness to the possibility of making sense of this life in this world—or the life and world into which things can become. And we find wonder*ing* in sustained acts of attention that tarry with the challenge of holding space around the things of this world and this life to find *more* sense and meaning in them, often through creative recombination.

The distortion vector of Post-Punk noise rock I've delineated is an example of an informal tradition of ritualistic quasi-acts of wondering. That is one, major thing that is noteworthy about it. The Post-Punkers we've considered here took noise and tarried with its negative, catching up society's angst and injustice within it, aiming especially at the gross inauthenticity and conformism repressing the negative. These rockers sought the beauty in confronting the sound, locating a zone of imaginative possibility deep within the dissonance. They created a ritual of wondering.

Post-Punk wonder is a *tougher, more enduring wonder* than neo-Humean flights of fancy. Post-Punk wonder helps people gymnastically enter the void: the distorted heart of an inauthentic, narcissistic, and abusive society where sense and meaning get crushed or die away neglected, falling through the cracks of structural injustice and actual cruelty and disregard.

Ancient, Spiritual Exercises of Wonder

If Schelling is the hoary soul who located the mind's groundlessness in the wake of Kant's exposure of the imagination as always moving in possibilities *beyond* what is grounded, it is Martha Nussbaum who brings us into practical life with her blend of ancient philosophy with modern concerns. When Nussbaum theorizes wonder from her Lucretian and psychoanalytic sources, she seeks the development of authentic, engaged human beings who can actively strive to fight for justice and to bring creative, non-narcissistic flourishing into the structures, patterns, and ethos of our societies. She is drawing on a tradition that goes back to the earliest roots of the philosophical tradition as it was formed out of Ionia (today, Turkey) and what we now know as Greece: the tradition of disciplined exercises *of the soul and the mind* to become a better human being, more fit for taking on the problems and challenges of this life. This is soul exercise, not just physical gymnastics.

Plugging into the vortex of positive anxiety of Post-Punk wonder is an inchoate spiritual exercise (the term comes from historian of ancient philosophy Pierre Hadot in *Philosophy as a Way of Life*) locating and refining the mind's openness to sense and meaning through sonic and emotional work. It connects Post-Punkers' misgivings about inauthenticity, their malaise, and their angst with the power of their imagination and their spirit to make better sense of things. Here to wonder is a sustained *act of self*. In this way, Post-Punk wonder can be seen as a garage-based, DIY philosophical practice, not far from the makeshift, streetwise manner of, say, the Stoics—from *stoa*, porch—who set up on the porch, just like that. And didn't the Cynics cause all manner of confusion in the market with their punked out antics of paradox?

So, we might see Post-Punk wonder not as a "speed trial," but as a trial of the arts of mental capaciousness. Strange freaks of sound stake our imaginations on ways of being in the world at ease in unease because our minds are mentally excited to make something out of the dissonance. This reading of Post-Punk noise rock, space rock, and guitar based ambient music angles toward a cast of mind that can help us be more authentic in a society's social dis-ease.

Authenticity as Something Messy to Fight For

As exercises staking ourselves in confronting negative anxieties, the stakes of Post-Punk wonder come to concern authenticity. Philosophers such as Charles Larmore (*The Practices of the Self*) have argued that authenticity is a quality of *the process of being yourself*. Being yourself is not a static thing; it is a practice in which we come to commit to what makes sense to us both in how we think about it and in what we intend to do about it. The practice of the self, as Larmore calls it, involves surfacing and acknowledging how you feel so that you are responsible to the ways in which your behavior and beliefs or intentions can come apart, distort. If our societies keep us from surfacing our angst or pressure us to conform in ways that don't actually make sense to us, then they contribute to the real need for us to become authentic.

Post-Punk Wonder can be seen as one response to such a situation, where society sets up inauthenticity, but authenticity is needed. When the vortex of positive anxiety clears our mind from negative, narcissistic thoughts to being open to finding the possibilities of sense and meaning in things, this affirms our power to figure out what makes sense and to be free enough inside our minds to affirm it, even to have the spirit to commit to it. Post-Punk Wonder, spacing out amidst distortion while tarrying with the negative and confronting angst, plays a needed role in authenticity for those attuned to it who get it.

This leaves an appealing reverberation. The openness of Post-Punk wonder at ease in unease discloses an authenticity that is messy and honest, worth fighting for. Rather than being some pristine and narcissistic thing about having a pure identity, authenticity becomes identified essentially with *searching* and *imagining* a way to remain in touch with what truly matters to us, not avoiding our angst, fears, anger, or the injustice and inauthenticity of our society. As Kierkegaard wrote in one of his last pseudonymous works, *Concluding Unscientific*

Postscript to Philosophical Fragments (1846), the truth here is in "subjectivity," in the process of striving to find a truth that truly makes sense to you. For three generations, Post-Punk wonder's made a sonic contribution to this vital, existential project.*

---

* Thanks: Saleem Dhamee for introducing me to Thela, Windy and Carl, Flying Saucer Attack, and Salomé in the late 1990s, Chicago, including their iconic album series *am/pm* (amen music/party music) from Chicago of the same period. Listen, especially, to their song, "lower Wacker" on *pm* (Dutch Courage Records, 2001). Lars Helge-Strand for mix taping me Swans' "Blind Love" in 1989, Rouen, France. A forgotten-named record store in Utica, New York, for carrying *Confusion Is Sex* and *Speed Trials* around 1984. Alex Shakar for sending me Bauhaus's "Antonin Artaud" (1982) as if to prove the point about Swans.

18
Post-Punk and Socratic Philosophy

ROBERT KÖNIG

Anyone asked what a theory of Punk looks like should probably respond: there *is* no such thing as a theory of Punk. Punk inherently rejects straightforward theorization. Or, as Jesse Prinz puts it "there is no way to give an inclusive aesthetics of punk" (*Prinz 2014*, p. 584).

Yet, this is paradoxically the driving force behind why we theorize about Punk: a philosophy of Punk is *punkish itself*—it does not simply accept the claim that there is no theorization of Punk. With this in mind, it's worth considering the first of three ideals that Prinz works out for the aesthetics of punk: *irreverence*. Punk defies presumed norms. And, the second and third ideals follow from this: *nihilism* and *amateurism* (Prinz 2014, 585 ff.) which is why Punk rebels against categorization, standardization, mainstream, and theory. And that's why we, in turn, theorize about it.

Yet, at this early stage of theorizing, we can already be engaging in what can be called *Post-Punk*. Post-Punk essentially entails expressing irreverence, as does Punk. But, in addition to this, Post-Punk employs irreverence against itself. It becomes an aesthetic form of Punk's self-overcoming. This is an unappreciated significance of the "Post" in Post-Punk.

Post-Punk is not simply "after" Punk in a temporal or cultural sense; it represents the most radical execution of Punk with its own unique means. If all Punk embodies irreverence, denial, and resistance, then so does Post-Punk. However, Post-Punk embodies the unique ability of Punk to reflect inwards and to apply each of these themes onto itself. Thus, it provokes a development within (or because of) its own essence.

In some philosophical frameworks, such as the Hegelian school, such a thing is called *negation of negation*. Such self-negation leads to self-transcendence by self-abolishment. This is what Post-Punk does by punkish means. In Post-Punk, Punk becomes inherently active, constructive and creative, while maintaining a bitter sense of nihilistic seriousness. This also creates its own irony, caricature, and parody and thus raises questions of authenticity. That's where Punk completes itself; when it finds its final form. Punk *must* evolve into Post-Punk. Otherwise, it has never been Punk in the first place.

Post-Punk as an Aesthetic Method

It seems as if Post-Punk is not solely as a mere artistic style, as it is a phase in modern music or a socio-cultural lifestyle. There are several studies on our subject from these perspectives (for instance those by Haddon, Batukan, Butt, Eshun, Fisher, Crossley, Reynolds, or the *Punk and Post-Punk Journal* and the Punk Scholars Network).

I view Punk and Post-Punk as avenues for exploring philosophical aspects within modern music. So, I'm talking about them as an *aesthetic method*. What is an aesthetic method? It's a way of expressing and depicting specific experiences and making them palpable for others by aesthetic means. Post-Punk not only becomes a subject of philosophy but also a method of philosophizing. This raises two important questions:

1. What specific experience is conveyed through Post-Punk?

2. In what particular manner is this experience represented in Post-Punk?

To answer these questions, we can turn to philosophy as a guiding companion, which will support us in illustrating the aesthetic method in its essence.

Socrates was a Post-Punk

As far as we know, the ancient philosopher Socrates did not compose any works of philosophy. Our knowledge of him stems primarily from the teachings of his student, Plato. In traditional depictions, Socrates emerges as a critic of prevailing societal norms and orders. He fearlessly delves into inquiries such as the true knowledge possessed by priests regarding the gods, the capacity of politicians to define justice, the understanding of knowledge by scientists, and the ability of artists to encapsulate beauty. In each instance, Socrates exposes the pretense of knowledge in his interlocutors, revealing their lack of true understanding. Socrates's arguments with other people are reported in Plato's dialogues, such as the *Republic Euthyphro*, and *Gorgias*.

By challenging the core concepts of ancient Greek society, Socrates dismantled proposed norms, dismissing them as (at best) a sort of *pseudo*-knowledge. At first glance, we might consider him a philosophizing Punk, deconstructing established notions. This is in part because he didn't approach his task as a traditional scholar by simply lecturing (as if he were some sort of authority figure). Instead, he positioned himself as their student, thus adopting an *amateurish* stance.

Socrates, however, cannot be classified as a typical Punk as understood by Jesse Prinz. While Socrates's relentless and irreverent deconstruction might suggest an inquisitive path towards *nihilism*, Socrates went beyond a mere nihilistic criticism of his interlocutors or the authorities of the day. He consistently engaged in the deconstruction of his *own* position. Famously, he acknowledged (in Plato's *Apology*) that the only knowledge he possessed was the knowledge that he knew nothing. Socrates subjected himself to his irreverent approach as much as anyone else.

According to Socrates, it's imperative that we dismantle our own asserted positions, rather than just scrutinizing the viewpoints of others. This approach is evident in his invaluable embrace of contradiction, paradox, and irony. We should actively seek out and apply these elements, Socrates would instruct us, not only when examining the perspectives of others but also in relation to our own critical standpoint. A philosopher must engage in self-criticism even of his own criticism alongside the evaluation of various viewpoints, integrating self-transcendence into their critical analysis. As a result, Socrates's deconstructive endeavors become profoundly ironic, self-confrontational, and inherently inadequate. It is in this important respect that Socrates embodies the essence of not just a Punk philosopher but a *Post-Punk* philosopher.

Existential Dissonance

Socrates encourages us not only to seek out contradictions but also to embrace them. And, his intention is not to simply resolve these contradictions but rather to continuously maintain a state of openness towards them, thereby constantly distancing himself from his own position. This approach results in a perpetual "post" quality within our own attitudes, leading to their self-overcoming through their own means.

A similar dynamic unfolds in the realm of Punk as a mode of expression, particularly when it turns its focus inward using its own punkish methods. In doing so, Punk transforms into Post-Punk and adopts an irreverent, nihilistic, and amateurish stance towards itself. As a result, it defies stylistic conventions, eschews fixed themes, and refuses to represent definitive attitudes. It dissolves into an ongoing *post*-state that influences its aesthetic and expressive essence, initiating a process of transformation. Post-Punk is the creative self-abolishment of Punk by expressively ironizing it. And, in addition to all of this, Post-Punk depicts this very irony. The entire aesthetic of Post-Punk assumes that we're familiar with the irreverence, nihilism, and amateurism of Punk and are therefore prepared to transcend it using its own methods.

Post-Punk is a highly demanding aesthetic. We can identify Post-Punkish expressions by their inherent self-deconstructive nature, continually expressing irony through their own deconstruction. For instance, though The Exploited created a Punk manifesto with *Punk's Not Dead*, this title marks a battle cry of Post-Punk. For Punk confronts itself with its own deconstruction of it.

This fundamental aesthetic experience can be thought of as *existential dissonance*. Post-Punk conveys a specific dissonance aesthetically, which also affects those who engage in its expression. From a philosophical perspective, this dissonance represents an existential experience that disrupts the very essence of something. In this sense, as Stuart Hanscomb explains, Post-Punk also inherits core philosophical concepts from existentialism, which seeks to grasp the originally jarring experiences that make up existence. It is an unwavering call to embrace aesthetic dissonance by engaging with the very forms it distances itself from in the process. In a similar vein, the German philosopher Nietzsche states in *The Birth of Tragedy* that after nihilistic deconstruction, only the aesthetic justification of the world remains. Post-Punk serves as a self-deprecating, confrontational, and individualistic expression of this notion. It urges us to embrace aesthetically expressed and experienced existential dissonance, even in relation to our own Punk attitudes. Existential dissonance is the grounding experience of Post-Punk.

The Aesthetic Characteristics of Post-Punk

The second question our thesis raised was: how is *existential dissonance* depicted and represented in Post-Punk? Which specific aesthetic method does it employ?

The fundamental Socratic attitude of existential dissonance towards ourselves finds expression through irony. In the realm of Post-Punk, this attitude takes on an aesthetic dimension. Rather than resorting to direct criticism, attack, or rejection, the Post-Punkish elements of deconstruction and irreverence manifest themselves through the irony of understated descriptions, statements, and indifferent portrayals. The anger inherent in Punk Rock undergoes a transformation, emerging as the assertive cynicism of Post-Punk. Again, there are numerous examples of this. However, before considering them, we can identify three distinct characteristics that define the experience of existential dissonance within Post-Punk as an aesthetic method. These characteristics stem from its initial Socratic attitude and align with the three traits outlined by Prinz in his definition of Punk Rock.

Aesthetic Cynicism

The primary method employed in expressing existential dissonance within Post-Punk is its pervasive aesthetic cynicism. This cynicism serves as the counterpart to Prinz's concept of *irreverence* and operates by presenting deconstruction through the medium of mere description and representation. In order to maintain its irreverent nature while adopting simply descriptive modes, Post-Punk must engage in an ever-evolving selection of themes and styles. As Simon Reynolds aptly points out, Post-Punk embodies an "imperative to constant change" encompassing themes, styles, and modes of expression. Nevertheless, this perpetual transformation is not arbitrary; it remains firmly rooted in the continuous depiction of existential dissonance.

Post-Punk claims the ability to traverse boundaries and provoke thought through its mode of mere depiction. On the one hand, it addresses taboos and forbidden subjects using straightforward and descriptive approaches. On the other hand, it exaggerates the essence of normality by employing overflowing and flamboyant depictions of it. The power of punkish deconstruction is effectively harnessed through cynical descriptions, particularly when tackling themes that are either suppressed or demand an extravagant means of expression. Thus, within Post-Punk, we encounter a juxtaposition of extreme subjects expressed through seemingly ordinary and normalized statements and styles, as well as the portrayal of simple or commonplace issues in disconcerting and thought-provoking ways.

Better known musical references for this include Siouxsie and the Banshee's "Happy House," depicting the terror of forced positivity:

> This is the happy house
> We're happy here in the happy house
> Oh, it's such fun, fun, fun, oh . . .
> This is the happy house . . .
> It's safe and calm if you sing along . . .
> We're happy here in the happy house
> To forget ourselves and pretend all's well.

Depeche Mode's "Everything Counts," cynically glorifying the horrors of capitalism:

> The handshake seals the contract
> From the contract there's no turning back . . .
> The grabbing hands grab all they can
> All for themselves—after all
> It's a competitive world
> Everything counts in large amounts.

Bauhaus's "She's in Parties," describing a merely staged life:

> She's acting her reaction
> She's in parties
> It's in the can.

Killing Jokes' "Wardance," overcoming punkish hedonism:

> Music for pleasure
> It's not music no more
> Music to dance to
> Music to move
> This is music to march to
> Do a war dance.

Kraftwerk's "Radioactivity" highlighted how Kraftwerk, among others, influenced the emergence of Post-Punk):

> Radioactivity
> Tune in to the melody
> Radioactivity
> Is in the air for you and me.

A later example of cynical exaggeration would be Pearl Jam's "Do the Evolution," depicting the attitude of a strong socio-psycho-ecological evolutionism:

I'm at peace with my lust
I can kill 'cause in god I trust, yeah
It's evolution, baby
I'm at peace, I'm the man
Buying stocks on the day of the crash, yeah
On the loose, I'm a truck
All the rolling hills, I'll flatten 'em out
It's herd behavior
It's evolution, baby
Admire me, admire my home
Admire my son, he's my clone
This land is mine, this land is free
I'll do what I want but irresponsibly
It's evolution, baby
I'm a thief, I'm a liar
There's my church, I sing in the choir
Hallelujah, Hallelujah . . .

Expertise in Insufficiency

Irreverence manifests as descriptive cynicism in Post-Punk. But, what (if any) role does amateurism play in Post-Punk? In Punk, amateurism serves as a form of negation, allowing individuals to withdraw from dominant norms and standardized expectations. However, amateurism is an *inclusive* negation, emphasizing that anyone can engage in Punk. It goes beyond being a beginner or a bungler; it actively rejects any form of aesthetic standardization. This attitude of inclusive negation can be observed in a variety of music genres, such as metal or hip-hop, which employ methods like escapism or ideas of social struggle.

What if anything does that tell us about Post-Punk? As an expression of existential dissonance, Post-Punk combines self-negation with amateurism. It goes beyond mere withdrawal and becomes a constructive negation that overcomes its own detachment from standards and norms. Aesthetically, this constructive negation means constantly reshaping forms of expression, even if it entails rejecting amateurism in favor of *professionalism*. A self-publishing author, an indie record label founder, or an active company works council can all embody the spirit of Post-Punk.

In the realm of pop music, this is reflected in a creative willingness to experiment with minimalism, dilettantism, and deliberately insufficient modes of expression, while simultaneously professionalizing them. Post-Punks are *experts in amateurism*, reminiscent of their philosophical counterparts, the

Socratics. They are not mere amateurs; they are profession-alizing their amateurism. Vivid and well-known examples of this approach in music include Joy Division, Einstürzende Neubauten, Skinny Puppy, The Cure, or New Model Army. They all express themselves through a masterful insufficiency. Later influences of this Post-Punk spirit can be found in almost every musical subculture, including techno, hip-hop, metal, and various forms of goth.

Ironic Authenticity

Creatively affirmed cynicism and expertise in insufficiency give rise to the question of authenticity, a topic that resonates within various aesthetic methods but is primarily relevant to Post-Punk. Whether it's the debate on *trueness* in metal or the pursuit of *realness* in hip-hop, authenticity remains a significant aspect. Ryan Moore emphasizes the importance of authenticity in all postmodern subcultures. In the context of Post-Punk, however, authenticity takes on an ironic character, serving as a mirror image of the *nihilism* described by Prinz in Punk.

Unchallenged nihilism often gives way to *hedonism*, as explored by Doomen. Nihilistic indifference implies that any-thing goes, leading to a radical focus on the present moment. Consequently, punk frequently results in a form of nihilistic hedonism.

However, in contrast to this, Post-Punk incorporates exis-tential dissonance, embracing its own punkish self-distancing. Thus, even nihilism is propelled toward transcendence, as com-plete hedonistic withdrawal or absolute indifference offers lit-tle solace. Self-transformative processes imbue nihilism with creative irony, akin to Socratic philosophy (other philosophical examples would be the lifestyle of *absurdism* in the thought of Albert Camus or the radical skepticism of René Descartes, which flips into affirmative thinking through excessive self-doubt about its own act of doubt).

Post-Punk does not eradicate nihilistic indifference and its hedonistic consequences; instead, it elevates them through ironic exaggeration, permeating every experience. This existen-tially dissonant self-ironization becomes the hallmark of Post-Punkish authenticity. Constantly ironizing one's own stance reveals an authentic self-relationship. This distinct aesthetic thematization of authenticity can be termed *Post-Punkish*.

Vivid examples of this include "No Time to Cry" by The Sisters of Mercy, ironizing the rationalization of emotions:

It's just a feeling
I get sometimes . . .
You've got to shake the hand that feeds you . . .
It's just like always coming down on
Just like Jesus never came and
What did you expect to find
It's just like always here again it's . . .
No time for heartache
No time to run and hide
No time for breaking down
No time to cry
Everything will be alright
Everything will turn out fine
Some nights I still can't sleep.

"Eine Symphonie des Grauens" by Monochrome Set, breaking the traditional romanticism of a lovesong by putting it in the imagery of gore and death, while the poetic self distances itself by constantly responding "I think I'm in love" to its own feelings:

I'm dead and dank and rotten
My arms are wrapped in cotton
My corpse loves you, let's marry
Get smart once, Every night at sleepy time
Get smart, twice, I hang my skin out on the line
Get smart, sing, Oh, darling, would you be, be mine
I'm in love, I think I'm in love [...]
I'm caught in a mesh of veins
My fingers and flesh and brains
My skull gives head, so let's wed
Get smart once, every night when all alone
Get smart, twice, I drape my flesh around the phone
Get smart, pray, Oh, darling, would you be my own
Don't cry, beautiful, it's just a phase.

"How Soon Is Now" by The Smiths, on social anxiety and being able to deal with it:

See I've already waited too long
And all my hope is gone
You shut your mouth
How can you say
I go about things the wrong way?
I am human and I need to be loved
Just like everybody else does.

"The Weeping Song" by Nick Cave and the Bad Seeds, ironically reflecting on a human life-span:

> Father, why are all the women weeping?
> They are weeping for their men
> Then why are all the men there weeping?
> They are weeping back at them
> This is a weeping song
> A song in which to weep . . .
> Father, why are all the children weeping?
> They are merely crying son
> Oh, are they merely crying, father?
> Yes, true weeping is yet . . . to come.

More recent examples, at least from our perspective can be
seen in Marilyn Manson's "Rock is Dead" and Nine Inch Nails'
"Hurt." The first song, using the term "Rock," ironically depicts
the inclusion of rock-framed protest and irreverence within the
very structures Rock protests against:

> Rock is deader than dead
> Shock is all in your head
> Your sex and your dope is all that we're fed
> So fuck all your protests and put them to bed . . .
> We're so full of hope and so full of shit
> Build a new God to medicate and to ape
> Sell us Ersatz dressed up and real fake
> Anything to belong
> Rock is deader than dead . . .
> God is in the TV.

"Hurt" tells the story of existential dread in distancing oneself
from existential dread,

> I hurt myself today to see if I still feel . . .
> You could have it all my empire of dirt
> I will let you down i will make you hurt
> I wear my crown of shit on my liar's chair
> Full of broken thoughts i cannot repair . . .
> The feeling disappears you are someone else
> I am still right here what have I become?
> My sweetest friend everyone I know
> Goes away in the end . . .
> If I could start again a million miles away
> I would keep myself I would find a way.

Confrontational Individuation

Post-Punk challenges us aesthetically, embodying the core essence of Punk. However, it also challenges its own methods of confrontation and incorporates them into a dissonant, cynical, insufficient, and ironic experience. Its aesthetic method is continuously reshaped through its experience of dissonance. Post-Punk resembles the philosophical approach of Socratic thought through aesthetic means. It transforms itself into an expressive act that constantly requires its own overcoming, perpetually embodying the "post" in a very punkish way of making experiences tangible. And so, just as all Punk must evolve into Post-Punk, no Post-Punk can ever remain simply Post-Punk. However, its own evolution into a multitude of forms is just as much unified by the inherent experience of existential dissonance in all of them. Only where the experience of existential dissonance ceases altogether do we move away from Post-Punk.

This tense aesthetic self-relation can have two consequences. It can either lead to expressive arbitrariness, resulting in nihilistic indifference and consumerism, or it can be combined with a call for active creativity and self-development. With this in mind, the experience of existential dissonance can lead aesthetically to cynical monotony or be seen as a provocation to create. The former position discards the potential for self-overcoming and retreats into a purely aesthetic quietism, while the latter sees dissonance as a motivation for active participation and personal individuation. This confrontation with one's own individuation is essential for both Punk and Post-Punk. While any Punk remains an invitation to seek, live, and embody your own individuality, classic Punk and Post-Punk differ in their specific approaches to this practice. Punk negates, whereas Post-Punk negates negation (affirming it throughout this process in constantly new forms).

And so, Post-Punk becomes an ongoing aesthetic demonstration of the problem of individuation. It embraces the fundamental concerns of Socratic philosophy, emphasizing self-thinking and the significance of one's own individual thought process. Simultaneously, Post-Punk focuses primarily on the aesthetically experienced dimension of dissonance, incorporating depictions rich in cynicism, insufficiency, and irony within the process of individuation. Through this, it can address its own constant failure as a purely aesthetic form by critiquing existential limits, taboos, and norms. It consistently transforms even the deepest critique into a new norm to be transcended all over again. Here, the constant "post" element manifests itself uninterruptedly. Post-Punk individuates itself both creatively and normatively. This inherent dissonant tension against itself remains the core experience expressed in any Socratic aesthetic method, with Post-Punk being one of them.

VI

Post-Punks Behaving Badly

19

Mark E. Smith—Guru of Post-Punk

MARTIN MUCHALL AND PAUL BREEDEN

The year is 1994, and erstwhile Fall guitarist and songwriter Brix Smith Start is facing a dilemma: should she become the new bass player in Hole, or reunite with her former band?

A tricky matter. As the second option would mean working with her ex-husband, the famously mercurial Mark E. Smith, and their separation had been fractious, the opportunity to play alongside Courtney Love might seem the more obvious choice.

Her decision may therefore come as a surprise, for as she wrote in her autobiography, "If it weren't for the Fall, there would be no Hole. There would be no Nirvana . . . There was really only ever one choice. I would rejoin The Fall."

Long before Brix first joined them, The Fall were already perceived as having set the standard by which other Post-Punk bands should be judged. Seminal albums such as 1983's "Hex Enduction Hour" influenced artistes such as Kurt Cobain, as well as groups like Pavement, Suede, Sonic Youth, The Pixies, and Franz Ferdinand.

Mark E. Smith's approach to life and music-making rings with philosophical significance. Take the fact that when the group was formed in Manchester in 1976, during the Punk Rock explosion, they were briefly known as "The Outsiders." The name alludes to the title of a novel (*L'Étranger*) by the French existentialist Albert Camus, as well as a bestselling book (*The Outsider*) by the British philosopher Colin Wilson. But Smith discovered there had already been a 1960s garage band called "The Outsiders," and he changed the band's name to mirror the Camus novel he preferred—*La Chute* ("The Fall").

Nietzsche and Schopenhauer, two German philosophers who anticipated existentialism, have also been cited as influences (though in his autobiography Smith confuses the latter with Kant). Then there's Jean-Paul Sartre, another existentialist, whose declaration that "Hell is other people" was one with which Smith concurred.

However Smith's personal philosophy has more in common with Stoicism, a much older Graeco-Roman school of thought, than with continental existentialism. Additionally, when it comes to his controversial working methods, Eastern mystical philosophy, as well as Wilson's uniquely optimistic brand of existentialism, may both be of greater help than Camus or Sartre, if we wish to understand what Smith was trying to achieve.

You Can't Expect to Feel Cock-A-Hoop Every Minute of Every Day

The founder of Stoicism was Zeno of Citium (334–262 B.C.E.), and the movement takes its name from the *Stoa*, a painted porch in Athens from which public lectures were given. Over the course of five centuries, this philosophy continued to be refined and it became championed in the Roman world.

Today, the adoption of a Stoic outlook is commonplace. For example, many troops in the US army now receive training in Stoic philosophy to help them stay calm in combat, deal with powerful emotions like anger and guilt, and endure captivity if they are taken prisoner. Cognitive Behavioral Therapy or CBT, which is reckoned to be effective for depression and anxiety, is also underpinned by this philosophy. Classic works by the likes of Epictetus, Cicero, Seneca, and Marcus Aurelius still enjoy healthy sales, and there are any number of popular introductions to Stoicism on sale.

So what does Stoicism have to offer, and what kind of personal impact did it have on Mark E. Smith?

Firstly, although the Stoics had distinctive ideas about Nature, logic, and knowledge, they are mostly remembered for their views on mental self-control: we now say that someone is "stoic" if they do not allow powerful emotions and adverse events to affect them.

The philosopher and former slave Epictetus (85–135 C.E.) argued that although we do not control most of the things that happen to us, we *do* have control over the way we *think* and *feel* about our experiences. For instance, we can't be sure that we will never suffer disease or a life-changing injury, that the people we love will never leave us, or that we will always have enough money to get by. Often, when things do not go our way, we end up feeling angry, fearful and frustrated.

Yet Epictetus asserted that we *always* have a choice about the way we react to things. In his *Discourses*, he states that if a tyrant threatens to put us in chains, we can respond by saying, "You can chain my leg, but you cannot chain my power of choice."

Having been a slave, Epictetus knew what he was talking about. It is claimed that he walked with a limp because his leg had been deliberately broken by his master, so this was no mere abstract philosophy that he was advocating.

Epictetus's tough philosophy of resilience continues to inspire others. One famous example is James Stockdale, a US fighter pilot who was shot down during the Vietnam war. Stockdale spent seven years in captivity, during which he was tortured fifteen times, and spent years in leg irons and solitary confinement. It was a memory of Epictetus's writings that helped him to survive, especially the sentence, "Some things are up to us, some things are not." Stockdale could not influence his environment, but he could still control how he thought about it. He was able to maintain his character and self-respect, and his Vietnamese interrogators failed to break him.

Stoic beliefs therefore really do seem to make a difference in coping with adversity, so it should come as no surprise that they have appealed to working class people, who often have to find ways to deal with poverty and hardship.

Coming from that kind of background himself, Mark E. Smith makes it clear, in his autobiography *Renegade*, that his older relatives had adopted the same phlegmatic mindset, and that this had rubbed off: "There was a lot to learn from that generation—the Stoic attitude . . . You can't expect to feel cock-a-hoop all the time."

Later in the book, he is critical of self-indulgent younger men who lack this kind of temperament and who are "going to the doctor's every five minutes telling them how depressed and distanced they feel. And they're not really depressed, not clinically—it's not even disillusionment. I think it's because they have too much time and space to think about themselves."

Reflecting on his own close relationships, Smith has this to say: "More often than not, they've left me. It's never bothered me, though. Most blokes go suicidal, but not me."

Finally, here he is looking back to the start of his musical career: "In the beginning, I was quite sensitive . . . That can be a real problem. As soon as I started to fill in tax forms and sort paperwork out, as soon as I didn't have five days to be artfully glum and existential, all that changed."

From these examples, it's evident that, in spite of his familiarity with Sartre and Camus, Smith does not conform to the stereotype of the typical existentialist. If that were the case, one would expect The Fall's lyrics to express existential themes, such as the intolerable burden of existence, or the sense that life is meaningless. But there is none of the angst or melancholy that one finds in the songs of, say, Ian Curtis or Morrissey. Instead, Smith's writing tends to consist of surreal, cryptic, belligerent narratives that are collage-like, often written from the perspective of a disturbed and brooding alter-ego. According to the critic Simon Reynolds, the songs evoke "a kind of Northern English magic realism that mixed industrial grime with the unearthly and uncanny."

Then there is Smith's remarkable work ethic to consider. Over their thirty-eight-year lifespan, The Fall released thirty-one studio albums, as well as numerous live albums and compilations, making them far more prolific than any other Post-Punk band. Later Stoics like Cicero (106–43 B.C.E.) and Seneca (1 B.C.E.–C.E. 65) believed that we should make the most of our lives and not expend energy on trivial tasks. Smith seems to have done just that. Allowing himself time to ruminate on the meaning of life does not appear to have entered the equation.

Though increasingly ill in his later years, he worked to the end: one of this article's authors waited in a packed Bristol music venue in November 2017 for Smith to lead his band out, aware that at recent gigs he had been in a wheelchair. Hours later, the band members, *sans* Smith, walked brokenly on stage for the last time to reveal that their leader was too ill to leave his hotel. Unbowed, Smith compared himself to a defeated English Civil War leader whose downfall came in the same city—"As I, like Prince Rupert, leave Bristol with my tail between my legs . . ." and promised to be back. But it was to be his last outing from Manchester, and he died weeks later.

Smith's philosophy therefore seems to be much more in accord with Stoicism than existentialism. However, as we shall see, this does not exhaust the possibilities.

You Don't Deserve Rock'n'Roll

Smith's *modus operandi* was combative. Firstly, he was notorious for hiring and firing band members, frequently on a whim, reasoning that, "If it's me and yer Granny on bongos, it's a Fall gig," an oft-misquoted phrase that is also illustrative of his lack of regard for whoever was playing alongside him.

For instance, long-serving guitarist Marc Riley unwittingly provoked his departure by disco dancing to the The Clash's "Rock the Casbah," while the services of drummer Karl Burns were procured and then dispensed with no fewer than nine times. Even ancillary staff were not immune: a sound engineer was dismissed for eating a salad.

Secondly, Smith was renowned for haranguing group members whose stage performances were deemed not up to par. Perhaps the most famous example is on the album "Totale's Turns," when one unnamed musician is berated with the aside, "Will you fuckin' get it together instead of showing off?"

Thirdly, Smith's propensity for interfering with his band's stage equipment could also be a source of friction, as was the case on the infamous occasion when he fought with Karl Burns and guitarist Tommy Crooks at the New York venue Brownies in April 1998. This culminated in their immediate departure, along with bassist Stephen Hanley.

These incidents raise some obvious questions: why did Smith do things like this, and why did so many musicians put up with this kind of behavior?

In his book *The Art of Losing Control*, Jules Evans writes about how, having embraced Stoic philosophy, he was still left with a desire for what he calls "ego-transcendence," to go beyond our ordinary selves and feel connected to something greater. For Evans this is a need that is increasingly unmet in our secular Western world. But he believes that the most charismatic performers are capable of inducing "ego loss" in themselves, their audiences, and their fellow musicians.

In *The Hit: Into the Rock'n'Roll Universe and Beyond*, the distinguished scholarly expert on Buddhist philosophy Andrew Rawlinson concurs, arguing that such performers are broadly engaged in the same enterprise as Eastern gurus. Here the term "The Hit," which usually refers to a bestselling song, acquires an additional, esoteric meaning. It functions as a cipher for the mystical experience of non-duality, of oneness with ultimate reality, that spiritual teachers are attempting to engender in their devotees.

Controversially, in Hinduism and Buddhism, considerable ethical latitude has been extended to this revered type of personage, who use wildly unpredictable behavior, in blatant violation of their faith's ethical precepts, to elicit an experience of awakening in their followers.

In Buddhism, such behavior is regarded as an *upaya*, a "skillful means," if it produces the desired result. For example, Japanese Zen masters are known to beat their students to trigger awakenings, a practice that flies in the face of the principle of *ahimsa* or "non-violence" so cherished in Indian Buddhism. Then there is the Buddhist text known as the *Skillful Means Scripture*, in which the Buddha sleeps with a woman who was threatening to commit suicide out of love for him, thus violating the monastic principle of chastity. Finally, from the 1970s, we have the example of Chogyam Trungpa, a Tibetan spiritual teacher of "crazy wisdom." Trungpa was known as a reckless drunk who ate and drank what he liked, smoked, took psychedelics, and enjoyed sexual relationships with his followers, in violation of foundational Buddhist values.

In the Madhyamaka school of Buddhist philosophy, pushing students beyond their psychological limits (usually in intensive meditation) is designed to demolish the conceptions of reality that the ego clings to in an effort to preserve itself, as only then can that reality be apprehended as it truly is.

Seen from this unusual angle, Smith's behavior becomes more comprehensible, even if it remains ethically suspect: by keeping his musicians off-balance and in a constant state of creative tension, by deliberately not pandering to their expectations or those of his fans (which other frontman would show his disdain by keeping his back to the audience, or ridiculing his middle-aged fans as "The League of Bald Headed Men"?), by intentionally choosing a drug and alcohol-fueled path of derangement, he could be plausibly regarded as having generated the optimum conditions for "The Hit" to occur.

But did he succeed with this approach? The testimony of former wife Brix certainly suggests so:

> I remember being on stage and . . . being transported. Chills would run up and down my body and I felt as if I were being lifted off the stage. I was so immersed in the music that I felt possessed by it. At the most powerful times when we were so on point, it was religious. It blew me away.

The majority of former members look back with fondness on their time in The Fall and regard it as having been of transformative value.

Some venerate Smith even when he royally abused them. Former guitarist Ben Pritchard's reverence for him has been described by journalist Dave Simpson as "boundless, almost religious," even though Smith opens his autobiography with a long section slamming Pritchard as "paranoid" and "an old-fashioned gentleman fraud." An early member, Eric McGann, suggests that "among some band members, Smith was known as 'God'." Simpson speculates that "perhaps there is something supernatural or mystical in the way Smith "takes the crap people do" and turns it into brilliance."

Have you been to the English Deer Park? It's a large type artist ranch This is where C. Wilson wrote Ritual in the Dark.

Is it still far-fetched to conceive of Smith as a guru-type character? The notion may not be as outlandish as it looks, given that he was an admirer of authors who were mystically inclined, such as Arthur Machen, Philip K. Dick, William Blake (the lyrics to the song "W.B." are based on his poem, "A Song of Liberty"), and Colin Wilson, the only philosopher to be name-checked in a Fall song.

Colin Wilson achieved fame at the age of twenty-four when his first book, *The Outsider*, "a study in existentialism, alienation, and extreme mental states," was published in 1956 to glowing reviews. Wilson attained celebrity almost overnight when his offbeat lifestyle was disclosed: much of the book had been written in the Reading Room of the British Museum while Wilson was sleeping rough on Hampstead Heath.

Yet the fame was short-lived, partly because he was identified as one of the "Angry Young Men," a group of iconoclastic working-class or lower middle-class novelists, playwrights and filmmakers that included John Osborne, Alan Sillitoe, and Lindsay Anderson. According to Wilson, the backlash against this movement was an expression of the British class system in operation, as the literary establishment quickly became bored with the novelty of this first collective of working-class writers. Wilson's follow-up work, *Religion and the Rebel*, was roundly dismissed by those who had previously feted him, and it was not until the release of *The Occult: A History* in 1971 that his reputation was restored.

That Wilson's writing should have had considerable appeal for Smith is unsurprising. Both were autodidacts from working-class backgrounds, and neither attended university. Wilson's conviction that adverse personal circumstances were of more value to a creative person than an easy life chimed with Smith, along with his view that overcoming such challenges helped to instill the virtue of resilience, and inoculate against an unduly self-indulgent, pessimistic view of the world. In fact, Wilson's "new existentialism" is distinctive for its optimism, and Smith might have found it congenial for this very reason.

What this philosophy retains from the existentialism of Camus and Sartre, and what it shares with Stoicism, is an emphasis on freedom. According to Sartre, the absence of a designing God means that human beings have no obvious purpose. However, this also means that we are free to decide for ourselves what we want to do with our lives. As with Stoicism, this freedom extends to the emotions. If we are miserable, that is a choice that we have made and we should take responsibility for it. However, the fact that we are here by accident rather than design confers a sense of what Sartre called "contingency" and Camus "absurdity" on our lives, as nothing that we choose to do with our freedom can have any lasting significance.

For Wilson, this conclusion is unwarranted. In *The Outsider* and later works, he repeatedly draws attention to "peak experiences," which are overwhelmingly positive and characteristically mystical. In these states, feelings of alienation and despair are dispelled, and everyday consciousness is shown to be a liar.

Even punk musicians are not immune from peak experiences. For example, former Zero Defex bassist Brad Warner reports that while on his way to work in Tokyo, suddenly,

> all my complaints, all my confusions and misunderstandings just kind of untwisted themselves and went *plop* on the ground . . . The universe was me and I was it. I looked up at the sky and that experience was exactly like looking at a mirror. "That's me" you think to yourself . . . Well I got that same feeling no matter where I looked . . . There was no doubt that this state was "true." It was far more true than the state I considered to be normal up until then.

For Wilson, the task of the new existentialism is to study the nature of consciousness and discover methods for evoking this type of experience, which bestows a profound apprehension of freedom and purpose on its recipients through an act of will.

In Wilson's later work he argued that occult or supernatural powers should be regarded as expressions of an expanded human consciousness. Again, the allure this might have for Smith is obvious. The name of his own record label, "Cog Sinister" alludes to his self-professed powers of pre-cognition. As he puts it in his autobiography, "having the ability to see into the future . . . I've always felt this. Countless times I've written something or said something and it's manifested itself in reality." In her autobiography, Brix Smith Start also testifies to Smith's psychic abilities. In an interview with Simpson, she claimed that after he felt "disrespected," Smith put a curse on a journalist, who two days later suffered a serious accident. It should be noted that no record of such a calamity can be found; nor have any psychic events been proven to the satisfaction of scientists; but the belief of both Smith and his former wife in his psychic powers is significant nonetheless.

We only know for certain that he read three of Wilson's books, but given Smith's interest in criminology and the occult (journalist John Doran has suggested that the album *Hex Enduction Hour* be regarded as a magic spell or occult ritual), it does not seem unreasonable to speculate that Smith was acquainted with Wilson's wider body of work. On occasions he even seems to share Wilson's optimistic outlook, making his reputation as an irascible curmudgeon a little less deserved.

Both Stoicism and Sartre's existentialism go too far in insisting that we choose our emotions. If this were the case, most of us would simply decide to feel happy. It is also a concern that "peak" or mystical experiences should be accepted as self-authenticating, and Wilson's tendency to often take paranormal abilities at face value is suspect.

Nevertheless, certain artists excite our respect when they succeed in preserving a high degree of freedom throughout their creative lives, and this, together with Mark E Smith's remarkable capacity for self-renewal, might best be explained by his Stoic and sanguine temperament, as well as his adoption of band management strategies comparable to the methods deployed by crazy-wise gurus to generate that elusive "Hit" in their followers.

20

Elvis Costello Raises Hell on SNL

DAVID LaROCCA

On December 17th 1977, Elvis Costello performed live on television with his band, the Attractions on *Saturday Night Live*, only two years into the sketch-comedy show's ongoing, nearly half-century operation.

Within a few bars of starting to play the band's debut single, "Less than Zero," Costello suddenly ceases to sing, and tells his band "Stop! Stop!," then turns back to the live audience (in the studio before him and watching and listening elsewhere) and declares: "I'm sorry, ladies and gentlemen, there's no reason to do this song here" <https://youtu.be/eD_24nDzkeo>. Then he addresses the band anew, whispering "Radio, Radio," and with that prompt the Attractions launch into a spirited rendition of the band leader's alternate selection.

For decades, the scene—amounting to only a dozen or so seconds—has proved a scandal, one on par, perhaps, with Sinéad O'Connor's daring act of ripping in half a photograph of Pope John Paul II on the same stage in Studio 8H after singing Bob Marley's "War." Assessing the professional fallout of such acts is a separate project—but in brief, we can see that Costello was invited back to perform at the *SNL* 25th anniversary, while O'Connor appears to have been more aggressively punished for her defiance (with her protest of the Catholic Church's scandal of sexual abuse only recently being vindicated).

Costello in 1977 was not a punk rocker himself, but a New Wave innovator in the presence of Punk, a musician who, on *SNL*, made a particularly Punk act in his self-appointed role as a proxy for bona fide Punk, living adjacent to and claiming for himself its energy and ethos. In those few seconds of shifting course, changing his mind, going off script, Costello borrowed a

Punk move and made it his own. For us, the drama encodes philosophical lessons about improvisation and invention, freedom and conformism, authority and creativity, constraint and authorship.

What does it mean to deviate from pre-planned television programming? Given the strictures of the Federal Communications Commission (FCC), we are familiar with the "bleep" that sonically covers over profanity, but what about stopping a line of thought altogether—and starting a different one? And while considering the freedom of such an act, what if the deviation was, in fact, planned? Does premeditation change the meaning of the detour?

With such questions, we are launched into a philosophical study of deprogramming and reprogramming on live television—and how such a moment may become emblematic (an icon for an age or a movement, or at the very least, in today's parlance, a meme that captures a quintessential temperaament). In those few seconds, Elvis Costello and his band provide a clinic on the aesthetics and ontology of Punk defiance and creativity, one whose philosophical significance still radiates through our musical and wider popular culture.

Making It New, Again

From our vantage, how do we know the act on live TV in 1977 sustains cultural significance, even if we are not yet sure what that significance might amount to? Consider that the iconicity of Costello's move was reinforced in a metareferential moment during *SNL*'s twenty-fifth anniversary show in 1999, in which Costello burst in on the Beastie Boys during their live performance of "Sabotage" and, after reprising his famous introduction of the song from the original performance, played, you guessed it, "Radio, Radio" with the obliging Beastie Boys as his back-up band <https://youtu.be/22wwbTQYKxc>.

This act of interior homage—where a show decides to celebrate itself, even its most controversial moments—is coupled with outside applications too, such as when fans and imitators make it their own: from a "Weird Al" Yankovic parody to the way indie rock musician, St. Vincent started a version of her song "Cheerleader" on *Conan*, again on live television, but interrupted herself to say, as you will by now expect, "I'm sorry ladies and gentlemen, there's no reason to play that song." And thereupon plays *not* an alternate selection from her own oeuvre, but Costello's "Radio, Radio."

During an opening monologue, when Jason Sudeikis hosted *Saturday Night Live* (October 22nd 2022), he stirred awe at all the talent that has graced the *SNL* stage, pointed to the place "where all the music happened"—and his short list was: "Elvis Costello, Kanye, Nirvana, The Rolling Stones."

At each moment of iteration and invocation, we may pause to wonder if the repetition or re-application of the act defangs it—in Costello's loaded lyric "anesthetizes" it—creating a gimmick, where once it was a potent marker of defiance. Reflecting on the incident many years later, Costello himself deflated the transgressiveness of the stunt when he said "It felt good, but it was hardly a revolutionary act" (*Unfaithful Music and Disappearing Ink*, p. 308). No doubt, we're left to parse what a "revolutionary act" is—what we mean by the phrase, or why we should care about creating one—when thinking of Costello's *SNL* hijinks.

We could say that the interruption-and-reprogramming's status as a Punk act may have nothing at all to do with its revolutionary quality. Better, perhaps to speak to Punk's capacity to agitate. And in 1977 Punk music did agitate; and Costello's defiant leap from his assignment made many unnerved. Perhaps by now—more than four decades later—even Costello himself has lost touch with the energy of the song-as-protest and the counter-programming as a Punk act of consequence.

Rather than the "revolutionary," a more fitting punk mentality may come from a different metaphor—unsettling. As Ralph Waldo Emerson, a Punk Transcendentalist wrote: "I unsettle all things. . . . People wish to be settled; only as far as they are unsettled is there any hope for them" ("Circles," pp. 318, 320). Bravery amounts to being sanguine about living in a condition of perpetual change, and in those endless "moments of transition" finding our orientation to taking "next steps." Still, we must be on guard, as Emerson also counsels, whether an act, say, of apparent norm-challenging risks yet another "foolish consistency"—this time of anti-social behavior, or the expression of a prevailing spirit of the *agon* (the contest, contesting, the contested) merely for the reaction one gets from others—stirring trouble as a *modus operandi*.

Costello's apology and, indeed, his formality ("I'm sorry, ladies and gentlemen, there's no reason to do this song here.") may hardly seem like a moment of Punk rudeness, but then there is often something paradoxically *polite* about Punk actions—like a friend who calls you on your stupidity, or a teacher or spouse who interrupts your speech to save you from what troubling thing you are about to say. And if in addition to seeming polite, the interruption is planned or staged, that's fine too! Such performativity—such meta-ness—adds yet more layers to the probity of the Punk gesture and its kind of care: yes, we can be *thoughtful* about such transgressions.

Some viewers have suggested that Bruce Thomas lets the "secret" out by halting too quickly, almost as if on cue (and to a lesser extent, so does Steve Nieve). Indeed, the band doesn't seem *that* surprised by their band leader's boldness. Others have intimated that it was Costello's own manager who recommended the stunt as a way for the British band to get the attention of an American audience. Yet, as we have seen elsewhere, even if it's fraud, it's still instructive. Consider Casey Affleck's heavily rehearsed stunt, *I'm Still Here* (2013)—a species of what I have called hoax *verité* and different from the fabrications found in Orson Welles's *F for Fake* (1973) and Sarah Polley's *Stories We Tell* (2012).

In Affleck's conspiratorial effort at performance art, the running time of the movie doesn't resolve the status of the film *as* fake. Likewise with Costello's radical interruption of his own work, all these decades on, we remain unsure how to understand the scene. And in that state of indeterminacy—admittedly, we remain unsettled—we are granted much latitude to explore the power of Punk behavior and its effects on the making and reception of art.

Inherited Order and Imposed Improvisation

As it happened, a genuine Punk band—the Sex Pistols—was scheduled to perform on *Saturday Night Live* that evening in 1977. However, drug convictions led to Visa problems that prevented the band from traveling to the United States from their home in Britain. (Take note how Attractions drummer, Pete Thomas's T-shirt reads "THANKS MALC"—a gesture of gratitude to the manager of the Sex Pistols, Malcom McLaren, who failed to get his band to the gig.)

Elvis Costello and the Attractions became a last-minute replacement, which in itself lends interest to the sense of Costello and his band as Punk, or better, as a suitable replacement for an emphatically, emblematically Punk band such as the Sex Pistols. Maybe Costello felt emboldened by the trade—and with it, anointed by a kind of peer-esteem baptism that filled him and his band with intentions and methods to unsettle the establishment. When Costello switched songs, the almost-always cool-headed producer of the show, Lorne

Michaels, was so incensed that he rushed to the side of the main camera filming the band and gave Costello the middle finger throughout the performance of the song—a strikingly Punk gesture on Michaels's part! History revealed that Michaels didn't mind "Radio, Radio" being played (the record company wanted Costello to do another song, though), but it was longer than the slot and so threw off the show's tight schedule; like a good arts manager, he was upset by threats to scheduling, not content.

The enemy of planning, then, appears to be spontaneity, so what we have in this case is a question about inherited order and imposed improvisation: something that was and remains at the core of live performance, perhaps especially live television, which is constrained by time, by marketing interests (such as commercials), and by the nature of rehearsal. *SNL* is an institutional exemplar of all of the above: the crew rehearses all week; sponsors are lined up and their advertisements are set in place; and yet in the open spaces of live presentation there is room for improvisation. Of course, there are moments when actors "break" (usually laugh, but smiling can be enough to show a seam) or drop a violating-and-bleep-commanding f-bomb. Yet, as the charge of the live broadcast also affords, there is space and time for the achievement of comedy of an order altogether different from the pre-recorded.

Cavell on Improvisation

As we think about Costello and the Attractions performing "in the place of Punk"—that is, as proxies (for the Sex Pistols) and perhaps as self-appointed emissaries from another genre—let's look to Stanley Cavell's still-generative reading of modernist music in a moment of modernist philosophy, his "Music Discomposed," which first appeared in 1967 (and was added to the Cambridge edition of *Must We Mean What We Say?* in 1976, the year before Costello's incident). Surprisingly, Cavell's own proto-punk instincts in this essay transform the familiar senses of "improvisation" such that we find ourselves thinking of Bach and Beethoven as *improvisers.*

> . . . an ethnomusicologist will have recourse to the concept [of improvization] as a way of accounting for the creation-cum-performance of the music of cultures, or classes, which have no functionaries we would think of as composers, and no objects we would think of as embodying the intention to art . ("Music Decomposd," p. 200)

Cavell speaks of "improvisation" in the work of music (the manner of its performance on a given occasion, for instance); and also on film (such as the way actors behave, showing, in fact "a natural dominance of improvisation over prediction" ("Cons and Pros," p. 53) as well as on television (where the "amount of talk" involved seems to demand a persistent improvisation of content) ("The Fact of Television," p. 253). So as Cavell has us consider "what is composition, what is it to compose," or for us to treat "compositions as objects *composed*," we're wondering about those moments—such as the live performance of music on live television—when improvisation intercedes on planning, rehearsal, and the assignments of the composition. Indeed, as Cavell puts it,

> reliance on formula should allow the fullest release of spontaneity . . . The context in which we can hear music as improvisatory is one in which the language it employs, its conventions, are familiar or obvious enough . . . that at no point are we or the performer in doubt about our location or goal . . . ("Music Discomposed," p. 201)

As Rosalind Krauss tells us, other options include "absolute mechanization of chance" (John Cage) or "utter submission to total organization" (Ernst Krenek's electronic programming) ("The Rock," p. 103). With Cavell, then, and in our scene with Costello, we have this productive coupling of being entirely sure of the context of the performance and yet also utterly unsure how the artist's interruption in that space—his improvisation—will turn out. And so we recognize the form, yet, for the way the content is treated (inserted, replaced, etc.), both realms are transformed: the venue is suddenly a space for countermanding the "programmed" (the fated, the composed) and an occasion in which the well-known song is given a radiant new valence of signification (What does this song mean now, played in this way?).

We are *suddenly in danger*, and that is precisely what Cavell recognizes in the performance of art: "Within the world of art one makes one's own dangers, takes one's own chances—and one speaks of its objects at such moments in terms of tension, problem, imbalance, necessity, shock, surprise . . . ("Music Discomposed," p. 199). It shouldn't be lost on us that being "in danger" when there is no genuine danger (say, to life and limb) is precisely how Kant understands the experience of the sublime. The aesthetic potential for improvisation, therefore, is as enormous as it is unpredictable.

Now consider that there is not just Costello, his song, the show *SNL*, but also the *audience* (in studio and at home).

Something crucial is happening *in relation to* those who would "receive" the act as one meriting comment, one somehow suffused with the capacity for impact—in a word, the power to unsettle. As Cavell puts it:

> in art, the chances you take are your own. But of course you are inviting others to take them with you . . . and your invitation incurs the most exacting of obligations: that *every* risk must be shown worthwhile, and every infliction of tension lead to a resolution, and every demand on attention and passion be satisfied—that risks those who trust you can't have known they would take, will be found to yield value they can't have known existed. ("Music Discomposed," p. 199)

At the time, of course, Costello himself couldn't know how the legacy of his act would cash out—what it meant in the moment or what it would still mean decades later, but then artists are rarely the best critics of their work, perhaps especially if the art in question is improvised, since they too are experiencing it for the first time, just like us.

Still, for Cavell, the meaning of the artistic act and the reflections a critic offers on those acts (her assessments and her judgments) are nevertheless productively and necessarily entwined, since "the modernist situation forces an awareness of the *difficulty* in avoiding prescription, and indeed of the ways in which criticism, and art itself, are ineluctably prescriptive—art, because its successes garner imitations . . . criticism . . . because the terms in which he defines his response themselves define which objects are and what are not relevant to his response" (p. 208). In turn, our criticism is creative too—its compositions generate the conditions in which art—even transgressive, or perhaps especially transgressive art—finds intelligibility for audiences, that is, as individuals coming to new work, groups seeking to find emblematic instances, or cultures gathering exemplars for future reference, repetition, reconceptualization, including for canonization.

TV Made the Radio Star

Think of the scene of Costello's interruption as also illuminating something distinctive about the medium of television, here in the light of Cavell's observation that each television format—such as the serial/program we have since October 1975 called *Saturday Night Live*—offers "the establishing of a stable condition punctuated by repeated crises or events that are not developments of the situation requiring a single resolution, but intrusions or emergencies . . . each of which runs a natural course and thereupon rejoins the realm of the uneventful" ("The Fact of Television," p. 253).

Costello's prank is just such an intrusion or emergency in the life of the live show. Even though we have always watched the show live—even if "behind" the protection of an FCC-imposed delay (that monitors for prohibited language, wardrobe malfunctions, and so forth)—we watch, in part, because of the particular charge all of this improvisation (however scripted and rehearsed it may be) reveals to us in novel moments, such as when, as noted, a comedian or guest "breaks," or a musical guest suddenly replaces a stage for repetition with a stage for innovation.

Indeed, according to Cavell's logic, when the show functions without "errors" it is, alas, "uneventful," much as a newscast that adduces things that have happened, one thing after another—leaving us with the paradoxical sense that the news is not, in a word, newsworthy. In our case, with this TV show, with this moment in its history, the notoriety of Punk actions—call them anarchist or anti-authoritarian—are beautifully and fittingly glossed by the Cavellian tandem "intrusion and emergency" in which we are faced with what amounts to news, to the new, to the shocking and thus eventful.

Costello said later that the inspiration for the last-minute song change did not originate with him, but came instead from a moment he saw on BBC's *The Lulu Show* in 1969 when Jimi Hendrix concluded his performance of "Hey Joe" by announcing on air, "We're going to stop playing this rubbish" (*Unfaithful Music and Disappearing Ink*, pp. 307–08). Unlike Costello, who played another of *his own* songs, Hendrix played Cream's "Sunshine of Your Love"—a band that had recently broken up—until his air was cut. Costello recalled, "It was like watching your television go out of control." And so, nested in what appeared to be Costello's seminal scene of television defiance is this autobiographical reflection that finds an even earlier instantiation. Though Hendrix's and Costello's are not identical acts, we are, with Costello, closer to the space of homage and imitation, the planned and pre-determined and not the nominally improvisatory. And yet, Costello's very pre-meditation—with a heavy dose of Punk-inspired appropriation—is generative, since, as Cavell notes about music generally, "Reliance on formula seems to allow the fullest release of spontaneity." Consequently, constraint itself can provide an artist pathways to creativity—including to provocation, and, indeed, to pedagogy in new forms and modes. Costello had set about applying or repurposing

Hendrix's act as a "formula" of a sort—call it an inspiration—in order to manufacture an "intrusion and emergency." Costello himself was obviously and strikingly impacted by Hendrix's interruption (was Hendrix's planned too?), and so sustained the energy in the guise of an imported Punk statement for American audiences.

When Costello forces his own show to "go out of control" in 1977, he doesn't denigrate the song like a self-effacing and self-knowing Hendrix ("We're going to stop playing this rubbish"), but instead suggests the song is inappropriate, out of place, a scandal: "there's no reason to do this song here." So we're invited to presume that there *is* a reason for him to sing "Radio, Radio" on live television, on *SNL*, and at that time in the history of music and of technology. The band The Buggles formed in that same year, and the following year, wrote "Video Killed the Radio Star,"—as legend has it, in an hour. The song, released in 1979, featured these lyrics:

> Video killed the radio star
> In my mind and in my car
> We can't rewind, we've gone too far
> Pictures came and broke your heart
> Put the blame on VCR
> You are a radio star.

Meanwhile, back in 1977, "Radio, Radio"—with its own duplication and repetition firmly in place—admonishes its listeners even as, in a moment of metamusic, Costello sings of listening to the radio himself ("With every one of those late night stations / Playing songs bringing tears to my eyes"). And yet, those are *not* tears of longing or joy (from listening to his favorites) but tears of frustration (from listening to the kinds of songs that get played by bottom-line driven station owners and programmers):

> And the radio is in the hands of such a lot of fools
> Tryin' to anesthetize the way that you feel
> Radio is a sound salvation
> Radio is cleaning up the nation
> They say you better listen to the voice of reason
> But they don't give you any choice 'cause they think that it's treason
> So you had better do as you are told
> You better listen to the radio.

"Radio, Radio" and "Video Killed the Radio Star" are late Seventies meditations on the emergence of new media—and on their contestation by New Wave performer-critics. MTV broadcast for the first time in 1981. Radio—the dominant live medium of the prior century—and especially the popular music of the post-World War II era, would be suddenly challenged for dominance, influence, and relevance. Soon enough, in the 1980s, a song often *needed a video* in order to be launched into wide circulation and rotation on the radio. The radio star, then, became the video star; the video star absorbed the radio star.

Given all the Punk and New Wave credentials of the song "Radio, Radio," and Hendrix's influence on the *SNL* act, it's surprising to learn that the song began in 1974 as "Radio Soul," a piece Costello described as Bruce Springsteen- inspired—especially by songs on *The Wild, the Innocent and the E Street Shuffle* (1973). Lyrically, this early version was, according to Costello, about "the idea that the radio broadcasting from within you was ultimately of more value than the radio in the dashboard or the wireless on the shelf" (*Unfaithful Music*, p. 306). An eerie premonition of the spiritual elements of the Walkman and iPod to come—the way we create soundtracks for our own lives, becoming our own "radio programmers." In 1977, however, Costello revised the song to make it more aggressive and a more pointed critique of British radio, especially in the wake of the BBC's attempt to censor the Sex Pistols' song "God Save the Queen." (And so we come full circle to the band that was originally set to appear on *SNL*, and does appear on the cover of this book's predecessor volume, *Punk Rock and Philosophy*.)

With the context of the song's compositional development, and the history of its release in mind, "Radio, Radio" presents as a pre-Clash "public service announcement" *and* as an homage to the Sex Pistols. Not surprisingly, it also served as an affront to Costello's own record label, Columbia: they insisted he play "Less than Zero" on *SNL*, but Costello wanted to assert more control over what he sang, and he believed "Radio, Radio" was a better fit for the occasion; not only was he writing his own songs, he was programming them too (another bid for becoming your own radio station, internal or otherwise). Perhaps, not surprisingly, the fate of "Radio, Radio" *on the radio* was dire: once the advertisers realized the song was *anti*-radio (that is, the problem with radio as status quo rather than radio as avant-garde), stations stopped playing it. "I want to bite the hand that feeds me. I want to bite that hand so badly," sings Costello. Ryan Prado declared "Radio, Radio" to be "Costello's punk-as-fuck dissertation on corporate radio," one that "still seethes as red-faced to this day" ("The 20 Best Songs by Elvis Costello").

Our lives are heavily repetitious, as the existentialist philosopher Søren Kierkegaard reminded us, and people—especially those in positions of authority: parents, schools, governments, and perhaps most of all, corporate entities—tell us what to do (and increasingly so these days via social media and other forms of digital surveillance, including algorithmically-informed directives, enticements, and monitoring). All the more reason to continue thinking about Costello's "punk-as-fuck" move to cancel a song, pick another, and play it loud, fast, and with conviction. Here we have a worthy aid to reflection in our own times: though our days are full of the same tasks, thoughts, and patterns, they can be interrupted, new things picked up, a new course chosen.

And this unsettling can be occasioned even if the move is itself rehearsed or faked. The act of improvisation within constraints remains us of the central functions of art, whether as artist or critic, performer or audience. We're all positioned to draw lessons from biting the hand that feeds us.

VII

In Search of the Essence of Post-Punk

21
Post-Punk Music—
Your Scene?

MIHAELA FRUNZA

> But I got a feeling things are about to get much worse
> Before it gets worse
> And I'm not too good at feeling good
> Least not the way I thought I would
>
> —"I'll Let You Down," FRANK IERO and the Patience

"I belong to this fandom," "It feels like family here," and "This is where I truly fit in" are commonly expressed phrases in the comments of Instagram posts, Reddit communities, and YouTube videos featuring songs from My Chemical Romance, the various musical projects initiated by Frank Iero, Palaye Royale, and L.S. Dunes. Being a part of a virtual community where personal encounters are unlikely requires sharing numerous similarities.

Can you truly claim to "belong" to a specific musical genre, such as Post-Punk? What does this assertion actually mean? Furthermore, why is it significant, aside from providing inspiration for someone sitting on a balcony on a spring night, clad in an old leather jacket, to write an article for a Post-Punk and philosophy compilation?

"First things first," as a verse from a peculiarly named band would proclaim. What does the term "belonging" truly entail? It's not a concept that typically resides within the grand gallery of philosophical ideas. It doesn't emerge as one of the appealing subjects that have captivated great thinkers throughout the past two and a half millennia, such as "freedom," "being," "truth," or "beauty." In fact, the *Stanford Encyclopedia of Philosophy* doesn't even feature a distinct entry dedicated to "belonging." Upon exploring its virtual pages, you may countlessly encounter the word as a relational element intertwined within the definition or articulation of various concepts, spanning nationalism to aesthetics, yet it lacks its own dedicated category. Ironically, "belonging" appears to be considered unworthy of belonging to a scholarly compendium.

So, let's pause our search for a moment and turn to a more fundamental one—the common dictionaries. Here, we discover that "belonging" generally encompasses several meanings, including: "to be in a proper situation," "to be suitable, appropriate, or advantageous," "to be the property of a person or a thing," "to be attached or bound by birth, allegiance, or dependency," or "to be a member of a club, organization, or set."

When asked, "where do you belong?" individuals of all ages typically respond with their homes, families/loved ones, places, or communities. Fandoms or musical genres are not habitually included in these common responses. Thus, once again, the author of these lines faces a dilemma: not only is "belonging" deemed unworthy of a comprehensive philosophical examination, but it also seems ill-suited for connecting people to a musical community. So, what other possibilities exist?

Perhaps my approach to "belonging to Post-Punk" was flawed from the beginning, and a more insightful perspective can be gained by examining the Post-Punk music itself. What, if anything, do bands like My Chemical Romance, FIATC, FIATP, FIATFV, Palaye Royale, and L.S. Dunes have in common, aside from being listed as top recommendations on the author's Spotify playlist?

Night Vision

Where do we belong? Anywhere but here.

—FIATC

As this song title anticipates, one common thread among these bands is the sense of displacement they convey through their lyrics and musical compositions. My Chemical Romance embarked on their musical journey in the aftermath of the tragic events of 9/11, and their early songs address the confusion and pain wrought by those events: "And in this moment, we can't close the lids, on burning eyes / Our memories blanket us, with friends we know, like fallout vapors / Steel corpses stretch out towards an ending sun / Scorched and black, it reaches in and tears your flesh apart / As ice cold hands rip into your heart" ("Skylines and Turnstiles"). In "Bombsquad," L.S. Dunes touches upon the Capitol riots following the 2020 presidential elections, expressing their perplexity and discontent towards the ensuing chaos: "I don't want to wait in purgatory / Televised evacuation airs / On the other side of every camera / This side won't be shared." However, the discontent and unease articulated and passionately shouted by these bands are not solely rooted in political crises.

MCR's popular track "I'm Not Okay (I Promise)" begins with a monologue that highlights a divergence in tastes and abilities from the mainstream: "You like D&D, Audrey Hepburn, Fangoria, Harry Houdini, and croquet. You can't swim, you can't dance, and you don't know karate. Face it, you're never gonna make it."

While mixing together a series of abilities and limitations, the whole monologue is tinted with a sense of resignation about the person's chances of success or fitting into societal norms. Similarly, in Palaye Royale's "Dying in a Hot Tub," the vocalist shouts during the pre-chorus: "Have you heard the news that you're on your own? / Have you heard the news you got nowhere to go?" The remainder of the song hits the audience with a mixture of images of self-destruction, hedonism, and the allure of a reckless lifestyle that emphasizes a sense of displacement and the struggle to find a place to belong in a world that feels indifferent.

Displacement can be interpreted as a reflection of the challenges in finding a sense of comfort and belonging. It draws its strength from a range of dark emotions and states of mind, which are notably reinforced by the visual style of album covers, costumes worn during performances, and music videos. Some key emotions included in this realm are anger, suffering, anxiety, depression, and a preoccupation with death. While contemplating these themes, I coincidentally found myself in a Zoom conference with a contemporary author, Mariana Alessandri, who penned a book titled *Night Visions*.

As I listened to Alessandri and her examples, and afterwards reading through her book, it became evident to me that she was essentially describing the universe inhabited by the bands I had chosen, albeit I suspect she had never heard of them. However, her book seeks to challenge the foundations of what she terms "toxic positivity" (the idea of maintaining a constant positive attitude, while dismissing or invalidating any negative emotions or experiences) and the five core pillars for describing these dark visions align precisely with the emotions previously mentioned: anger, suffering, anxiety, depression, and grief.

Night Visions commences by challenging the binary opposition of light and dark, which Alessandri associates with Plato's allegory of the cave in his work "The Republic." As many newcomers to philosophy discover, Plato portrays the human condition as that of prisoners confined within a cave, shackled, and facing a wall. They perceive shadows of objects projected by a fire situated behind them. Eventually, one of the prisoners escapes and, after enduring months of arduous effort, finally beholds the true brilliance of sunlight, having only known shadows and reflections.

While the prisoners are reluctant to break free from their chains, as the shadowy parade on the wall constitutes their sole reality, our genuine place does not lie within the dark cave. We, as beings of light, must not abandon our true calling. Consequently, reason, rationality, and clear vision are esteemed qualities, while agitation, turbulence, and irrationality are destined to remain in darkness. Nonetheless, Alessandri proposes reclaiming the realm of emotions and moods and seeking a proper approach to explore it. Rather than subjecting it to the flames of reason, she advocates employing what she terms "night vision." By drawing upon a range of philosophers who have delved into the depths of dark moods, such as Audre Lorde, bell hooks, Maria de Lugones, Miguel de Unamuno, and Søren Kierkegaard, she endeavors to enhance our vocabulary of the dark and explore the tools associated with these ill-famed feelings.

I find a compelling parallel between the concept of "night vision" presented by Alessandri and the rebellious anthem "Welcome to the Black Parade" by My Chemical Romance. The lyrics, "Do or die, you'll never make me / Because the world will never take my heart / Go and try, you'll never break me / We want it all, we wanna play this part / I won't explain or say I'm sorry / I'm unashamed, I'm gonna show my scars / Give a cheer for all the broken / Listen here, because it's who we are," echo the essence of Alessandri's conception.

The line "Give a cheer for all the broken" could signify the recognition and celebration of the challenges and hardships that have shaped individuals, aligning with the exploration and comprehension of profound emotions and moods. The lyrics of the song capture a remarkable strength, resilience, and willingness to navigate life's darker facets while staying true to oneself. Consequently, they share a profound resonance with the essence of "night vision" and its implications.

Exploring Anger

Power, there's so much power in realizing that you're going to die.

—Death Spells

Honestly, I'm convinced the best of me is the worst of me
Believe me, I've tried but I just can't seem to fight
Against the tide and undertow that drag me down
So low beneath the foam I can't feel the sun burn my eyes.
—"Oceans," Frank Iero and the Patience

Alessandri begins her book by exploring the complex emotion of anger. Instead of conforming to the traditional condemnation of anger as expressed in classical philosophy by figures like Plato, Aristotle, and Marcus Aurelius, she takes a different approach. Alessandri draws insights from influential thinkers like Audre Lorde, bell hooks, and Maria de Lugones to examine the concept of anger more deeply. In doing so, she uncovers the multifaceted nature of anger and its potential for empowerment and transformation. Alessandri firmly acknowledges anger as a valid and essential emotion that can act as a catalyst for meaningful change. She recognizes that when anger is channeled constructively, it becomes a potent tool to challenge oppressive systems and confront injustice.

When someone outside the fandom explores Post-Punk music, the most apparent aspect they are likely to encounter is its pronounced anger. The vocalists' screams, the relentless drumbeats, and the guitar rhythms all contribute to a pervasive expression of a potent and often visceral anger. The bands discussed in this chapter conform to this pattern. For instance, Palaye Royale's song "Nervous Breakdown" features lyrics in which the singer passionately bellows: "Twist the knife just a bit further / Don't look at me, I think about murder / I think I'm 'bout, about to explode / I think I'm goin' to have a nervous breakdown."

These lyrics evoke a boiling rage and an intense yearning for revenge or retribution, illustrating how anger has consumed the individual, driving them to the limits of their mental and emotional capacities. Likewise, the song "It's Not a Fashion Statement, It's a Fucking Deathwish" by My Chemical Romance encapsulates the band's fiery disposition. The very title itself conveys a strong sentiment. The lyrics proclaim: "I will avenge my ghost with every breath I take / I'm coming back from the dead / and I'll take you home with me / I'm taking back the life you stole." The chosen words and vivid imagery in these lyrics reflect an unwavering determination to confront and triumph over the cause of their anger, conveying a profound and intense emotional intensity.

According to Alessandri in her book, suffering is often downplayed or dismissed by those who adhere to a mindset of relentless positivity. However, she argues that simply denying or trying to cure suffering does not honor the experiences of those who undergo it. Instead, Alessandri suggests adopting the insights of Miguel de Unamuno, who views suffering as an opportunity to forge interpersonal connections. Unamuno's perspective encourages us to see suffering not as a toxic substance we inflict upon one another but rather "a cup of sorrow provided by nature that we pass around and sometimes drink from together" (p. 68).

Pain is a prevalent theme within the musical realm of the bands I analyze. Whether it is physical or emotional, the presence of pain is portrayed as a disruptive force that can overpower one's will. In the lyrics of Palaye Royale's song "Tonight is the night I die," for instance, pain is expressed as a dominating entity that holds one captive: "Surrender to my pain / Locked inside my cage / Could I be a prisoner / To the voices in my brain?" Similarly, in the song "2022" by L.S. Dunes, pain is depicted as an overpowering presence that cannot be escaped except at the cost of your life.

The lyrics convey the sentiment that if the narrator cannot endure until the year 2022, they will at least witness how much pain they can withstand: "If I can't make it 'til 2022 / Least we'll see how much I can take. Sometimes, I wish she had just let me drift away, free from any pain, all at once." Moreover, pain can be likened to a net that traps and isolates one from external stimuli, until it becomes the only familiar and even desired reality. The lyrics of "Choke on One Another" by Death Spells capture this notion: "My pain is safe and sound / (You'll be the end of me, you'll be the end of me) / This world just brings me down / (You'll be the end of me, you'll be the end of me) / Hypnotizing, paralyzing, awe-inspiring, sterilizing."

In these songs, pain is portrayed as a formidable force that swamps individuals, shaping their existence and potentially leading them to contemplate their own mortality. The lyrics vividly illustrate the overwhelming and all-consuming nature of pain, resonating with listeners who have experienced similar emotions.

The remaining dark moods explored comprehensively by Alessandri in her book are similarly depicted in the lyrics and melodies of the Post-Punk representatives discussed in this chapter. Alessandri endeavors to restore the inherent human dignity associated with the grieving process, drawing inspiration from the works of Montaigne and Cicero. In parallel, the song "Record Ender" acknowledges the contrast between mere conversation and the constant grieving of lost affections and animosities, as expressed in the lyrics: "You're only talking / I'm always grieving the loss of my loves and my hates / If the air is heavy, you can hold my breath and I'll hold yours" (Frank Iero and the Future Violence).

Alessandri refrains from romanticizing depression and anxiety but instead, armed with ideas expressed by Gloria Anzaldua and Søren Kierkegaard, she explores the possibility that these states of mind offer insights into our finite existence. This sentiment resonates in lyrics like "I've felt this bad for so long / I'm scared I'm fine" (FIATC, "Guilt Tripping") or the explicit song title "Anxiety" by Palaye Royale, which declares: "A Band-Aid on a bullet hole that's still bleeding / Numb you up until you can't feel a goddamn thing / A generation full of anti-sobriety / A generation that is full of anxiety."

These lyrics mirror Alessandri's exploration of depression and anxiety, emphasizing their pervasive nature and the struggles associated with them. The songs neither glamorize nor diminish these experiences, but rather acknowledge their profound impact on individuals and society at large.

Coming Home

Yes, it comforts me much more to lay in the foundations of decay.

—My Chemical Romance

Where do we go?
Where is our home?
Where do we go my love?
You know, my love
I can see
If you just follow me
You'll be the queen and I'll be
I'll be the king of the damned. ("King of the Damned," Palaye Royale)

Anger, pain, grief, depression, and anxiety are intrinsic aspects of our lives that many struggle to navigate. Our society often attempts to diminish these emotions, encouraging us to bury them beneath a facade of positivity. However, minimizing these emotions does not make them disappear. Fortunately, the songs of these bands offer a respite for fans, as they provide a space where these unsettling and dark moods are openly expressed and articulated.

When fans listen to these songs, they find solace in knowing that they are not alone in confronting these challenging emotions. The musicians themselves are brave enough to acknowledge their own vulnerabilities and adept enough to express them in ways that resonate not only with the intellect but also with the heart. Through this shared experience of listening and participating in the music, fans establish a profound connection to their own vulnerabilities, resulting in a sense of validation and understanding.

This connection creates a profound feeling of belonging and a sense of being at home. It is through this emotional resonance that fans find comfort and a reassurance that their experiences are not isolated or abnormal. The music becomes a medium through which they can fully embrace their own emotions and find a sense of acceptance and kinship with others who have embarked on a similar emotional journey.

22
Rip It Up and Start Again

GEORGINA H. MILLS

Lenny Kaye once said that the Sex Pistols "rode the punk force right off the edge of the cliff, and then it was time for something new." What came next was a wave of musical and artistic contributions unlike anything that had come before it. The "something new" that arrived with Post-Punk was quite a departure from what the pre-Punk eras had to offer.

What Post-Punk tells us about Punk is that the Punk movement was a *paradigm shift*. Thomas Kuhn explained that most of the time science proceeds by solving puzzles, without any basic assumptions being questioned. But occasionally, there is a scientific revolution which thoroughly transforms the way scientists conceive of their research. Everything looks different, and the revolutionary new scientists can't seem to talk to the old, traditional scientists, who often die off without accepting the new way of seeing the world. Classic cases are the revolution which switched from the Earth to the Sun as center of the universe and the revolution which replaced Newton's theory of gravity with Einstein's.

Kuhn describes this by saying that scientific thinking is governed by a paradigm, a very general and deep-rooted way of understanding. In a scientific revolution, *the ruling paradigm shifts*, and suddenly everything is perceived differently. Stylistic differences in the arts come and go, but Punk is something more fundamental. Kuhn argues that a new paradigm does not represent progress itself—rather, it represents starting again from scratch. Punk was the starting point of the new paradigm, by breaking apart every convention that it could get its hands on, it allowed for the creativity and contrast of the Post-Punk era.

Using Kuhn's shifting scientific paradigms as an analogy lends itself well to this particular aesthetic revolution because of the rebellion inherent in Punk's philosophy. From Iggy Pop performing shirtless and covered in glitter to Poly Styrene shouting "Oh bondage, up yours!" at the top of her lungs, the Punk movement sought not only to push the boundaries of musical expression, but to demolish them entirely.

Essential features of the Punk movement included an explicit rejection of rigid norms of musical style, performance, and composition. This is where we can see what Punk did for Post-Punk. Post-Punk was unique in its juxtaposition of contrasting elements of music from diverse sources and genres, such as Blondie incorporating disco elements into their rock album, Nina Hagen using a classical voice to make unsettling sounds, or David Byrne drawing his lyrics from Dadaist poetry.

Kuhn's structure of revolutions can be applied to aesthetic revolutions as well as scientific ones. While artistic movements may come and go without necessarily representing a paradigm shift, the Punk to Post-Punk pipeline makes an excellent case for the existence of aesthetic paradigm shifts. Punk was characterized by accessibility, simplicity, and rejection of restrictive norms—a fresh start unconfined by the precedents set by previous decades of musicians. This paradigm shift allowed the music scene to explore all the possibilities such freedom allowed. The result was Post-Punk, an eclectic, unpredictable, and ever-changing genre that would have been unthinkable in the pre-Punk era. Thanks to Punk's paradigm shift, Post-Punk was able to play by Punk's new rules—no rules whatsoever!

The Punk Revolution

Everyone has a different opinion on when Punk was "over." For Legs McNeil, it was over when the Sex Pistols came to America (*Please Kill Me*). For Viv Albertine, it was over one night in the 100 Club when Sid Vicious blinded a woman in one eye by smashing a glass on the ground. For Rob Symmons of Subway Sect, it was the day he, along with various others of the Punk scene, were denied entry to a boat on the Thames where the Sex Pistols were playing for "record company people" (*Clothes, Clothes, Clothes*, p. 185).

For many, it was never over, and the Punk Rock of today is as much a part of Punk as anything ever was. There's no clear demarcation between Punk and Post-Punk, either in terms of timeline or in terms of genre. If we eliminate all potentially Post-Punk bands from the Punk lineup, Punk seems like a flash in the pan, lasting only a couple of years while its legacy continued for decades. We can see the progression of Punk to Post-Punk and beyond as a kind of aesthetic revolution, with Post-Punk operating on a paradigm established by Punk. In the case of Punk, especially, we have indeed seen something of a Kuhnian paradigm shift. The musical and visual accomplishments of the Punk movement represented a brand new paradigm and, more importantly, a tossing out of the old paradigm.

One of the most impactful accomplishments of Punk was to bulldoze through genre and style and allow a blank canvas for music and musicianship to build on top of. Punk does not appear as the next stage in a style, but an abandonment of previous style conventions. Not progress, but a paradigm shift. In this analogy Post-Punk would represent the progress within the new paradigm. Punk broke all the rules of music so that Post-Punk could be limitless in its scope and possibility. I will argue that Post-Punk illustrates the value of the Punk movement. Punk moved the goalposts and changed the structure of our aesthetic reality, and gave Post-Punk the framework it needed to create without inhibition.

We're on the Road to Nowhere

The phrase "paradigm shift" is most commonly associated with scientific enquiry, where a new paradigm radically changes the kinds of scientific questions that are pursued, and the enquiry as a whole takes an entirely different set of assumptions as its premise.

There is such a thing as an aesthetic paradigm shift or an aesthetic revolution. While an aesthetic paradigm shift may not work in quite the same way as a scientific one, there are some structural similarities. A paradigm shift represents a significant change in the foundational assumptions of the scientific community, or in the case of an aesthetic paradigm shift, the artist. In both the scientific and the aesthetic case, what is possible and the norms of enquiry are determined by the paradigm. If we believe that the Sun rotates around the Earth, our calculations of its movement or position in relation to planets will reflect that assumption. If we assume that the Earth revolves around the Sun, however, we will approach such enquiries in an entirely new way.

Punk specifically bears a resemblance to Thomas Kuhn's account of paradigm shifts in science because of the start-from-scratch approach that the Punk movement used. In *The Structure of Scientific Revolutions* Kuhn's account of scientific paradigm shifts contains an important feature that often seems counterintuitive: that a shift in paradigm itself is not progress, the progress occurs after the paradigm shift. This feature often does not sit comfortably for beginners in philosophy of science.

According to Kuhn's account of progress, the shift from, for example, bad air theory of disease transmission to germ theory would not represent progress. However, the shift would facilitate progress now that a new paradigm has been adopted. Knowing about the existence of germs is not, in itself, progress, but learning about germs and how they are transmitted, how they may cause illness, how to combat such illnesses, this would represent progress in Kuhn's account. Now that new assumptions have been adopted, we can use them for the real progress.

According to Kuhn's account, a paradigm shift represents a break from tradition, something of a blank slate. When we have a new paradigm we do not have new knowledge as such, but a new set of assumptions upon which we can build knowledge. What has been achieved in a paradigm shift is not progress, but new possibility. Not all eras of aesthetic style have this paradigm shift as their catalyst. For example, we can see the change from art nouveau to art deco as a change in style, but not a paradigm shift. The rules of artistry such as pattern, realism, and medium remained the same but the style changed. Similarly, in the descendants of Punk themselves, we can see a clear progression in mood and content from the pop-punk of the late 1990s onwards, to the emo subculture of the mid-2000s. Changes took place from one to the other, and while many bands from that time curated an original and distinctive style within their respective genre, the shift was not as momentous as a paradigm shift. There was continuity as well as fluctuation, and a chain of creation instead of destruction of previous rules and norms.

So when is an aesthetic movement a paradigm shift? Music and art movements come and go often, with new elements and developments that build on the old. For something to catch the status of aesthetic revolution or paradigm, shift, as in science, there must be a change in the background assumptions that shape the artist. I would like to posit that, for art and music, there are a number of ways this can take place. An important one might be the purpose of the art work. For example, is our background assumption that the music ought to be danced to, listened to, or witnessed as a performance? Another possibility might be whether we value beauty or realism in visual arts.

Should art be beautiful? Should it be realistic, fantastical, or abstract?

In music, genre can represent the basic assumptions of the paradigm, as can norms of tonality. This kind of assumption might be the basis for your musical paradigm. Background assumptions surrounding composition might be features of the paradigm. One striking example of a musical paradigm shift might be Stravinsky's *Rite of Spring*, first performed in 1913 and choreographed by Vaslav Nijinsky. The composition contained dissonant elements that defied expectations set by the previous Classical and Romantic eras of classical music, and the choreography was characterized by unsettling movement, some considered indecent at the time. The score was so unprecedented that, during rehearsals, it was said that Stravinsky became irritated by the frequent interruptions from musicians sure that he had made an error. Composer Julius Harrison described it as "abhorrence of everything for which music has stood these many centuries . . . all human endeavour and progress are being swept aside to make room for hideous sounds."

Though *The Rite of Spring* was criticized widely, it was groundbreaking. It ushered in new possibilities for composers and choreographers by changing the limits of what was acceptable. The Modern era of classical music allowed for ugly but expressive music and irregular tonality, music filled with surprises and dissonant layering. We can see this as a kind of dramatic paradigm shift. At first, it sounds wrong to listeners of classical music. None of the styles and traditions that they were used to were being obeyed. However, after the new paradigm is formed, one that changes the rules of composition, new progress can be made. Choreographers were no longer bound by the assumption that emotion must be portrayed through clean and controlled gestures, but Nijinsky's angular and primal choreography showed that dancing doesn't need to be pretty and proper in order to be moving and impactful.

Is this a paradigm shift in the same way as a scientific revolution? Well, it was initially unpopular, as was the notion that the Earth revolved around the sun when it was new, but what these changes also had in common was a change in the way things are done. At one point, we thought we knew what the rules were, but after the paradigm shift, we have to experiment a little and make the rules anew, or indeed, do without them. An aesthetic paradigm shift differs from a scientific one in that it is easier to work within previous paradigms than it is for science. There's nothing stopping anyone from composing a chorale so paradigmatically Baroque that Bach himself could have written it, but these days you might have trouble doing any meaningful astronomy on the assumption that the sun revolves around the Earth.

So what does this have to do with Post-Punk? Well, if Punk represents the rite of spring, Post-Punk represents the wealth of atonal composition and angular choreography that the twentieth century provided. While rock genres and subgenres have shifted and developed consistently since their inception, the intentional subversiveness of Punk created an opening for experimentation, and broke the illusion that the conventions of rock performance ought to be obeyed.

Search and Destroy

According to Simon Reynolds (*Rip It Up and Start Again*), "punk had declared 1976 to be year zero." While this might be something of an exaggeration—Punk retained its influences from pre-Punk days—Punk did represent a significant change in how artists approached music and musicianship. Up until the early 1970s there had been rules and norms governing who can be a musician and how to be a musician. The Punk movement represented a change on all fronts. The gatekeepers of musicianship were circumvented, the norms of how to make music were demolished, and the roles of who can be a musician were abandoned and made anew. As Viv Albertine says of Johnny Rotten:

> I look up at him twisting and yowling and realise it's everyone else who's wrong, not him. How did he make that mental leap from musically untrained state-school-educated, council-estate boy, to standing on stage in front of a band? I think he's brave. A revolutionary. (*Clothes, Clothes, Clothes, Music, Music, Music, Boys, Boys, Boys*, p. 86)

Aside from the question of *who* could access musicianship during Punk, *how* musicianship was accessed was also subject to a paradigm change that developed through the Post-Punk era. DIY was a large part of Punk's new paradigm, and Post-Punk extended this from making music through recording and rethinking relationships with record labels. Many in the Post-Punk movement turned away from major labels, fearing that this would confine them and ruin their sound, and instead sought to make music through small labels that were part of their own movement or had a high level of creative input from the musicians themselves. The DIY movement started in the Punk era continued into Post-Punk, with independent labels such as Mute Records and Factory Records functioning as both record label and all-around creative hub and giving autonomy to the artists that worked with them.

There may be some dissent from this view of Punk. Reynolds argues that "For the Post-Punk vanguard, punk had failed because it attempted to overthrow rock's old wave using conventional music." Whilst it's true that many Punk legends such as the Ramones played re-upholstered versions of rock-'n'roll classics, or created new music from the same timbre and tonality, the same bits and pieces of the old, this does not make music conventional.

One of the hallmarks of Punk as an aesthetic movement is juxtaposition. Taking the traditions of genre and generations of legacy and putting it in the hands of the irreverent and unexpected. It's the Ramones singing "Baby I love you," the Sex Pistols putting the Queen of England on their album covers. Iggy Pop covered in glitter, leather, and tulle all at once. Masculinity without dominance, femininity without deference. Its raw musicality and tits on the outside of your T-shirt. A few of the parts might be conventional, but the configuration is jarring and unexpected, or at least it would be to a Punk novice. Part of the novelty of Punk music requires that it take elements of conventional music and destroy its connection with genre and tradition through performance. This set the stage for Post-Punk as an anarchic and limitless genre of possibilities.

Post-Punk as Progress

Simon Reynolds claims that "Destroying is always more dramatic than building. Post-Punk was constructive and forward-looking." One of the characteristics of a Kuhnian paradigm shift is the fact that progress is possible after the paradigm shift. What demarcates Punk as a Kuhnian aesthetic revolution is the progress that Post-Punk represents. Impossible under pre-Punk conditions, but encouraged by the new paradigm. Once the impetus to counter-culture had been established, then the constraints on possibility were gone, and this manifesto for music became the stage for inventive Post-Punk creativity.

This time in music saw art rock from the likes of Talking Heads, PiL turning their eclectic mix of influences into an avant-garde sound wall, and Gang of Four creating aggressive political rock. Post-Punk represents a diversification of style and mixing of influences that would have found little traction in previous decades. The blends of disparate influences and methods meant experimentation could lead to an explosion of micro-genres in pop and rock music. The mission was no longer to create a great example of a pop or rock song, but to find out what is possible. Punk's drive to make something shocking lead to Post-Punks drive to make something new.

Some interesting examples of this include Talking Heads' use of Dadaist poetry to create lyrics that's sole meaning appears to be their rhythmic value. Another might be Adam and the Ants incorporating rhythms from Burundi drumming into their music, creating an unusual contrast with their whimsical lyrics about pirates and highwaymen. Post-Punk shows us progress that is only possible because of the paradigm shift that Punk represented. Adam Ant would never have been able to pull off Prince Charming if he and Jordan Mooney hadn't performed together in the 100 club with "Fuck" carved into his back as a fashion statement. Public Image Limited would have seemed atonal and off-putting if the Sex Pistols hadn't blown the norms of genre and decorum wide open.

Post-Punk as a genre is hard to characterize because of its diversity. Endless subgenres of pop and rock seem to fall under the umbrella of Post-Punk. This is an excellent illustration of the progress that punk's new paradigm allowed. Punk music and the movement that made it was about rejecting constraint and tradition, which allowed Post-Punk to embrace anarchic curiosity about what kind of music can and should be made. With this progress, Post-Punk left few stones unturned for artistic expression.

The Catalyst

Simon Reynolds characterizes Punk as having failed in its mission to exact change, and Post-Punk as a much more successful driver for change. I disagree.

Punk was the catalyst needed to allow Post-Punk to make the kind of progress that Punk desired. Punk was the revolution, and Post-Punk was the practice of building a new type of music. Punk rejected the old paradigm and created the groundwork for a new one. Whilst there may have been many Punk bands like the Sex Pistols that existed as a flash in the pan, and burned out before they had a chance to define the sound of a new genre, they opened the door for a world of progress. Post-Punk took every opportunity that Punk had left for them and used it to grow something new.

Whilst I would not like to give a mission statement for Punk, it was only meant to blow the doors off. The rest was up to the musicians who came next. If we think of Punk as essentially a paradigm shift, Punk was an extremely successful movement. An aesthetic revolution need not make progress; it need only change the assumptions and traditions of the aesthetic past, or parameters within which art is created.

23

Post-Punk as Democratic Mass Culture

MINDY CLEGG

What do we mean when we say "Post-Punk"? It's far more than the genres that followed Punk. To understand it, we must come to grips with the formlessness of 1970s Punk and how Post-Punk took on that chaos.

Punk as a genre of music never disappeared—Punk's not dead, as the kids say. Rather, Punk hardened into hardcore in the early 1980s. While the genres clustered under the umbrella of Post-Punk share a common musical root found in the 1970s, they also share a belief that making music should be a truly community-based, democratic process.

The Rise of Hardcore

Since its inception, the term "Punk" was born of debate starting with those boisterous music critics working at *Creem* magazine. There was not much consistency in how "punk" was used initially. Dave Marsh gets the credit for coining the term "punk rock" and Lester Bangs and Greg Shaw for popularizing the term more broadly. Shaw dubbed garage rock bands of Southern California "punk" while Bangs focused on a few bands out of Detroit. Bangs later zeroed in on the growing scene around Max's Kansas City and CBGBs in New York City as *the* defining Punk scene (Clegg, *Punk Rock*, p. 51).

Bands began to describe themselves as Punk, too. The earliest use of the term "punk" by a band seems to be by Suicide in late 1970. By the time *Punk* magazine began publishing in 1976, a broader cultural phenomenon was evident. By the end of the 1970s, academics began to explore the topic of Punk, cementing its cultural import. Since the 1950s, teen culture had become a focus of cultural studies and by the late 1970s Punk was starting to be seen as the next big youth culture.

Dick Hebdige discusses Punk in his book *Sub-culture*, published in 1979. Hebdige took an aesthetic ap-proach to Punk and compared Punks to earlier cultural rebels such as author Jean Genet. In the 1970s, Punk was not a coherent genre of music. Rather, the definition was being worked out between different groups in society—musicians, fans, critics, academics, the mass media, the recording industry. For those involved in these scenes, active participation mattered and drove the definition from within, even as it evolved among critics. Active engagement was a key component of Punk.

Today, when discussing the genre, we tend to mean hardcore Punk, a subgenre that emerged in the late 1970s. A new wave of Punks embraced the term, giving the music a new, faster, more aggressive life. In LA, Black Flag led a suburban adden-dum or a violent challenge to Punk in Hollywood (depending on whom you ask). In Washington DC, Bad Brains heard the Ramones, abandoned funk for Punk, playing it harder and faster than anyone before them. Some of the first wave bands like the New York Dolls, the Ramones, the Sex Pistols, the Clash, X, and the Germs retained the term 'punk'. But they retroactively become progenitors of the hardcore scene, as if that was the plan all along. A variety of bands that were part of the original Punk scenes were re-categorized. In that sense, far too often, Punk is still defined by the metrics of the main-stream music industry with its preoccupation with sorting artists into genres for the sake of marketing.

Reclassifying bands based on new understandings of the past is not inherently problematic. But some problems emerge with the first wave to hardcore narrative. The "no true punk rocker" debate serves nothing but historical erasures. Women, people of color, and queer people often struggled to find accep-tance within hardcore Punk, despite being critical participants of these scenes. Lauraine LeBlanc described how young men felt young women "invaded" "their" scenes while "girls in male-dominated youth subcultures such as Punk continually con-front ideologies of gender that remain largely invisible" (*Pretty in Punk*, p. 8).

James Spooner discussed his experiences as a Punk who was Black in his foreword to the book *White Riot*. After discovering Punk, a punk who was white, at his school told Spooner that he was only "cool" because he was Punk. Spooner recalled "that day

I was asked to make a choice: punk or black" (p. xiii). Members of the LGBQT+ community also often felt marginalized in hardcore scenes, with queer Punks' contributions being ignored or categorized as Post-Punk. Those invested in that perspective argued that Punk Rock should be an apolitical yet countercultural space. This meant avoiding progressive and intersectional politics. The experiences of women, people of color, or queer people came to be construed as divisive and too political by some.

Despite attempts at gatekeeping, women, people of color, and LGBQT+ people made important contributions to Punk. Sam Sutherland argued that early Punks in Toronto found a safe space to develop within LGBQT+ spaces. Bands like the Dishes and the art collective General Idea were early influences. In the city of Chicago, queer and Black spaces allowed for the first flowering of Punk culture. Yet, in his recent book, Kevin Mattson's history of hardcore Punk in the 1980s focused on young white men, despite the diverse nature of Punk scenes across time and space. Hardcore came to be understood as the "most true" form of Punk, and that which did not fit into it was relegated to the realm of Post-Punk or new wave. Only some Punks were "true" Punks.

In other words, many bands now classified as Post-Punk have actually been *reclassified* due to our tendency to revise the past. I mentioned the band Suicide above, possibly the first band to describe their music as punk. This experimental electronic band is sometimes called Post-Punk likely because their first album was not released until 1977. Nina Corcoran called them "proto-punk" in an article in *Pitchfork*. This stems from the modern definition of punk as primarily describing American hardcore. These critics parsing what is "pure" Punk and what is not often gloss over the absolute diversity of sound found in early Punk.

Bands like the Ramones and Sex Pistols are considered the bellwether of punk. But bands like Suicide, the Talking Heads, Blondie, the Screamers, X, Black Randy and the Metro Squad, Catholic Discipline, and Jayne County among many other artists were also part of these early scenes. These bands embraced experimentation with music, which now defines our understanding of Post-Punk. Suicide—the first band to call themselves punk—were no longer Punk, but adjacent to it. But can a better understanding of Post-Punk help us to change these erasures and help us to understand music as more than just a commodity to be marketed to particular demographics?

Beyond Hardcore

Post-Punk also developed in the discourses of music critics. Their disagreements imagine temporal overlap with Punk and reveal just how little unity there is as to when Punk gave way to Post-Punk. British critic Simon Reynolds called 1978 to 1984 "the prime years of Post-Punk," a period of creativity to rival the Sixties (*Rip It Up and Start Again*, p. xiv). During this period, Punk moved outside of insulated "bohemian" urban communities and into "the suburbs and the regions" of England. It included a collection of genres inspired by Punk such as "no wave, punk-funk, mutant disco, and industrial" (p. xvi). Notably, he treated hardcore and the British Oi! scene as distinct phenomena (p. xvii).

Clinton Heylin argued that the term originated in 1978 with the music press, such as when Charles Shaar Murray used that term to describe Howard Devoto's second band Magazine, which he formed after his first band the Buzzcocks. Murray argued that Devoto's new band was not Punk "but was referenced against 'punk'" (*Babylon's Burning*, p. 426). Heylin noted that during this time "a whole new set of Post-Punk journalists" emerged on the scene (p. 429). Heylin argued that ultimately, Post-Punk as a terminology "failed to catch on" (p. 458). That might come as a surprise to the authors in this book! George Gimarc argued that "in the early 1980s, what was once a sharply focused music scene called Punk shattered into a dozen different factions." He included Oi! and hardcore as part of Post-Punk, in contrast to Reynolds (*Post Punk Diary*, Foreword).

Meanwhile, historian Bradford Martin noted that "Post-Punk has wrought greater concern with the authenticity of musical expression and diversified approaches to songwriting, and has emerged as a culturally venerated music that is fundamentally about something" (*The Other Eighties*). He called Post-Punk an underground phenomenon. Post-Punk musicians and fans developed "an identity as a community" based on "opposition to the era's dominant music, social, and political institutions" (p. 96). Martin's view had the advantage of a few extra decades of music and cultural history to consider. But it also offers up a communal and democratic explanation of Post-Punk.

The genres of music swept into the category of Post-Punk were hotly debated and not always clear. But hardcore punks pioneered a set of strategies that people making other kinds of music would embrace: an active kind of cultural democracy. The bands that fall under the Post-Punk label share an approach to production, distribution, and consumption of music along with a leveling between fans and artists. Rather than viewed through the lens of corporate professionalism—with a strict division between producer and consumer—Post-Punk genres tend to embrace DIY (do-it-yourself) ethics.

First-wave punks obliterated the line between fans and musicians, encouraging those watching in the audience to learn a few chords and start their own bands. Building on that, Post-Punks embraced that notion of democratic cultural production, whatever genre of music they played. The democratic nature of Post-Punk can be seen in how those bands embraced independence.

Independent music labels were not unique to Post-Punk. Ed Ward argued that independent labels put rock music on the map in the post-war period (Volume 1, p. 39). But rock indies were commercially-oriented. According to David Szatmary, by the mid-1950s, independent companies had a large market share of the R&B market, showing the centrality of profitability (*Rockin' in Time*, p. 15).

First-wave Punks were not necessarily anti-commercial; some of the bands of the era achieved commercial success. Some signed to major labels or to commercial indies. The Sex Pistols were signed to EMI in the UK. Alan O'Connor noted that the Ramones signed to Sire Records, a commercially oriented indie label founded by Seymour Stein to license European artists in 1966. Stein ran the label like a major and their artists were distributed by Warner Brothers (*Punk Record Labels,* pp. 1–2). By the time the Ramones were signed, it seems that the mainstream industry sought to distance itself from the term "Punk." Sire played an important role in the rise of the "Punk is dead" trope. They refused to market the Ramones (and other bands they signed) as Punk, but insisted on the term New Wave (Gordon, "Fossils").

During this period, the recording industry was highly centralized. O'Connor argued that hardcore labels were founded in part as a response to this centralization as major labels controlled about ninety percent of the market in 1977 (p. x). As a result, the negative reaction of the industry towards Punk during the 1980s was driven in part by a wave of new independent labels that emerged out of Punk scenes. These indies would rival the rock wave of the 1950s. According to Pierre Perrone, some labels were commercially oriented, such as Virgin Records in the UK, who picked up the Sex Pistols once they were dropped by EMI ("Forty Years of Virgin").

Other new labels were artist-run and less commercially focused. They prioritized creative freedom of their artists, forging an alternative to the mainstream industry, and a sustainable model of music production. Necessity was indeed a mother of invention here. O'Connor discussed the experiences of the UK Subs on GEM Records, a subsidiary of RCA, which resulted in the band losing control of their early recordings. O'Connor noted "all the old punk bands were not on major labels. Many first-generation bands issued their records themselves or were on small labels . . . Apart from a small number of famous bands in England most of the early punks existed on the margins of the record industry." O'Connor called DIY production "a necessity" (p. 2). Hardcore punks experimented with independent production driven by that necessity. Black Flag initially planned to release *Damaged* on their own label SST but with distribution by Unicorn, who had a distribution deal with major label MCA. A legal dispute between MCA and Unicorn and then with SST stalled the release. As a result *Damaged* could not be released until Unicorn went bankrupt in 1983 (pp. 2–3).

Such experiences drove a new wave of independence. O'Connor argued that hardcore Punk scenes existed as "a cultural field" as theorized by Pierre Bourdieu. He explained that "a field is a relatively autonomous space in society where a specialized activity takes place." Further, "they exist within the field of power" meaning state regulation "and the economic field" meaning corporations. "A field exists when a struggle has taken place for its autonomy." Bourdieu advocated understanding art via "fields" because he believed that art was best when "judged by their peers and rewarded on that basis" rather than on the profits they generate for corporations. This took time to evolve within Punk as the majors had to lose interest in bands from Punk scenes (p. 4).

Hardcore bands lost access to an audience directly outside of their scenes once the majors changed their tune on Punk. The harder-edged style favored by bands that made up hardcore meant that they "removed themselves from the field of commercial rock music" as the majors saw hardcore as unmarketable. Many Post-Punks would wear that unmarketability as a badge of honor, and not just hardcore bands. But O'Connor argues that independence was sometimes a conscious choice of conviction. This was built on the anti-commercial tendencies found in some first-wave Punk music. Ian MacKaye of Teen Idles, Minor Threat and Fugazi started Dischord Records as a political choice (p. 5). The DC punks did more than just copy what independent labels of the past had done, rather "they invented their own way of doing things." For example, they hand-folded the covers for their early releases. In doing so "Dischord Records was setting the standard for the field of hardcore punk labels. Quite a number of DIY labels today mention Dischord as an example of how to do it" (p. 6).

In Britain, the band Crass shaped a political meaning of Punk as well. The band "operated as a collective" influenced by their anarchist politics. They started Crass Records very early on (p. 8). O'Connor argued that labels like Dischord and Crass continued to influence Post-Punk artists. He stated that "each generation of punks discovers that it is not difficult to record songs and have them pressed." They have even reconfigured the meaning of success. "Getting to 10,000 is punk-rock gold," he wrote (p. xi).

Not all hardcore bands embraced DIY production, but enough did to make this more democratic form of cultural production an important definer of Post-Punk culture—not just bands, either. Bradford Martin argued that Post-Punks prized independence. "Post-Punk fans," he noted, "believed they were making important consumer choices by buying independently produced records, and musicians believed they were challenging major label hegemony by making their music available through the independents." Distributor Rough Trade touted their independent bona fides as well as the breadth of genres they distributed including "import and domestic Hardcore, Experimental, Industrial, Dance, and the Undefinable" in their marketing (*The Other Eighties*, p. 100).

During the 1980s, several such networks emerged: Mordam Records, Dutch East India, and the aforementioned distributor Rough Trade. Martin argued that the existence of these distributors signaled "the incomplete nature of the majors' hegemony over distribution." These distributors and the labels they serviced embraced a deliberate strategy as articulated by Ruth Schwartz, founder of Mordam. She argued that those who worked for indies cared about the music and the community, not just profits (p. 101). The mode of production and distribution was what mattered, not blind adherence to genre. But there were connections there, too. Martin noted how the sound of first-wave Punk ran through Post-Punk. We can draw a straight line from the Ramones or Sex Pistols to bands like Sonic Youth via "a jangling, aural buzzing, cacophony" (p. 101).

Post-Punks also embraced shocking subject matter. Band names sought to "shock middle-class sensibilities," such as Circle Jerks, Crucifucks, and Butthole Surfers. Bands like the Minutemen wrote lyrics which challenged the militarism of the era, such as "Themselves." These bands embraced anticommercialism. There were layers of transgression, questioning traditional social values of American society, underpinned by independent production. Most importantly, Post-Punk culture was democratic in its reach and access. Independently produced music erased the line between musicians and fans. Martin argued that "Punk bequeathed to Post-Punk a tradition of performers who tried to reduce the distance between themselves and their fans both literally and figuratively" (pp. 101–02). First wave punks embraced DIY cultural production, and Post-Punks followed that to its logical conclusion.

This explosion of indie production needed a media support system. So Post-Punks forged a globe-spanning media landscape to support their growing scenes, embracing zines as an alternative to the mainstream music press. Stephen Duncombe described zines as "independent and localized, coming out of cities, suburbs, and small towns across the USA, assembled on kitchen tables." He argued that zines represented a form of resistance to mass culture, "a different possibility" (*Notes from Underground*, p. 2). Duncombe argued that zines were "a true culture of resistance," an "organic" form of cultural resistance, "an indigenous strain of utopian thought" of the 1980s and 1990s. Post-Punk zines grew out of similar conditions that drove DIY Post-Punk labels—a lack of music press attention—even as they were self-consciously anti-commercial (p. 7).

Zines were critical to building Post-Punk translocal communities. We can see that in the hardcore paper of record, *Maximumrocknroll* (*MRR*). O'Connor argued that the zine "combines intelligent articles and reviews, leftist politics, and support for a non-commercial hardcore punk scene." It provided space for ongoing, interactive discussions on a variety of topics among its readers via articles, scene reports, letters, and classified ads. Reader participation was key. Small punk labels were encouraged to place ads for their artists to directly address their community and support the zine. *MRR* circulated globally, which helped make hardcore into a global, translocal community (p. 7). *MRR* and its editor Tim Yohannon "had a huge influence on shaping the practices and values of DIY punk" (*Punk Record Labels*, p. 8). Duncombe argued that the rise of zines was a byproduct of "democratized consumption of culture" in the early twentieth century, though he conflates "democratize" and "commercialize." Entire industries emerged to "entertain" the masses, he argued, but in the process "something was lost." Duncombe noted that with the rise of mass culture, "people were—and are—less and less connected to what they consume" (p. 107–08).

Zines like *MRR* helped to inject more democratic principles into the production and consumption of culture, making culture an active form of consumption. Zines also allowed people to work out what it meant to be a punk. Martin noted how the "letters to the editor" section was a key location of ongoing discussions and debates. "Often letter writers responded to letters from previous issues, allowing for whole dialogues." He noted how the editors often weighed in on debates found in the letters section, such as a discussion of racism in the hardcore scene. One highly controversial band on this issue was New York City's Agnostic Front whom many viewed as racist. Their fans offered up a defense of the band. Though he allowed space for the band's defense, Yohannan pushed back and expanded on the problematic aspects of the band's politics and how that contributed to violence in hardcore spaces (*The Other Eighties*, pp. 107–08).

Yohannan expected and understood that what constituted the Post-Punk landscape was diverse, and not everyone would agree with his views. In true democratic fashion, he embraced discussion over him imposing his views on the scene. Taken together, independent production and distribution of Post-Punk artists and the centrality of zines in shaping Post-Punk culture reflect the democratic values at the heart of that culture.

Post-Punk: Cultural Democracy in the Wild

People who grew up on Post-Punk culture have promoted more democratic thinking in the mainstream culture in recent years. Monopolistic corporations have come to dominate cultural production and distribution, making our experiences with cultural engagement measurably worse. In response, author and activist Cory Doctorow recently coined a new phrase: "enshittification." The term emerged in the ongoing discussion in his new book with Rebecca Giblin, *Chokepoint Capitalism*. Giblin and Doctorow focus on the culture industries to explain how modern capitalism has created chokepoints which benefit only monopolistic corporations, not the producers or the consumers. Post-Punks anticipated some of these arguments, as many understood the problems of corporate control of culture examined in the book. To a large degree, it is a tale as old as capitalism. But we should pay attention to the specificity of how capitalism functions in the here and now.

As Doctorow explains, major tech and social media firms have created a monopoly on "content creation" despite touting online communities as bulwarks of democratic engagement. In an interview with Adam Conover, Doctorow noted that these firms have been operating in a post-regulatory landscape, allow-ing them to create a monopoly over "creative markets." People have become accustomed to thinking of cultural production—or content, as big tech would have us understand it—not as a critical aspect of human life, but as another cheap commodity. Just call-ing the various forms of culture being shared online "content" really gives the game away.

Would a better understanding of Post-Punk culture help us to think through the problem of commodification and mono-polization that Giblin and Doctorow wrestle with in their book? Could it show us alternative strategies for fostering more democracy in our culture? Absolutely! In fact, the final chap-ters explore just such solutions. It comes down to empowering communities with democratic cultural production and con-sumption (*Chokepoint Capitalism*, pp. 142–259). That sounds quite Punk!

Living in a capitalist economy necessitates being able to make a living. For artists, that need not mean "selling out" their principles. We should dig out from under the mythologies of rock and Punk history in order to better see the warts-and-all stories of that history. Post-Punk culture shows us another way to make culture in our society. Rather than focusing on attaining wealth and stardom, an artist can seek to build a democratic, community-based approach to music production that supports their work.

The paths trodden by several decades of Post-Punk com-munities illustrate that a non-commercial option is not just viable, but can thrive, especially because music represents one of the most universal and human of all endeavors. All culture works as a social glue that holds human communities together. Subjecting music production primarily to market forces rather than understanding its social function devalues human creativity.

As Doctorow noted in his discussion with Conover, a "pro-gressive shock doctrine" can help us to give a set of solutions when we reach crisis points caused by the capitalist system. Understanding the democratic nature of music production in the Post-Punk ecosystem and how they built alternatives to the mainstream corporate music industry can be an important part of that shock doctrine.

24
Adventures Close to Home

JESSE J. PRINZ

Much of metaphysics is concerned with distinguishing kinds of kinds. It asks, what is the basis for grouping things together in a category? For example, many of the categories in sciences (particles, elements, minerals, cell-types) are believed to be unified by features that are intrinsic and essential: protons, for example, are particles with a charge of +1.

The idea of intrinsic essences may have some applicability outside of science as well, even in the arts. As a first pass, we might think that impressionist paintings can be defined by their palette, subject matter, and application of paint, and ballet may be defined by a vocabulary of dance moves. In music, intrinsic essences may also do some work in classification. A fugue, for example, can be defined as a specific musical form.

But what about the categories we use to classify music in record stores, award ceremonies, and streaming services? Do categories such as classical, reggae, disco, hip-hop, heavy metal, and punk have inherent essences? Here we often use the word 'genre', and sometimes also 'style'. In some cases these categories also refer to movements and to subcultures. Punk is a style, a genre, a movement, and a subculture.

In contrast, there are common musical categories that are none of these things: oldies, world music, and, arguably, alternative. Here we will be concerned with Post-Punk. What kind of kind is it? Does it have an inherent essence? Is it a style, a genre, a movement, and a subculture? What, in any case, are those things?

Post-Punk is a different kind of kind than Punk. It is not a style, movement, or subculture.

Is Post-Punk a Style?

The term 'style' can be defined as repeatable and recognizable manner of production in art. To call style repeatable means can recur across works, either by the same artist or across artists, and can thus serve as a guideline, conscious or not, for creating new works. We can perform "Happy Birthday" in the style of the Bee Gees or the Sex Pistols, or in a funk or hardcore version. To say that style is recognizable means that it is something we can perceive in music. This can mean that style inheres in factors such as the instruments used, the formal qualities of the music (rhythm, tempo, texture, harmonies), and the moods evoked (such as playful, somber, serene, anxious). Arguably, style can also include signifiers or semiotic features, provided they are perceivable (exotic, space-aged, dreamy, creepy). Listeners do not passively pick-up on what's there to be heard, but rather attend to different features based on interests and prior experience. You can listen for features of style that might not by immediately apparent.

Styles appear at different scales. It can be identified in individual musicians, across bands with similar pedigree, and across music subgenres and genres. Music theorists sometimes use linguistic analogies here, with the style of an artist being called an idiolect, and styles shared at larger scales being given designations such as dialects, or languages (Meyer, "Toward a Theory of Style"). The language of Punk, for example, might include speed, distortion, and snarling vocal styles. Within this language, each act will have its own distinctive style (Patti Smith versus Sham 69), and there will be clusters of bands that are recognizably similar (the Dead Boys and the Pagans versus the Rezillos and the Undertones versus Social Distortion and Bad Religion). There is variation, but also overarching similarity.

When it comes to Post-Punk, however, the variation is less unified. To see this, we need to remember how Post-Punk emerged. According to a standard telling, Punk quickly became a cliché of itself after receiving mainstream recognition in the mid-1970s. By 1977, when the term Post-Punk emerges, Punk already seemed limited and formulaic to many listeners. There were also those who felt that Punk had not lived up to its own ambition to break away from prior musical forms. Grounded in rock, Punk was more musically conservative than its take-no-prisoners ethos seemed to demand. There was, therefore, an active search for new modes of expression (the term "new musick" was used before "Post-Punk" took hold). Against this background, performers with a Punk sensibility began to experiment, break Punk's rules, and move in new directions. Now here's the rub: the directions were highly varied.

Some bands began to actively incorporate other types of music. In the UK, Punk had already mingled with Jamaican music, and leading bands had recorded reggae tracks (the Clash, Generation X, the Ruts). Emerging bands took this further, not simply emulating reggae, but more subtly and thoroughly incorporating selective aspects of reggae instrumentation and dub recording techniques, to create original forms of hybrid music (the Slits, Gang of Four, Joy Division). Other bands brought in elements of disco (Blondie, Public Image Ltd., New Order) and funk (ESG, Liquid Liquid, Maximum Joy). There were also band that placed emphasis on avant-garde experimentation (Pop Group, Theoretical Girls, This Heat), bands that brought in saxophones (the Contortions, LiLiPUT, Essential Logic), and bands that brought in synthesizers (the Screamers, Magazine, Devo). Some Post-Punk is sparse and angular (XTC, Wire), some is dense and atmospheric (Siouxsie and the Banshees, Cocteau Twins), some is gloomy (Glorious Din, DA!), and some is energetic and upbeat (the Teardrop Explodes, Bush Tetras).

There was some order in this variety, but little unity. Instead, a number of distinct, identifiable musical styles emerged. There was synth-punk, no wave (an experimental movement based in New York), and Goth. Some music scenes had shared characteristic, like the Leeds bands, who played a stripped down, repetitive descendent of Punk (Gang of Four, Mekons, Delta 5). The Fall, from Manchester, had a similar sensibility, but other Manchester Bands, like Magazine, did not. Likewise, Birmingham's Au Pairs pair easily with the bands from Leeds, but other Birmingham bands, like the Swell Maps, do not. Despite the variety, all of these are considered Post-Punk. That label subsumes (at least some) new wave, no wave, art-punk, Goth, cold wave, dark wave, two-tone ska, and industrial music, along with many artists who resist classification (Pere Ubu, the Birthday Party, Young Marble Giants, the Raincoats).

Unlike Punk, then, which enjoys considerable stylistic cohesion, Post-Punk subsumes a wide, and open-ended range of styles. The main source of unity is a shift away from Punk, without losing something of Punk sensibility. What gets retained from Punk varies, from (snarl and song structures in Magazine; irreverent lyrics in the Manchester scene, and noisiness in no wave). There is some overlap in what Post-Punk bands abandon. For example, there is a widespread tendency to shift away from blues-based rock, but, for some bands, that means a shift away from black music more generally, and for others it means a shift to funk, disco, and dub (Haddon, *What Is Post-Punk?*). If instructed to play "Happy Birthday" in a Post-Punk style, you would be overwhelmed by options: Add synths? Strip things down? Merge snarl and dub? Go Goth? It's not that Post-Punk lacks recognizable styles; rather, it has too many. Post-Punk is defined by its point of departure, not its destination. It travels multiple ways at once.

Is Post-Punk a Genre?

If Post-Punk is not a style, might it nevertheless qualify as a genre? These two terms are sometimes used interchangeably, but music scholars recognize that they are different (Moore, "Categorical Conventions in Music Discourse"). Genre includes style, but extends far beyond what music sounds like. One of the most influential recent definitions owes to the musicologist Franco Fabbri. He defines genres as sets of rules defined over a number of dimensions: formal, semiotic, ideological, behavioral, and economic ("A Theory of Musical Genres," pp. 54–59). The sociologist, Jennifer Lena adds to this story, emphasizing the importance of community, and introducing multiple aspects of social activity associated with genres, including slang, drug use, press coverage, and typical income sources for artists (*Banding Together*, p. 9).

Building on such work, I would define a genre as a set of communal norms, practices, and expectations that govern the production, consumption, and differentiation of musical works. I say "norms, practices, and expectations" rather than just "rules," because some rules are not explicitly codified, and the actual practices play an important role in determining a genre's conventions. Under "production" and "consumption," I would include many dimensions, including aims, attitudes, themes, techniques, musical styles, performance styles, venues, audience behavior and fandom, distribution, and attendant aesthetics. Punk, for example, is not just a musical style: it has associated political beliefs, dancing styles, fanzine production, and fashion. Each of those contributes to the genre.

The term "differentiation" in my definition refers to the fact that each genre is often understood in relation to other genres, with which is it presumed to compare or contrast. Lena (p. 7) uses the term "boundary work" and the ethnomusicologist, Heather Sparling ("Categorically Speaking") uses a term from literary theory: intertextuality. Sparling cites Jocelyne

Guilbault (*Zouk*) who talks of each genre emerging in a field and existing within a sociomusical ecology. I will use the term "field" to refer more specifically to the genres against which a given genre differentiates itself. We can use the term "core" to refer to the aforementioned positive characteristics of a genre (styles, themes, and so forth).

For every genre, there is a core of features and a field of salient comparison genres. For each comparison genre, there is also a principle of comparison: for example, the core might be understood as an extension of the genres in the field or as a rejection. Punk tends to be understood as rejecting other genres: amphitheater rock, prog rock, and disco, along with related aesthetic ideals. Other genres—those we call subgenres and offshoots—are understood as extensions. Oi! and hardcore can be defined as extensions of Punk, while grunge and riot grrrl can be defined as offshoots. Each shares many core features of Punk, while also changing emphasis, dropping some, and adding others.

Here we might distinguish two kinds of extension: those that overlap in time with the comparison genre, and those that appear after it declines. This temporal difference can impact field salience: the association between hardcore and Punk is stronger than the association between grunge and Punk. Beyond subgenres and offshoots, there are also so-called revivals, which, when aim to resuscitate rather than extend. Notice that Punk has a diffuse field (it contrasts with several genres) and a unified core (it has a fairly cohesive set of positive features). Extensions of punk have cohesive fields (they are mainly defined in comparison to punk itself) and cohesive cores (hardcore and grunge have recognizable styles and fashions).

With this machinery in place, we can ask whether Post-Punk is a subgenre or offshoot of punk. We also ask if it even qualifies as a genre. Here again, we are immediately confronted with the diversity of Post-Punk styles. Goth, no wave, and synth punk differ musically. They also differ in the associated attitudes, aesthetics, and other positive features. Using the language of core and fields, we can say that Post-Punk has a relatively unified field (it is defined in comparison to Punk), but a highly diffuse core. In this respect it differs from subgenres and offshoots, which are more cohesive. Coining a phrase, we might call Post-Punk an "excursive genre": its diffuse core can be characterized as a collection of excursions from the field of Punk. The field is cohesive, the core is diffuse, and the relation is one of excursion. Unlike subgenres, which merely change emphasis and add features, excursions can depart more decisively, dropping central tenets or adding new ones that are harder to align with the original genre. This can be a matter of degree, and classification is therefore open to debate. Some might say that Post-Punk's sub-genes, such as Goth and no wave, also qualify as sub-genres of punk.

Growing up in the era of Post-Punk I can say that this boundary is very porous. I regarded Wire, Magazine, and the Slits as Punk bands, though I would have been happy to call them Post-Punk. No wavers, such as James Chance and Lydia Lunch, struck me as belonging to a different genre, as did Goths. Sometimes, we would make finer distinctions: the Slits' early recordings were Punk, but the albums are Post-Punk; the Cure's first single is Punk but then they went Goth; the Damned, too, went Goth (regrettably); and so on. One could also say things like Siouxsie Sioux is a Punk (a famous member of the Bromley Contingent), but her music is Post-Punk.

Such blurriness is a feature, not a bug. The approach to genre that I am recommending captures the way in which these categories are contestable. For example, it always seemed up for debate whether a given new wave band qualified as Post-Punk. The Cars and Lena Lovich didn't qualify in my mind, perhaps because they were not edgy enough or because they didn't establish Punk pedigree.

The idea of pedigree captures the importance of the idea that genuine Post-Punk must trace roots back to Punk, either musically or biographically. Back in the day, I didn't count New Romantic bands as Post-Punk, but Adam Ant was an exception, because he was inspired by the Sex Pistols. Pedigree was never enough, however, since artists with Punk roots could stray too far to retain the Post-Punk epithet: Billy Idol, Buster Poindexter, and Madonna all illustrate. Too much pop could break the trail back to punk. There were, of course, borderline cases; Bow Wow Wow made it onto my mix tapes, but with some hesitancy.

The idea of tracing back to Punk does not require actual contact with a seminal Punk scene. As sociologists teach us, cultural forms can span great distances though touring bands, record distribution, media coverage, and word-of-mouth (Fine and Kleinman, "Rethinking Subculture"). By the early 1980s, Post-Punk was global. There were great artists in Mexico (Size, Synptoma), Belgium (Nacht und Nebel, Red Zebra), France (Edith Nylon, KaS Product), The Netherlands (Flue, Poison Ivy), Greece (Libido Blume, Metro Decay), Poland (Kryzys, Maanam), Yugoslavia (Idolii, Paraf), Russia (Kino, Vova Blue and Brothers in Reason), South Africa (Dog Detachment,

National Wake), and Japan (Earthling, Zelda). There is vast variety in this music, but palpable Punk influence earns each the Post-Punk honorific.

The lesson that I've been trying to distill is that Post-Punk behaves differently than both Punk and offshoots of Punk. Where Punk has a diffuse field and cohesive core, and offshoots have a cohesive core and a cohesive field, Post-Punk has a cohesive field and a diffuse core. Completing this taxonomy, we might say that "musical periods" have diffuse fields and diffuse cores, and "precursor genres," have cohesive fields and diffuse cores (proto-punk has a shared comparison genre—Punk—but a diffuse range of bands that inspired that genre). In cases where the core is diffuse, one might ask whether the term genre is appropriate. Are precursor genres and excursive genres really genres? I am inclined to say yes, but in an unusual sense of the word. Whereas most genres are unified by their positive features, the unity of these is found in their principle of differentiation. Post-Punk's various forms are all excursions from a shared starting point (and proto-punk has a shared outcome).

Is Post-Punk a Movement?

Genres exist in time. They have beginnings, and many decline and end. Some authors even go so far as to define genre as essentially historical (Gracyk, "Heavy Metal"). I prefer to say that genres have histories. Sometimes those histories lack cohesion, as in the case of proto-punk: bands such as the Stooges and the Velvet Underground, along with many minor Garage bands, were doing their thing independently of each other. Put differently, proto-punk was not a movement. Punk, in contrast, was. Though there were many Punk scenes, each had some awareness of what others were doing, and, by the time the term "punk" was introduced, information flow allowed members of different scenes to recognize a shared cause.

Like "style" and "genre," "movement" can be defined in different ways. The account I prefer derives not from music but from art history and the philosophy of art. Michael Baxandall (*Patterns of Intention*) proposes that artists approach each work with a "charge and brief," corresponding to the problems they are trying to solve. Adopting the word "brief," Jonathan Gilmore uses this idea to characterize art movements, such as like cubism. A "brief" is "the set of problems" that a group of artists "collectively see as important to address in their work" (p. 52). From this perspective, the history of genres can be seen as a history of problem solving, though the problems are sometimes inchoate, rather than explicit, and may take some time to discover. Movements produce works that satisfy their briefs, and, at a certain point that exercise may lose momentum, because the brief has been adequately addressed. Cubists wanted to make the two-dimensional surface of pictures salient, by representing three-dimensional objects as constellations of two-dimensional planes, arrayed atop the pictorial surface. After several years of intense experimentation, this brief seemed to have run its course, and cubism became passé. Gilmore links the end of art movements to these moments when briefs exhaust themselves.

By parity, we can define a musical movement as united by shared or overlapping briefs. The life-course of a movement will be impacted by perspectives about the extent to which those briefs have been explored to a point of diminishing returns. Punk reflected exasperation with both society and the music industry. It lives on in locations where those frustrations remain, and where Punk is regarded as a useful tool in coping with them. For some this brief lost steam almost immediately. Punk was co-opted by the music industry and popular culture, losing its subversive edge. Musically, Punk began to feel formulaic. As a movement, Punk fizzed, or at least dissipated. Its periodic offshoots and revivals are measured against the incipient brief, with diehard fans embracing sociopolitically potent successors, such as the riot grrrl movement, and scoffing at mainstream variants, like pop punk.

What about Post-Punk? Is it a movement? Here we face a dilemma. On the one hand, there does seem to be a brief: where to go musically after Punk's original incarnations seemed ready to expire? On the other hand, each manifestation of Post-Punk seems to have its own brief, be it the musical hybridization of the Slits, the experimentation of no wave, or the Victorian melancholia of Goth. One might see each of these as solutions to the overarching brief of Post-Punk, but each of these approaches came to have a life of its own, occupied with internal goals rather than referring back to Punk. It belittles each of the sub-genres of Post-Punk to suppose that justified their musical choices by constantly reminding themselves how they had managed to break free from Punk's rigid template.

Here the metaphor of excursion helps once more. If we see Post-Punk as a collection of excursions away from a common starting point, there is no reason to suppose that each will expend much energy looking backward. Each, can be defined as its own adventure, with new challenges as discoveries along the way. It's not that they entirely lose sight of their Punk roots. As a teenage punk rocker living in the era of Post-Punk, I shared my lunch table with Goths. We recognized each other as cousins—members of the same family. I listened to every form of Post-Punk and would happily combine them on my mix tapes. Post-Punk is a series of adventures, but they are adventures close enough to their origin point to retain a sense of relatedness. They are adventures close to home.

"Adventures Close to Home" is the title of a track that appeared on the Raincoats' first album (self-titled), as well as the first album of the Slits (*Cut*). The lyrics were written by Spaniard, Paloma McLardy (a.k.a. Palmolive), who played drums for both bands. The song begins with expresses of frustration followed by searching: "Through alleys of mysteries / I went up and down / Like a demented train." It's all about finding oneself and determining one's own fate. But this declaration of independence is qualified: "Full of myself / I left you behind / as if I could." Interpreted as a parable for Post-Punk, "Adventures Close to Home" captures the pursuit and discovery of new modes of expression, which lead to new kinds of music without ever really forgetting the place or origin.

Rather than calling Post-Punk a movement, then, perhaps we can call it a movement away: a constellation of trajectories, branching in all directions away from Punk, but never losing sight. The shared desire to break free from Punk launches these adventures, but that brief gets superseded by the demands of each individual quest.

Is Post-Punk a Subculture?

There is a final question to consider, one that has considerable relevance for the present time. Punk, famously, is a subculture as well as a musical genre. What about Post-Punk? Subcultures can be defined as groups whose values, behaviors, and styles differ from the dominant culture. Style, here, can refer to fashion, hairstyles, demeanor, slang, and taste (Mike Brake, *The Sociology of Youth Culture*).

Membership in a subculture is characteristically experienced as identity and often subject to gatekeeping with tests for authenticity and commitment. The modern history of subcultures walks in lock-step with music. There have been jazz-crazed beatniks, mods, rockers, rude boys, rastas, skins, hippies, headbangers, b-boys/b-girls, and punks. Post-Punk continued this trend in some ways, but also marks a significant change. There is no Post-Punk look, as such. Rather, some of Post-Punk's sub-genres were also subcultures. The most

obvious case is Goth, which inculcated a specific sensibility and
fashion sense (though some bands that presaged Goth, like Joy
Division, did not sport the associated regalia). Other sub-genres were less identifiable, and less linked to identity. People
didn't call themselves new wavers or no wavers, for example.
By the 1980s, many of the people who sported music-themed
looks were retro, hanging on to Seventies styles (as with Punk
and hip hop) or looking even further back (there were ostentatious revivals of mod and rockabilly). Nowadays, such identities seem quaint. It is sometimes said that the age of music-
themed subcultures is over. We could argue that Post-Punk
played a role in this change; it helped sever the tie between
music and subcultures.

That separation was a gradual process. Some Post-Punk
sub-genres that did not make visible demands on attire nevertheless had devoted scenesters. But my impression is that people's musical predilections were less linked to identity than
they had been in previous generations. It's not to say that visible subcultures died in the 1980s. Far from it. You could still
read taste off of couture in any high school cafeteria during
that decade, and new musical subcultures emerged, such as
rave culture and emo. Both of these continued into the 1990s,
and others have emerged since: scene, grunge, riot grrrl,
AfroPunk, and grime are salient examples. It's noteworthy,
however, that many of these are outgrowths or amalgams of
earlier subcultures. Since the 1990s, there is no longer any pre-
sumption that new music will usher in new identities.

Post-Punk created a conundrum. For anyone into Post-Punk,
in all its multiplicity, identifying with a single sub-genre would
feel like a betrayal to the others. Of necessity, there can be no
subcultural identity linked to the full range taken as a whole.
Post-Punk is too varied to allow that. This very fact served to
weaken the link between music and subcultures, and may have
even set the stage for an ultimate end of that association.

To see this, it helps to recognize Post-Punk as a manifestation of another cultural trend—postmodernism. The two terms
emerged around the same time. Modernism is an outlook that
got its footing during the Enlightenment. It believes in the sta-
bility of meaning, in essentialism, in progress. It sees history as
a great march forward, and also embraces the idea of great
intellects and creators, who guide innovations *ex-nihilo*.

Postmodernism sees meaning as unstable, rejects essentialism and progress narrative, and announces "the death of the
subject." That is, individuals are neither coherent entities nor
self-determined. In the arts, postmodernism marks the rejec-

tion of stylistic uniformity. Postmodern architects, for example, mix and match elements from different traditions. Post-Punk slots neatly into these philosophical perspectives. Whereas previous genres expected or demanded consistency and purity of taste, Post-Punk encourages the opposite.

To make this even more vivid, consider how the sociologist, David Muggleton, characterizes the difference between modern and postmodern approaches to identity. He offers the following list of contrasts (*Inside Subculture*, p. 52):

MODERN	POSTMODERN
Group identity	Fragmented identity
Stylistic homogeneity	Stylistic heterogeneity
Strong boundary maintenance	Boundary maintenance weak
Subcultural provides main identity	Multiple stylistic identities
High degree of commitment	Low degree of commitment
Membership perceived as permanent	Transient attachment expressed
Low rates of subcultural mobility	High rates of subcultural mobility
Stress on beliefs and values	Fascination with style and image
Political gesture of resistance	Apolitical sentiments
Anti-media sentiments	Positive attitude towards media
Self-perception as authentic	Celebration of the inauthentic

Glancing at this list, it should be apparent that enthusiasm for Post-Punk, as a genre, is better characterized by the postmodern column.

Heterogeneity, multiplicity, transience, and mobility all characterize those who have an excursive approach to popular culture. Those who like to adventure, to follow new paths and stray from points of origination, are likely to have a postmodern conception of their own subjectivity. We see this in the music as well. Post-Punk bands often meander, shifting styles, experimenting. They also moved further away from politics that their predecessors. Post-Punk ushers in a diminished sense of commitment, musically speaking, and less concern about maintaining boundaries. In these respects, it contrasts markedly with punk. Muggleton regards both Punk and Post-Punk as postmodern (pp. 44-45), but his own list of features indicates otherwise. Punk is notorious for its narrow range of uniforms, demands for commitment, political posturing, contempt for media, and valorization of authenticity (Fox, "Real Punks and Pretenders"). Punk is also unequivocally an identity as much as musical genre. Some Post-Punk subgenres, especially Goth, retain many of these features, but, as a whole, Post-Punk departs from the modernist model. Post-Punk, as such, is not a subculture, and it may well signal the decline of musical subcultures more generally.

A Template for Our Age

On November 26, 1977, *Sounds* magazine published a cover story on "New Musick," by music critics Jon Savage and Jane Suck. The part written by Savage contains what may be the first use of "Post-Punk" in print, though I suspect there are earlier uses in fanzines. Both authors are remarkably prescient. Suck alludes to an escape from the stranglehold that the Clash and the Sex Pistols had recently enjoyed, citing the rising influence of the Velvet Underground, Kraftwerk, Robert Fripp, Brian Eno, and David Bowie's album, *Low*. Savage mentions "more overt reggae/dub influence," "synthemesc nouveau pop," "withdrawal from our acceleration," and "integration of avant-garde techniques." As examples, he explicitly mentions. Pere Ubu, Throbbing Gristle, Devo, Subway Sect, the Prefects, Siouxsie and the Banshees, the Slits, and Wire (Subway Sect may look like an outlier, since they are associated with old school Punk, but they had recently performed, "We Oppose All Rock'n'Roll" on the John Peel radio show, and had called for a break from rock music in the September issue of *ZigZag*.)

Looking at these prognostications, we can see that the blueprints of Post-Punk were clearly in place by 1977—the year that the Sex Pistols released their first Album. Suck and Savage were not announcing the death of Punk—Savage tells us that a "healthy future of mainstream punk is assured"—but new musical forms were emerging. These new forms did not reject Punk entirely.

With Savage, they recognized that "in the energy of punk lies some kind of life-force." But they branch out in different directions. Suck and Savage mention Krautrock, synths, space sounds, reggae, experimental music, and even "somnambulism" (Suck) and "catatonic bleakness" (Savage)—perhaps their sense of Goth on the horizon. There is no unity here, only different paths away from a common point of origin. Different adventures close to home.

We might expect such meandering trajectories to fractionate the Punk scene, and, to some extent, that happened. But the pivotal point of Punk preserves a sense of connection. As Savage puts it, "the several strands delineated . . . will be able to coexist happily or otherwise in the record shops, 'zines, and your hearts." Despite its diversity, its lack of essence, Post-Punk continues to be recognized as a meaningful category. Post-Punk is a metaphysical and musical anomaly, but that makes it a fitting kind of kind for postmodern times. It may be described as a template for this current age of cultural eclecticism.

Bibliography

Ackerman, J.S. 1962. A Theory of Style. *Journal of Aesthetics and Art Criticism* 20.

Adamson, Peter. 2018. *Philosophy in the Hellenistic and Roman Worlds: A History of Philosophy Without Any Gaps, Volume 2.* Oxford University Press.

Adorno, Theodor W. 1973. *The Jargon of Authenticity.* Northwestern University Press.

———. *The Culture Industry: Selected Essays on Mass Culture.* Routledge.

Agger, Ben. 1992. *Cultural Studies as Critical Theory.* Falmer Press.

Albertine, Viv. 2014. *Clothes, Clothes, Clothes. Music, Music, Music. Boys, Boys, Boys: A Memoir.* St. Martin's.

Alcoff, Linda Martin. 1997. The Problem of Speaking for Others. In Patrick Colm Hogan, ed., *Cultural Politics and the Problem of the Author.* University of Pennsylvania Press.

Alessandri, Mariana. 2023. *Night Vision. Seeing Ourselves through Dark Moods.* Princeton University Press.

———. 2023. Living with Dark Moods: Mariana Alessandri in conversation with Kieran Setiya. *The Philosopher* YouTube Channel. <www.youtube.com/watch?v=HT7NwhOkzbc>.

Amplified. 2021. Joy Division: The Poster Children of Post-Punk. <https://www.youtube.com/watch?v=du_5Iij5CAE&t=605s>

Arinze, Ambrose T., and Ignatius N. Onwuatuegwu. 2020. The Notion of Absurdity and Meaning of Life in Albert Camus's Existentialism. *Open Journal of Philosophy* 10.

Arkush, Allan, director. 1979. *Rock'n'Roll High School.* DVD. Shout! Factory.

Bag, Alice. 2011. *Violence Girl: East LA Rage to Hollywood Stage: A Chicana Punk Story.* Feral House.

Bakunin, Mikhail. 1990. *Statism and Anarchy.* Cambridge University Press.

————. 2010. *Selected Writings from Mikhail Bakunin*. Red and Black.

Banks, Iain M. 1998 [1984] *The Wasp Factory: A Novel*. Simon and Schuster.

Barthes, Roland. 1967. The Death of the Author. *Aspen* 5–6.

Batukan, Can. 2018. Deleuze, Punk, and Post-Punk. *E-flux Journal* (May) <www.academia.edu/39921720/Deleuze_punk_and_post_punk>.

Baudrillard, Jean. 1994 [1981]. *Simulacra and Simulation*. University of Michigan Press.

Baxandall, M. 1985. *Patterns of Intention: On the Historical Explanation of Pictures*. Yale University Press.

Belsito, Peter. 1985. *Notes from the Pop Underground*. The Last Gasp of San Francisco.

Bookchin, Murray. 2022. *The Modern Crisis*. AK Press.

Boone, C. 1991. Has Modernist Music Lost Power? In Ingeborg Hoesterey, ed., *Zeitgeist in Babel: The Postmodernist Controversy*. Indiana University Press.

Bradley, J. 1992. *Czechoslovakia's Velvet Revolution: A Political Analysis*. East European Monographs.

Brake, Michael. 2013 [1980]. *The Sociology of Youth Culture and Youth Subcultures: Sex and Drugs and Rock'n'Roll?* Routledge.

Brown, Timothy S. 2004. Subcultures, Pop Music, and Politics: Skinheads and 'Nazi Rock' in England and Germany. *Journal of Social History* 38:1.

Burton, Robert. 2009. *The Anatomy of Melancholy*. Penguin.

Butt, Gavin, Kodwo Eshun, and Mark Fisher. 2016. *Post-Punk: Then and Now*. Repeater.

Campbell, John. 2000. *Margaret Thatcher*. Volume I. Cape.

Camus, Albert. 2006. *The Fall*. Penguin.

————. 2013. *The Outsider*. Penguin.

Caraballo, Ed. 1997. There's a Riot Goin' On: The Infamous Public Image Ltd. Riot Show, The Ritz 1981. *Perfect Sound Forever* (blog) <www.furious.com/perfect/pil.html?utm_source=pocket_saves>.

Carlin, George. 1997. *Brain Droppings*. Hyperion.

Cavell, Stanley. 1976. Music Discomposed. In Cavell, *Must We Mean What We Say? A Book of Essays*. Cambridge University Press.

————. 1981. Cons and Pros: *The Lady Eve*. In Cavell, *Pursuits of Happiness: The Hollywood Comedy of Remarriage*. Harvard University Press.

————. 1984. The Fact of Television. In Cavell, *Themes Out of School: Effects as Causes*. North Point Press.

Cixous, Helene, et al. 1976. The Laugh of the Medusa. *Signs* 1:4.

Clegg, Mindy. 2022. *Punk Rock: Music Is the Currency of Life*. SUNY Press.

Cohen, Lizabeth. 2003. *A Consumer's Republic: The Politics of Mass Consumption in Postwar America*. Penguin Random House.

Conover, Adam. 2023. Chokepoint Capitalism with Cory Doctorow. <www.youtube.com/watch?v=vluAOGJPPoM>.

Corcoran, Nina. 2022. New Suicide Compilation, *Surrender: A Collection* Announced. *Pitchfork*. <https://pitchfork.com/news/new-suicide-compilation-surrender-a-collection-announced>.

Costello, Elvis. 2016. *Unfaithful Music and Disappearing Ink*. Blue Rider Press.

Cox, Harvey. 1969. *The Feast of Fools: A Theological Essay on Festivity and Fantasy*. Harvard University Press.

Cummins, Kevin. 2018. *Alone and Palely Loitering*. Hachette.

Crenshaw, Mic, Celina Flores, and Erin Yanke. 2021. It Did Happen Here. Podcast. <https://kboo.fm/program/it-did-happen-here>.

Crosby, Donald A. 1988. *The Specter of the Absurd: Sources and Criticisms of Modern Nihilism*. SUNY Press.

Crossley, Nick. 2015. *Networks of Sound, Style, and Subversion: The Punk and Post-Punk Worlds of Manchester, London, Liverpool, and Sheffield, 1975–80*. Manchester University Press.

Curtis, Deborah. 2014. *Touching from a Distance: Ian Curtis and Joy Division*. Faber and Faber.

Curtis, Ian. 2014. *So This Is Permanence: Joy Division Lyrics and Notebooks*. Chronicle Books.

Davis, Angela. 1990. *Women, Culture, and Politics*. Vintage.

Derrida, Jacques. 1978 [1967]. *Writing and Difference*. University of Chicago Press.

Descartes, René. 1996. *Meditations on First Philosophy*. Cambridge, University Press.

Doctorow, Cory. 2023. Tiktok's Enshittification. Pluralistic.net <https://pluralistic.net/2023/01/21/potemkin-ai/#hey-guys>.

Doomen, Jasper. 2012. Consistent Nihilism. *Journal of Mind and Behavior* 33.

Doyle, Tom. 2011 [1998]. *The Glamour Chase: The Maverick Life of Billy Mackenzie*. Polygon.

Duncombe, Stephen. 1997. *Notes from Underground: Zines and the Politics of Alternative Culture*. Verso.

Duncombe, Stephen, and Maxwell Tremblay, eds. 2011. *White Riot: Punk Rock and the Politics of Race*. Verso.

Dunn, Kevin. 2016. *Global Punk: Resistance and Rebellion in Everyday Life*. Bloomsbury.

Eliot, Marc. 1989. *Rockonomics: The Money Behind the Music*. Omnibus Press.

———. 2005 [1998]. *To the Limit: The Untold Story of the Eagles*. Da Capo Press.

Emerson, Ralph Waldo. 1904. Circles. In *Essays: Second Series*, Volume II of *The Complete Works of Ralph Waldo Emerson*. Houghton Mifflin.

Ensminger, Ian. 2013. *Left of the Dial: Conversations with Punk Icons*. PM Press.

Esslin, Martin. 1961. *The Theatre of the Absurd*. Anchor Doubleday.

Evans, Jules. 2013. *Philosophy for Life and Other Dangerous Situations*. Rider.

———. 2019. *The Art of Losing Control: A Philosopher's Search for Ecstatic Experience*. Canongate.

Fabbri, F. 1981. A Theory of Musical Genres: Two Applications. In D. Horn and P. Tagg, eds., *Popular Music Perspectives*. International Association for the Study of Popular Music.

Feuerstein, Georg. 1992. *Holy Madness: The Shock Tactics and Radical Teachings of Crazy-wise Adepts, Holy Fools, and Rascal Gurus.* Penguin.

Fiiller, Tabbert, dir. 2018. *The Public Image Is Rotten.* Verisimilitude. <www.youtube.com/watch?v=9KOwCy0rcm4&t=5008s>.

Fine, G.A., and S. Kleinman. 1979. Rethinking Subculture: An Interactionist Analysis. *American Journal of Sociology* 85.

Fletcher, Tony. 2012. *A Light that Never Goes Out: The Enduring Saga of the Smiths.* Crown Archetype.

Fong-Torres, Ben. 1998. *Hickory Wind: The Life and Times of Gram Parsons.* St. Martin's.

Forbes, Robert, and Eddie Stampton. 2015. *The White Nationalist Skinhead Movement: UK and USA 1979–1993.* Feral House.

Fox, K.J. 1987. Real Punks and Pretenders: The Social Organization of a Counterculture. *Journal of Contemporary Ethnography* 16.

Francis, James A. 1995. *Subversive Virtue: Asceticism and Authority in the Second-Century Pagan World.* Pennsylvania State University Press.

Frank, Joseph. 2010. *Dostoevsky: A Writer in His Time.* Princeton University Press.

Frank, Thomas, and Matt Weiland. 1997. *Commodify Your Dissent: Salvos from the Baffler.* Norton.

Frith, Simon. *Sound Effects: Youth, Leisure, and the Politics of Rock'n'Roll.* Pantheon.

Gall, Gregor. 2022. *The Punk Rock Politics of Joe Strummer: Radicalism, Resistance, and Rebellion.* Manchester University Press.

Garfield, Simon. 2016. This Charming Man. In P. Woods, ed., *Morrissey in Conversation: The Essential Interviews.* Plexus.

Gergen, Kenneth. 2011. The Self as Social Construction. *Psychological Studies* 56.

Giblin, Rebecca, and Cory Doctorow. 2023. *Chokepoint Capitalism: How Big Tech and Big Content Captured Creative Labor Markets and How We'll Win Them Back.* Beacon.

Gilmore, J. 2000. *The Life of a Style: Beginnings and Endings in the Narrative History of Art.* Cornell University Press.

Gimarc, George. 1997. *Post-Punk Diary: 1980–1982.* St. Martin's.

Girard, René. 2023. *All Desire Is a Desire for Being: Essential Writings.* Penguin.

Goddard, Simon. 2013. *Songs that Saved Your Life:The Art of The Smiths 1982–87.* Titan.

Goethe, Johann Wolfgang von. 2017 [1774]. The *Sorrows of Young Werther and Selected Writings.* Signet.

Golsen, Tyler. 2021. The Wild Three Months of the Sex Pistols EMI Contract. *Far Out* <https://faroutmagazine.co.uk/sex-pistols-emi-contract-timeline>.

Gordon, Keith A. 2016. Fossils: Sire Records' Don't Call It Punk. *That Devil Music.* <www.thatdevilmusic.com/2016/08/fossils-sire-records-dont-call-it-punk.html>.

Gracyk, Theodore. 1996. *Rhythm and Noise: An Aesthetics of Rock*. Duke University Press.

———. 2016. Heavy Metal: Genre? Style? Subculture? *Philosophy Compass* 11.

Guilbault, J. 1993. *Zouk: World Music in the West Indies*. University of Chicago Press.

Gutman, Herbert. 1987. *Power and Culture: Essays on the American Working Class*. Pantheon.

Haddon, Mimi. 2020. *What Is Post-Punk? Genre and Identity in Avant-Garde Popular Music, 1977–82*. University of Michigan Press.

Hadot, Pierre. 1995. *Philosophy as a Way of Life: Spiritual Exercises from Socrates to Foucault*. Blackwell.

Hale, Grace Elizabeth. 2014. *A Nation of Outsiders: How the White Middle Class Fell in Love with Rebellion in Postwar America*. Oxford University Press.

Hanley, Paul. 2020. *Have a Bleedin Guess: The Story of Hex Enduction Hour*. Route.

Hanscomb, Stuart. 2010. Do It Yourself: Existentialism as Punk Philosophy. *Café Philosophy* <http://eprints.gla.ac.uk/54598>.

———. 2020. Shot by Both Sides: Punk Attitude and Existentialism. *Existential Analysis* 31:2.

Harrison, Julius. 1934. The Orchestra and Orchestral Music. In A.L. Bacharach, ed., *The Musical Companion*. Gollancz.

Havel, Vaclav. 1989. *Living in Truth: Twenty-Two Essays Published on the Occasion of the Award of the Erasmus Prize to Vaclav Havel*. Faber and Faber.

———. 1990. *Disturbing the Peace: A Conversation with Karel Hvizdala*. Knopf.

Hawkins, Stan. 2011. 'You Have Killed Me': Tropes of Hyperbole and Sentimentality in Morrissey's Musical Expression. In Eoin Devereux, Aileen Dillane, and Martin Power, eds., *Morrissey: Fandom, Representations, and Identities*. Intellect Ltd.

Hebdige, Dick. 1979. *Subculture: The Meaning of Style*. Routledge.

Hegel, G.W.F. 1998. *Aesthetics: Lectures on Fine Art, Volume II*. Clarendon.

———. 2004. *Introductory Lectures on Aesthetics*. Penguin.

———. 2010. *The Science of Logic*. Cambridge University Press.

Heidegger, Martin. 1999. *Contributions to Philosophy (From Enowning)*. Indiana University Press.

———. 2008 [1927]. *Being and Time*. Harper and Row.

Heylin, Clinton. 1993. *From the Velvets to the Voidoids: A Pre-Punk History for a Post-Punk World*. Penguin.

———. 2006. *All Yesterday's Parties: The Velvet Underground in Print*. Da Capo.

———. 2007. *Babylon's Burning: From Punk to Grunge*. Canongate.

———. 2017. *Anarchy in the Year Zero: The Sex Pistols, the Clash, and the Class of '76*. Route.

Hook, Peter. 2013. *Unknown Pleasures: Inside Joy Division*. It Books.

hooks, bell. 1981. *Ain't I a Woman? Black Women and Feminism*. South End.

———. 1989. *Talking Back: Thinking Feminist, Thinking Black*. South End.

Hopps, Gavin. 2009. *Morrissey: The Pageant of the Bleeding Heart*. Continuum.

Horkheimer, Max, and Theodor W. Adorno. 1982. *Dialectic of Enlightenment*. Continuum.

Hunt, Julia, and Ken McCormick. 2018. The Fall Singer Mark E. Smith Dies, Weeks After Bristol Gig Cancelled on Health Grounds. <www.bristolpost.co.uk/whats-on/music-nightlife/fall-singer-mark-e-1115159>.

Irigaray, Luce. 1985 [1977]. *This Sex which Is Not One*. Cornell University Press.

Johns, Brian. 1989. *Entranced: The Siouxsie and the Banshees Story*. Omnibus Press.

Kierkegaard, Søren. 1987. *Either/Or: A Fragment of Life*. Princeton University Press.

———. 1992 [1846]. *Concluding Unscientific Postscript to Philosophical Fragments*. Princeton University Press.

———. 2009. *Two Ages: The Age of Revolution and the Present Age, a Literary Review*. Princeton University Press.

———. 2015. *The Concept of Anxiety: A Simple Psychologically Oriented Deliberation in View of the Dogmatic Problem of Hereditary Sin*. Liveright.

Kohl, Markus. 2022. The Post-Punk Struggle for Authenticity. In Joshua Heter and Richard Greene, eds., *Punk Rock and Philosophy*. Open Universe.

Krauss, Rosalind. 2005. 'The Rock': William Kentridge's Drawings for Projection. In Chris Gehman and Steve Reinke, eds., *The Sharpest Point: Animation at the End of Cinema*. YYZ Books.

Kuhn, Thomas S. 1962. *The Structure of Scientific Revolutions*. University of Chicago Press.

Lachman, Gary. 2016. *Beyond the Robot: The Life and Work of Colin Wilson*. Tarcher Perigee.

Langer, Susanne. 1996 [1942]. *Philosophy in a New Key: A Study in the Symbolism of Reason, Rite, and Art*. Harvard University Press.

Larmore, Charles. 2010. *The Practices of the Self*. University of Chicago Press.

LaRocca, David. 2009. The Limits of Instruction. *Film and Philosophy* 13.

———. 2015. Were We Educated for This? In Richard Greene and Rachel Robison-Greene, eds., *Girls and Philosophy: This Book Isn't a Metaphor for Anything*. Open Court.

———. 2017. A Reality Rescinded: The Transformative Effects of Fraud in *I'm Still Here*. In LaRocca, ed., *The Philosophy of Documentary Film: Image, Sound, Fiction, Truth*. Rowman and Littlefield.

LaRocca, David, and Sandra Laugier, eds. 2023. *Television with Stanley Cavell in Mind*. University of Exeter Press.

Leblanc, Lauraine. 1999. *Pretty in Punk: Girls' Gender Resistance in a Boys' Subculture*. Rutgers University Press.

Lena, J.C. 2012. *Banding Together: How Communities Create Genres in Popular Music*. Princeton University Press.

Letts, Don, director. 2002. *The Clash: Westway to the World*. 3DD Entertainment.

Li Zehou. 2019. *A History of Classical Chinese Thought*. Routledge.

Lorde. Audre. 1984. The Uses of Anger: Women Responding to Racism. In Lorde, *Sister Outsider: Essays and Speeches*. Crossing Press.

Lyotard, Jean-Francois. 1994. *The Postmodern Condition: A Report on Knowledge*. University of Minnesota Press.

Marcus, Greil. 1989. *Lipstick Traces: A Secret History of the Twentieth Century*. Harvard University Press.

Marmysz, John. 2003. *Laughing at Nothing: Humor as a Response to Nihilism*. SUNY Press.

McKay, Iain. 2020. Anarchist: FAQ <https://theanarchistlibrary.org/library/the-anarchist-faq-editorial-collective-an-anarchist-faq-full>.

Maginnis, Tom. 2023. Review of Damaged Goods. Allmusic. <www.allmusic.com/song/damaged-goods-mt0004913936>.

Marcus, Greil. 1989. *Lipstick Traces: A Secret History of the Twentieth Century*. London: Faber and Faber.

———. 1999. *In the Fascist Bathroom: Punk in Pop Music, 1977–92*. Harvard University Press.

Marino, Gordon. 2004. *Basic Writings of Existentialism*. Modern Library.

Martin, Bradford. 2011. *The Other Eighties: A Secret History of America in the Age of Reagan*. Hill and Wang.

Mattson, Kevin. 2020. *We're Not Here to Entertain: Punk Rock, Ronald Reagan, and the Real Culture War of 1980s America*. Oxford University Press.

McCormack, Jerusha. 2007. From Chinese Wisdom to Irish Wit: Zhuangzi and Oscar Wilde. *Irish University Review*.

———. 2017. Oscar Wilde: As Daoist Sage. In M. Bennett, ed., *Philosophy and Oscar Wilde*. Palgrave.

McNeil, Legs, and Gillian McCain. 2016 [1986]. *Please Kill Me: The Uncensored Oral History of Punk*. Grove Press.

Melly, George. 1970. *Revolt into Style: The Pop Arts in Britain*. Allen Lane.

Meyer, L.B. 1979. Toward a Theory of Style. In L.B. Meyer and B. Lang, eds., *The Concept of Style*. University of Pennsylvania Press.

Middles, Mick. 2010. *The Fall: Wall of Pain*. Updated Edition. Omnibus.

Middles, Mick, and Lindsay Reade. 2006. *Torn Apart: The Life of Ian Curtis*. Omnibus.

Moore, Ryan. 2004. Postmodernism and Punk Subculture: Cultures of Authenticity and Deconstruction. *The Communication Review* 7, 2004.

Mullen, Brendan. 2002. *Lexicon Devil: The Fast Times and Short Life of Darby Crash and The Germs*. Feral House.

Murray, Isobel. 1971. Oscar Wilde's Absorption of 'Influences': The Case History of Chuang Tzu. *The Durham University Journal* 64:1 (December).

Murray, Robin. 2009. Gang of Four: Track by Track. *Clash*
    <www.clashmusic.com/features/gang-of-four-track-by-track/>.
Moeller, Hans-Georg. 1999. Zhuangzi's 'Dream of the Butterfly': A Daoist
    Interpretation. *Philosophy East and West* 49:4.
Moore, A. 2001. Categorical Conventions in Music Discourse: Style and
    Genre. *Music and Letters*, 82.
Morgan, Robin. 2014. *The Anatomy of Freedom: Feminism in Four
    Dimensions*. Open Road Media.
Morley, Paul. 2016. *Joy Division: Piece by Piece. Writing about Joy
    Division 1977–2007*. Plexus.
Morrissey. 1984. *The Morrissey Collection*. Smash Hits.
———. 2013. *Autobiography*. Penguin.
Muggleton, D. 2004. *Inside Subculture: The Postmodern Meaning of
    Style*. Berg.
Nancy, Jean-Luc. 1993. *The Birth to Presence*. Stanford University Press.
Nussbaum, Martha C. 2001. *Upheavals of Thought: The Intelligence of
    the Emotions*. Cambridge University Press.
Nietzsche, Friedrich. 1961. *Thus Spoke Zarathustra: A Book for
    Everyone and No One*. Penguin.
———. 1968. *The Will to Power*. Vintage.
———. 1975. *The Gay Science: With a Prelude in Rhymes and an
    Appendix in Songs*. Vintage.
———. 1980. *On the Advantage and Disadvantage of History for Life*.
    Hackett.
———. 1994. *The Birth of Tragedy Out of the Spirit of Music*.
    Penguin.
———. 1999. *The Genealogy of Morals*. Vintage.
———. 2003. *Beyond Good and Evil: Prelude to a Philosophy of the
    Future*. Penguin.
———. 2003. *The Twilight of the Idols and The Anti-Christ: Or, How to
    Philosophize with a Hammer*. Penguin.
O'Connor, Alan. 2008. *Punk Record Labels and the Struggle for
    Autonomy: The Emergence of DIY*. Lexington Books.
Ogg, Alex. 2009. Beyond Rip It Up: Toward a New Definition of Post-
    Punk? *The Quietus*.
    <https://thequietus.com/articles/02854-looking-beyond-simon-
    reynolds-rip-it-up-towards-a-new-definition-of-post-punk>.
Padgett, Ray. 2017. *Cover Me: The Stories Behind the Greatest Cover
    Songs of All Time*. Union Square.
Parsons, Lucy. 1905. *The Principles of Anarchism*. The Anarchist
    Library. <theanarchistlibrary.org/library/lucy-parsons-the-princi-
    ples-of-anarchism>
Perrone, Pierre. 2013. Forty Years of Virgin: How Richard Branson's
    Eccentric Record Label Changed the Charts. *The Independent*.
    <www.independent.co.uk/arts-entertainment/music/features/forty-
    years-of-virgin-how-richard-branson-s-eccentric-record-label-
    changed-the-charts-8629363.html>.
Picardie, Justine, and Dorothy Wade. 1990. *Atlantic and the Godfathers
    of Rock and Roll*. Fourth Estate.

Pippin, Robert B. 2018. *Hegel's Realm of Shadows: Logic as Metaphysics in 'The Science of Logic'*. University of Chicago Press.

Power, Martin J. 2011. The 'Teenage Dad' and 'Slum Mums' are Just 'Certain People I Know': Counter-Hegemonic Representations of the Working/Underclass in the Works of Morrissey. In Eoin Devereux, Aileen Dillane, and Martin Power, eds., *Morrissey: Fandom, Representations, and Identities*. Intellect.

Prado, Ryan J. 2014. The 20 Best Songs by Elvis Costello. *Paste* <www.pastemagazine.com/music/best-songs/the-20-best-songs-by-elvis-costello>.

Pringle, Steve. 2022. *You Must Get Them All: The Fall on Record*. Route.

Proudhon, Pierre-Joseph. 1994. *What Is Property?* Cambridge University Press.

Punk Scholars Network. 2023. <www.punkscholarsnetwork.com>.

Punter, David. 1996. *The Literature of Terror: Second Edition, Volume 1—The Gothic Tradition*. Longmans.

Ramone, Johnny. 2012. *Commando: The Autobiography of Johnny Ramone*. Abrams.

Rawlinson, Andrew. 1998. *The Book of Enlightened Masters: Western Teachers in Eastern Traditions*. Open Court.

———. 2014. *The Hit: Into the Rock'n'Roll Universe and Beyond*. 99 Press.

Reed, Lou. 1991. *Between Thought and Expression: Selected Lyrics of Lou Reed*. Machine Music, Inc.

Reynolds, Simon. 2005. *Rip It Up and Start Again: Post-Punk 1978–1984*. Faber and Faber.

Rorty, Richard. 1989. *Contingency, Irony, and Solidarity*. Cambridge University Press.

Russell, Bertrand. 1972. *A History of Western Philosophy*. Touchstone Books.

Savage, Jon. 1991. *England's Dreaming: Sex Pistols and Punk Rock*. Faber and Faber.

Sebestyen, V. 2010. *Revolution 1989: The Fall of the Soviet Empire*. Vintage.

Skilling, G. 1981. *Charter 77 and Human Rights in Czechoslovakia*. Allen and Unwin.

Scheler, Max. 1972. *Ressentiment*. Schocken.

Schelling, F.W.J. 2006. *Philosophical Investigations into the Essence of Human Freedom*. State University of New York Press.

Schütte, Uwe. 2022. Krautrock and British Post-Punk. In Schütte, ed., *The Cambridge Companion to Krautrock*. Cambridge University Press.

Seneca, Lucius Annaeus. 1987. On Leisure. In A.A. Long and D.N. Sedley, eds., *The Hellenistic Philosophers*, Volume I. Cambridge University Press.

———. 2010. *Selected Letters*. Oxford University Press.

Simpson, Dave. 2009. *The Fallen: Life In and Out of Britain's Most Insane Group*. Canongate.

Sinker, Daniel. 2001. *We Owe You Nothing: Punk Planet, The Collected Interviews*. New York: Akashic.

Smith, Mark E. 2009. *Renegade: The Lives and Tales of Mark E. Smith*. Penguin.

Sparling, H. 2008. Categorically Speaking: Towards a Theory of (Musical) Genre in Cape Breton Gaelic Culture. *Ethnomusicology* 52.

Spencer, Amy. 2008. *DIY: The Rise of Lo-Fi Culture*. Marion Boyars.

Spencer, Neil. 1992. Public Image Limited. *Volume Three*. Magazine packaged with compilation CD.

Spitz, Marc, and Brendan Mullen. 2001. *We Got the Neutron Bomb: The Untold Story of L.A. Punk*. Three Rivers Press.

Start, Brix Smith. 2016. *The Rise, the Fall, and the Rise*. Faber and Faber.

Stone, Merlin. 1978. *When God Was a Woman*. Harvest.

Storr, Anthony. 1997. *Feet of Clay: A Study of Gurus*. HarperCollins.

Strange, Richard. 2002. *Strange: Punks and Drunks and Flicks and Kicks. The Memoirs of Richard Strange*. André Deutsch.

Strauss, Leo. 1995. *Liberalism Ancient and Modern*. University of Chicago Press.

Stubbs, David. 2015. *Future Days: Krautrock and the Birth of a Revolutionary New Music*. Melville House.

Suck, J., and J. Savage. 1977. New Musick: FOR LIFE ON REWIND/FAST FORWARD/PLAY/RECORD/STOP/ . . . *Sounds* 23 (November 26th).

Sutherland, Sam. 2912. *Perfect Youth: The Birth of Canadian Punk*. ECW Press.

Svenonius, Ian F. 2006. *The Psychic Soviet and Other Works*. Drag City.

Szatmary, David P. 2010. *Rockin' in Time: A Social History of Rock-and-Roll*. Prentice Hall.

Thomas, Mark J. 2023. *Freedom and Ground: A Study of Schelling's Treatise on Freedom*. SUNY Press.

Thompson, Dave. 2002. *The Dark Reign of Gothic Rock: In the Reptile House with The Sisters of Mercy, Bauhaus, and The Cure*. Helter Skelter.

Trendell, Andrew. 2019. Robert Smith on the Power of The Cure's 'Boy's Don't Cry' on Gender Norms—and Never Being Goth. *New Musical Express* (October).

Varga, Somogy. 2012. *Authenticity as an Ethical Ideal*. Routledge.

Vasalou, Sophia. 2016. *Wonder: A Grammar*. SUNY Press.

Warburton, Nigel. 2012. *A Little History of Philosophy*. Yale University Press.

Ward, Ed. 2016. *The History of Rock and Roll: Volume 1, 1920–1963*. Flatiron.

———. 2019. *The History of Rock and Roll: Volume II, 1964–1977*. Flatiron.

Warner, Brad. 2005. *Hardcore Zen: Punk Rock, Monster Movies, and the Truth about Reality*. Wisdom.

Whatley, Jack. 2020. Riot at the Ritz: The Moment John Lydon's Public Image Ltd. Were Booed Offstage in New York. *Far Out Magazine* (May 15th). <https://faroutmagazine.co.uk/john-lydon-public-image-ltd-booed-off-stage-new-york>.

Wikipedia. The Fall (band) <https://en.wikipedia.org/wiki/The_Fall_(band)>.

———. Totale's Turns <https://en.wikipedia.org/wiki/Totale%27s_Turns>.

Wilde, Oscar. 2007 [1891]. The Critic as Artist. In J. Guy, ed., *The Complete Works of Oscar Wilde, Voume IV*. Oxford University Press.

Wilkinson, David. 2016. *Post-Punk, Politics, and Pleasure in Britain*. Springer.

Williams, J.P. 2011. *Subcultural Theory: Traditions and Concepts*. Polity.

Wilson, Colin. 1987 [1956]. *The Outsider*. Tarcher.

———. 2007. *The Angry Years: A Literary Chronicle*. Robson.

———. 2019. *Introduction to the New Existentialism*. Aristeia.

Woods, Paul A., ed. 2016. *Morrissey in Conversation: The Essential Interviews*. Plexus.

Yanosik, J. 1996. The Plastic People of the Universe. *Perfect Sound Forever*: online music magazine (furious.com).

Young, Edward. 2017. *Night Thoughts: With Life, Critical Dissertation, and Explanatory Notes*. University of Michigan.

Zhuangzi. Translations from Legge's version on the *Chinese Text Project* <https://ctext.org/zhuangz>.

Public Philosophy Ltd.

CHELSI BARNARD is a professional writer hailing from Ogden, Utah. She holds a bachelor's degree in Creative Writing and an MFA in English Literature. Throughout her career, Chelsi has made her mark specializing in pop culture and celebrity news. She has written for SpinMedia, Open Court, and US Weekly. She has contributed to *Boardwalk Empire and Philosophy*, *Girls and Philosophy*, *Orange is the New Black and Philosophy*, *Peanuts and Philosophy*, and *The Princess Bride and Philosophy*. Her articles in the digital sphere have been featured in Business Insider, PopCulture.com, and Decider, to name a few. Chelsi is a consultant to brands seeking unparalleled talent in crafting persuasive content. Chelsi possesses a deep appreciation for the musical artistry of Post-Punk, favoring iconic bands such as Siouxsie and the Banshees, The Cure, Talking Heads, Echo and the Bunnymen, Bauhaus, The Slits, and the Cocteau Twins.

WALTER BARTA is a graduate student and principal investigator at the digital research commons in the M.D. Anderson Library at the University of Houston. He liked Post-Punk *after* it was cool. Some of his favorite Post-Punk bands are The Smiths, The Fall, and Fugazi.

JEREMY BENDIK-KEYMER's latest book is *Nussbaum's Politics of Wonder: How the Mind's Original Joy Is Revolutionary*. His previous four books are now OA, including *The Wind—An Unruly Living*. As a professor at Case Western Reserve University, he lives with his family in Shaker Heights, Ohio, where they still play Swans, Sonic Youth, Windy and Carl, Thela, and Flying Saucer Attack on the stereo.

THORSTEN BOTZ-BORNSTEIN is currently Professor of Philosophy at the Gulf University for Science and Technology in Kuwait. In the area of film, he published a book on Béla Tarr (*Organic Cinema*) and the "Philosophy of Film" entry in the *Internet Encyclopedia of Philosophy*. His favorite Post-Punk bands are The Fall, The Smiths, and Violent Femmes.

PAUL BREEDEN is a journalist and psychology graduate with an enduring interest in the legacy of Punk and new wave. His favorite new wave bands include The Fall, Lena Lovich, X Ray Spex, XTC, and The Cramps.

OCEAN CANGELOSI, holding a PhD in philosophy from the University of Arizona and MAs from New York University and San Diego State University, has over a decade of interdisciplinary teaching experience in philosophy, communication studies, and English. Residing in San Diego with their amazing wife, Ocean surfs and plays a variety of instruments, including the theremin and Native American flutes. Currently, they are seeking the ideal academic position close to the waves while they adjunct, speak, and research: "Will teach for surf." Ocean urges readers to discover the following must-see musicians: Tamar Korn and a Kornucopia (best singer on the planet), Jake Sanders Music (best guitarist ever), the Cangelosi Cards (my only claim to fame), Jay Wang and Davey Titlwheel with Come Closer (slaying it in San Diego), and DJ Adam Henslay (best scratcher alive).

PETER J. CHURCH has a BA in Philosophy and Theology from Oriel College, Oxford University; a MLitt in Viking Studies from the University of the Highlands and Islands; and a PhD in early Victorian Gothic literature from the University of Exeter. He is currently the Bursar of Wellington College in Bangkok, Thailand. Some of his favourite Post-Punk bands are Joy Division, Magazine, New Model Army, and The Wedding Present.

MINDY CLEGG is a historian and writer living in Metro Atlanta with her husband and daughter. She holds a PhD in history from Georgia State University and currently teaches at Georgia Perimeter College part-time. Her most recent works include *Punk Rock: Music Is the Currency of Life* from Suny Press and bi-monthly essays at *3 Quarks Daily*. Her musical tastes run the gamut thanks to Post-Punk including the Velvet Underground, Throbbing Gristle, Blondie, Bad Brains, the Bags, Talking Heads, Pigface, Chris Connelly, This Mortal Coil, Low—among many others.

MATTHEW CRIPPEN holds a professorship at Pusan National University in Korea and a research position at the Berlin School of Mind and Brain. He's extensively published on widely varying matters in top journals and has a Columbia University Press book. He considers basically everything to be philosophical and doesn't have favorite Post-Punk bands. But some songs he likes are National Wake's "International News," The Pogues' "Lorca's Novena" and The Levellers' A38 live performance of "Sell Out.'

GEORGE A. DUNN is the editor or co-editor of eight books, including the recent *A New Politics for Philosophy: Perspectives on Plato, Nietzsche, and Strauss* and the forthcoming *René Girard and the Western Philosophical Tradition*. Having taught philosophy in both the United States and China, he is currently working with colleagues to establish a center for the study of global civilization affiliated with Hangzhou City University. His favorite Punk and Post-Punk bands include the Ramones, the Clash, Jason and the Scorchers, X, Social Distortion, Joe Strummer and the Mescaleros, and Yee Loi.

MIHAELA FRUNZA is currently a professor at the Department of Philosophy, Babes-Bolyai University, Cluj, Romania. She teaches courses in Ethics, Applied Ethics, and Philosophy for Children and she is the editor of the Review of Applied Philosophy (Revista de Filosofie Aplicat). Some of the Post-Punk bands she can't stop talking about include My Chemical Romance, Frank Iero and the Future Violents, Palaye Royale and L.S. Dunes.

CATHERINE VILLANUEVA GARDNER is Professor of Philosophy and Women's and Gender Studies at the University of Massachusetts, Dartmouth. Her area of specialization is in the history of women philosophers. However, she is pleased to have the opportunity to harness her misspent youth for a philosophical purpose. Some of her favorite Post-Punk bands include Joy Division, Young Marble Giants, the Cure, and Gang of Four.

SCOTT GORDON is currently pursuing his PhD in philosophy at Binghamton University in Binghamton, New York. His research is primarily in existentialism and hermeneutical phenomenology, with an additional research interest in Buddhist philosophy. Some of his favorite Post-Punk bands are Talking Heads, Adam and The Ants, The Clash, and Elvis Costello and The Attractions.

RICHARD GREENE is a Professor of Philosophy at Weber State University, where he also directs the Richard Richards Institute for Ethics. He is the author of *Spoiler Alert: It's A Book about the Philosophy of Spoilers*, a co-author of *Conspiracy Theories in the Time of Coronavirus*, and the editor of twenty or so books on philosophy and pop culture. He is a co-host of the popular podcast I Think, Therefore I Fan. His favorite Post-Punk bands are The Jam, Devo, and Talking Heads.

MITCH R. HANEY is an Associate Professor of Philosophy at the University of North Florida. He has published essays and edited volumes on work, leisure and the quality of life; ethics in social media, as well as organizational responsibility. His Punk and Post-Punk play lists always include Devo, Talking Heads, Dropkick Murphys, NOFX, and the 'ever-transcendent' Iggy Pop.

JOSHUA HETER is an Associate Professor of Philosophy at Jefferson College in Hillsboro, Missouri. He is the co-editor of *Punk Rock and Philosophy*, *Better Call Saul and Philosophy*, and *The Godfather and Philosophy*. Some of his favorite Post-Punk (and Post-Punk revival) bands are Joy Division, Arctic Monkeys, and Tokyo Police Club.

MARKUS KOHL received his PhD in philosophy from the University of California, Berkeley in 2012. He is Associate Professor of Philosophy at the University of North Carolina, Chapel Hill. Some of his favorite Post-Punk (and Goth) bands are (early) Cocteau Twins, Coil, Cranes, (early) The Cure, Mors Syphilitica, Lycia, Monumentum, Pink Turns Blue, The Sisters of Mercy.

ROBERT KÖNIG is a lecturer in Philosophy at the University of Vienna, and co-founder of the Archive of Post-Neokantianism and Critical Idealism at the University of Wuppertal, Germany. He also worked as a

DJ in the Viennese underground scene for over 10 years. Some of his favorite Post-Punk bands are Einstürzende Neubauten, The Sisters of Mercy, The Cure, The Monochrome Set, and She Wants Revenge.

S. EVAN KREIDER received his PhD in philosophy from the University of Kansas in 2005. He is currently Professor of Philosophy at the University of Wisconsin Oshkosh Fox Cities campus. His recent publications include "Knowledge and Imitation in Hutcheson's Aesthetics" (*Philosophical Forum*). Some of his favorite Post-Punk bands are the Cure, Joy Division, Siouxsie and the Banshees, and the Cocteau Twins.

DAVID LAROCCA, PhD, studied philosophy, film, rhetoric, and religion at Buffalo, Berkeley, Vanderbilt, and Harvard. He is the author or contributing editor of more than a dozen books, including *Metacinema* from Oxford University Press. He also wrote about music in "Suicide Machines: Bruce Springsteen, Ballard, and Broken Heroes on a Last Chance Power Drive." Like so many others, he remains devoted to Post-Punk living legends, The Talking Heads, The Pixies, Billy Bragg, and of course, Elvis Costello and the Attractions. www.DavidLaRocca.org

GEORGINA H. MILLS is a PhD researcher at Tilburg university working in Philosophy of Science. She has also written about philosophy of emotions, philosophy of medicine, and popular culture. She has been interested in Post-Punk for as long as she can remember and her favorite Post-Punk bands include Talking Heads, The Slits, Siouxsie and the Banshees, Television, and many, many more.

CANDACE MIRANDA-BARTA is a contributing author to *Anthony Bourdain and Philosophy* and a graduate of English at the University of Texas at Austin with a certification in creative writing. She is currently a healthcare professional that hosts Post-Punk concerts intraoperatively by blasting her favorite Post-Punk bands like the Talking Heads, Siouxsie and the Banshees, and, pun intended, The Cure through the operating room speakers.

MARTIN MUCHALL recently retired from teaching in the Philosophy and Theology Department at the Royal Russell School in South London. His previous publications include chapters in *David Bowie and Philosophy: Rebel Rebel* (2016), and *Blade Runner 2049 and Philosophy: This Breaks the World* (2019*)*. He maintains the popular website philrsblog.com, and has also contributed to some side-projects organized by the editors of *Philosophy Now* magazine (podcasts, lectures, workshops, balloon debates). His favorite Post-Punk bands are The Fall, Nick Cave and The Bad Seeds, The Slits, and Public Image Ltd.

JESSE PRINZ is a Distinguished Professor of Philosophy at the City University of New York, Graduate Center. Along with US/UK favorites, he's into Post-Punk from outside the Anglosphere: Serbia: Boye "Kafe Na Dnu Okeana" and Elektri ni Orgazam "Dokolica"; Russia: Yanka Dyagileva "From a Big Mind" and Vova Blue And Brothers Of The Mind "Industry"; Spain: Lavabos Iturriaga "Guasimira" and Oviformia SCI "Fashion magazines"; Greece: Libido Blume "In My Room" and T.V.C.

"With You"; Sweden: Global Infantilists "This Music" and Pink Champagne "Ögon"; Denmark: Tee Vee Pop "Garbage Man" and Sods "Ice Age for a While"; Iceland: Tappi Tíkarrass "Óttar" and Q4U "Creeps"; Netherlands: Poison Ivy "Ulster: Hate" and Pure Ace "Disposed"; Belgium: Chow-Chow "Mekka" and Absolute Body Control "Is There an Exit?"; France: KaS Product "So Young But So Cold" and Edith Nylon "Cinémascope"; Switzerland: LiLiPUT "Die Matronsen"; The Kick "I Got a Gun"; Germany: Bärchen und die Milchbubis "Ich Will Nix Älter Werden" and Ja Ja Ja "I Am an Animal"; Latin America: Picassos Falsos (Brazil) "Carne E Osso," Celeste y la Generation (Argentina) "Seré Judia," Nadie (Chile) "Ausencia," and Size (Mexico) "Tonight"; Japan: Plastics "Top Secret Man," Zelda "Darkness the Sight of One Day," and The Lautrec "Canaly."

CASEY RENTMEESTER is Professor of Philosophy at Bellin College in Green Bay, Wisconsin. He is author of *Heidegger and the Environment*, co-editor of *Heidegger and Music*, and has written numerous peer-reviewed articles and book chapters on philosophy. His favorite Post-Punk bands include Joy Division, Violent Femmes, Talking Heads, The Cure, Television, and Bauhaus.

MICHAEL RINGS is currently Teaching Assistant Professor of Philosophy at Siena College. He has published articles on cross-cultural art appreciation, the ethics of personal authenticity, and the aesthetics rock and pop music. Some of his favorite Post-Punk bands are The Birthday Party, Killing Joke, The Contortions, Cocteau Twins, The Fall, and Mission of Burma.

MARTY SULEK received his PhD in Philanthropy and Philosophy from Indiana University in 2011 under the direction of Laurence Lampert. His research interests are in philanthropy and civil society from the perspective of the humanities and normative theory. He is a faculty member of LCC International University in Klaip da, Lithuania. His current favorite Post-Punk and Punk-influenced bands are: Nirvana, Rage Against the Machine, Foo Fighters, Green Day, The Strokes, Audioslave, and The Pretty Reckless.

Index

India, 126
Instagram, 217
Invisible Records, 80
Ionia, 175
Irigaray, Luce, 136–37
Italy, 128

Jarboe, 172
Jayne County, 237
Jesus. *See* Christ, Jesus
The Jesus and Mary Chain, 167
Jirous, Ivan, 77–80
Joan of Arc, 115
John Paul II, Pope, 203
Jones, Mick, 39, 89
Joplin, Janice, 24
Joy Division, 3, 5, 10–11, 14, 17–18,
  36, 45–50, 63–64, 69–70, 97,
  105–06, 150–51, 153–55,
  160–62, 164–66, 170, 186, 247,
  254
  Closer, 11, 69, 154
  New Dawn Fades, 69
  Unknown Pleasures, 49, 63–64,
  68, 105–06, 151, 153

Kafka, Franz, 16, 80
  The Trial, 80
Kant, Immanuel, 172, 174, 175, 194,
  208
  Critique of Judgment, 174
KaS Product, 250
Kaye, Lenny, 225
Keane, 164
Khan, Genghis, 131
Kierkegaard, Søren, 3, 7, 10, 23,
  171–73, 176, 212, 220,
  223
  *Concluding Unscientific
  Postscript to Philosophical
  Fragments*, 176
  Either/Or, 10
Killing Joke, 184
King, Jon, 16, 25, 101, 163
Kino, 250
Klímová, Rita, 81
Kohl, Markus, 23–24, 26, 29
Kojak, 94
Kojève, Alexandre, 91, 92
Kraftwerk, 184, 255
Krauss, Rosalind, 208
Kryzys, 250
Kuhn, Thomas, 225–28
  *The Structure of Scientific
  Revolutions*, 227

L.S. Dunes, 217–19, 222
Langer, Susanne, 149–150, 152–54,
  157
Larmore, Charles, 176
LaRubia, Kyra, 110
Latino Rockabilly War
  Earthquake Weather, 93
The League of Bald Headed Men,
  198
LeBlanc, Lauraine, 236
Led Zeppelin, 24
Lee, Jeanette, 21
Leicester Square, 160
Lena, Jennifer, 248
Lesser Free Trade Hall, 160
Letts, Don, 89, 100
  The Clash: Westway to the World,
  89, 91
The Levellers, 126–28, 131–32
  Levelling the Land, 129, 130
Levene, Keith, 21, 24, 26, 28, 34
Lewis, Matthew, 98
Libido Blume, 250
LiLiPUT, 247
Lillywhite, Steve, 99
Liquid Liquid, 247
Live Skull, 170
LMC. *See* London Music Collective
London, 24, 86, 89, 94–95, 101, 142
London Music Collective, 24
Lopez, Trini, 94
Lorca, Federico Garcia, 126, 130
Lorde, Audre, 137, 146, 220–21
Los Angeles, 236
Love, Courtney, 193
Lovich, Lena, 250
Lucretius, 171
Lugones, Maria de, 220–21
  The Lulu Show, 210
Lunch, Lydia, 170, 250
Lydon, John, 5, 11, 21–22, 24, 26–
  31, 34–38, 48, 100, 164. *See
  also* Rotten, Johnny

Maanam, 250
Machen, Arthur, 199
MacKaye, Ian, 40–41, 240
Madonna, 250
Magazine, 165, 238, 247, 250
Maginnis, Tom, 16
Magor's Wedding, 78–79
Mair, Victor, 126
Manchester, 101, 105–06, 117, 160,
  193, 247
Manson, Marilyn, 107, 188
Marcus, Greil, 30, 100